# Freedom and Dialogue in a Polarized World

# Freedom and Dialogue in a Polarized World

## Sharon Schuman

UNIVERSITY OF DELAWARE PRESS
Newark

Published by University of Delaware Press
Copublished with Rowman & Littlefield
4501 Forbes Boulevard, Suite 200, Lanham, Maryland 20706
www.rowman.com

10 Thornbury Road, Plymouth PL6 7PP, United Kingdom

British Library Cataloguing in Publication Information Available

**Library of Congress Cataloging-in-Publication Data**

Schuman, Sharon, 1946–
Freedom and Dialogue in a Polarized World / Sharon Schuman.
pages cm.
Includes bibliographical references and index.
ISBN 978-1-61149-462-4 (cloth : alk. paper) -- ISBN 978-1-61149-463-1 (electronic)
1. Liberty in literature. 2. Decision making in literature. 3. Autonomy in literature. I. Title.
PN56.L47S38 2014
809'.933581--dc23
2013035243

Printed in the United States of America

# Contents

# Acknowledgments

This book would not have been written without the opportunities afforded by a career teaching literature at Deep Springs College, Willamette University, the University of Oregon, and Oregon State University. Collaborating with faculty and students in literature and political theory has led to a lifelong examination of the problem of freedom. At Deep Springs, the Seminar in Problems of Community and Authority, created by Randall Reid, introduced me to the writings of Hannah Arendt and to team-teaching opportunities with political theorists John Schaar and R. Jeffrey Lustig. At Willamette University, I team-taught with political theorist Robert Hawkinson, who found practical applications for our theoretical discussions by creating the Kaneko Commons Learning Community. Bakhtin scholars Caryl Emerson and Gary Saul Morson read my earliest essay about dialogic freedom and responded with enthusiasm. In 2007, Emerson summarized with my permission key aspects of dialogic freedom for the Moscow journal *Voprosy literatury* (*Questions of Literature*), for the first time launching the concept into a world beyond my study. Shakespearean David Bevington, an encouraging voice since my days as a doctoral student at the University of Chicago, read an early version of the essay that led to this manuscript. Political theorist Hanna Pitkin read an early version of the complete manuscript and at her kitchen table gave me my own private seminar in the difficulties of writing about freedom.

I would like to thank the editors at *Modern Philology* for publishing my essay, "Dialogic Freedom: In the Sideshadow of Bakhtin," which in 2009 introduced the concept of dialogic freedom to the English-speaking world. My chapter on *The Merchant of Venice* draws heavily on another essay, "Authorizing Meaning in *The Merchant of Venice*," published in *Text and Performance Quarterly* in 2002, which is quoted here by their permission.

The editorial board at the University of Delaware Press, especially Senior Editor Julia Oestreich, helped make this book much more readable. Thanks also to undergraduates Jessica Frazier, Carly Bradshaw, and Joel Reynolds of the Clark Honors College at the University of Oregon, and to undergraduate Matt Bradley of Oregon State, who read an early version of this manuscript and convinced me that students could enjoy reading literature for and with dialogic freedom. The participants in the Telluride Association Summer Seminar "Freedom, Dialogue, and Polarization," at the University of Michigan in 2011, also energized me for this project, as did political scientist Joan Sitomer, who team-taught it with me.

Beyond the classroom, an eclectic combination of friends, from composer John Chowning to bicycle shop owner Paul Nicholson and pro-life activist Nancy Hansen, encouraged me to believe that general readers could understand and respond to my ideas about freedom. The many people who have contributed to this conversation, from specialists to students to friends and family from a variety of backgrounds, have all coauthored the analysis in these pages by being receptive, encouraging, and questioning. I would also like to thank Henry Wonham, Chair of the University of Oregon English Department, for extending to me the courtesy appointment in English that has enabled me to enjoy faculty library privileges in this final phase of writing; University of Oregon Professor of Classics and UNESCO Chair Steven Shankman, who invited me to lead a seminar about dialogic freedom, and who can always be counted on for a spirited discussion of literature; and Jack Wilson, editorial page editor of the Eugene *Register Guard*, who has published a number of my opinion editorials, including one about dialogic freedom. Above all, I would like to thank my husband, David Schuman, my personal Fulbright and Guggenheim, for encouraging me to take time off from teaching to finish this project, and my children, Rebecca, Ben, and Lani, who never waver in their faith that what I choose to do must be worthwhile.

is also reprinted by permission of International Creative Management, Inc., copyright 1989 by Toni Morrison.

The *Iliad* of Homer, tr. Richard Lattimore, copyright 1951, is reprinted by permission of the University of Chicago. All rights reserved. Published 1951. First Phoenix edition 1961. Printed in the United States of America.

*The Inferno of Dante: A New Verse Translation* by Robert Pinsky, translation copyright 1994 by Robert Pinsky. Excerpts from Canto XIII and Canto V are reprinted by permission of Ferrar, Straus & Giroux, LLC.

"Me and Bobby McGee," words and music by Kris Kristofferson and Fred Foster, copyright 1969 TEMI Combine, Inc. All rights controlled by Combine Music Corp. and administered by EMI Blackwood Music, Inc. All rights reserved. International copyright secured. Used by permission. Reprinted by permission of Hal Leonard Corporation.

"The Merchant of Venice" by William Shakespeare, *The Oxford Shakespeare*, ed. Wells and Taylor, copyright 1987 Oxford University Press. Used by permission of Oxford University Press.

*Paradise Lost* (1674), by John Milton, quoted with permission, Thomas H. Luxon, ed., *The Milton Reading Room*, http://www.dartmouth.edu/~milton, updated March 2008.

"In the Penal Colony," from *Franz Kafka: The Complete Stories of Franz Kafka,* by Franz Kafka, ed. Nahum Glatzer, copyright 1971 by Schocken Books, is reprinted by permission of Schocken Books, a division of Random House, Inc. Any third party use of this material, outside of this publication, is prohibited. Interested parties must apply directly to Random House, Inc., for permission. "In the Penal Colony," from *Franz Kafka: The Complete Short Stories of Franz Kafka*, published by Vintage Books, is reprinted also by permission of The Random House Group Limited.

# Preface

This book arises from three convictions: that prevailing concepts of freedom are inadequate; that writing about literature should not be shrouded in jargon; and that literature, philosophy, political theory and history create intersecting arenas for better understanding the choices we make. These convictions seem to me so tame that I need to remind myself that they are controversial. By now it is almost heretical to argue that freedom is more than the ability to do as we please (as long as we don't hurt anyone else), and more than emancipation from ignorance. I argue that whatever freedom is, it is something that we experience not just by being left alone, or by gaining access to the truth, but by making decisions and taking action within a context of other people. The concept of dialogic freedom focuses on this aspect of freedom as something we coauthor.

In my particular field, the study of literature, to claim that we should write without jargon is another kind of heresy. Jargon separates the learned from the ignorant, and in truth, for those who understand it, jargon is both efficient and precise. To the uninitiated, though, it carries a menacing message: "Do your homework before you presume to ask me what I think! Learn my language if you hope to deserve to hear what I have to say!" It's as if to appreciate a baseball game, you had to be able to hit a 90-mile-per-hour pitch, or to drive a car, you had to be able to tune its engine. I argue that what we have to say about literature should be comprehensible, intriguing, and enjoyable to the average intelligent reader.

Beyond these heresies lies a third. I presume that we study works of literature not just for their craft, for the conditions of their creation or reception, for the ideologies that run through and against them, for the theoretical orientations that they reveal, or for the ways in which they subtract meaning even as they create it. For me, works of literature are created worlds that invite us to reflect on how we go about living and making decisions. It is at this level that literature puts us into contact with a wide range of disciplines and with questions about dialogic freedom.

I am the first to admit that the whole subject of freedom is fraught with problems, that my writing is not entirely jargon-free, and that the myriad approaches to literature developed over the centuries have only enriched how we read. Nonetheless, the three convictions listed above have shaped this manuscript, which is intended for the widest possible audience of students, professors, and general readers. To that end, chapter 1 clarifies the need for and nature of dialogic freedom, avoiding jargon as much as possible. I include a glossary to explain the few terms I could not do without. Chapters 2 through 9 explore works of literature, reading them both for and with dialogic freedom. Homer's *Iliad* shows how pleading for the release of a son's corpse hinges on a Trojan king's dialogic ability to get a volatile warrior to think about his own father. Dante's *Inferno* shows how decision-making processes involve a multitude of voices that we answer to, and that it is a matter of life and death that we not shut out the wrong voices. Shakespeare's *Merchant of Venice* shows what happens when a person's need to be heard elicits only deafness from others. Milton's *Paradise Lost* presents the dark side of dialogic freedom, in the virtuosity of Satan, who can always say what his listener most needs to hear. Dostoevsky's "Grand Inquisitor" explores the dialogic power even of silence. Melville's "Benito Cereno" explores how racism debilitates judgment in ways that can be exploited by rebelling slaves. Kafka's "In the Penal Colony" goads readers both to reexamine comforting bromides about neutrality and to want to intervene in a terrifying situation. Morrison's *Beloved* presents the emergence of dialogic freedom under the most impossible conditions. These works all reveal different aspects of dialogic freedom and probe the complexity of its operations, emphasizing that we need not wait for conditions to be perfect to enact it. Indeed, the two-sidedness of life within a context of other people makes dialogic freedom a constant possibility and an imperative. The last chapter presents a practical application of this concept of freedom to the ongoing debate about abortion, suggesting that we can reduce polarization by exercising freedom from a dialogic perspective.

For specialists in literature and theory, appendix A presents a supplementary discussion of the theoretical roots of dialogic freedom in the thinking of Mikhail Bakhtin, Aristotle, Hannah Arendt, Isaiah Berlin, and others. For general readers, students, teachers, and book groups, appendix B presents a guide to discussions about the works of literature this book explores, as well as exercises in dialogic freedom and suggestions about discussing hot-button issues of our day from a dialogic perspective. I have in mind the reader Franz Kafka describes, "crouching forgotten in a corner of the room where he can participate all the more intensely in what is happening there."[1] I ask myself,

"How do we invite that reader inside the room?" Part of the problem involves the turf battles not just between schools of thought within disciplines, but also between disciplines themselves. A reader of Dostoevsky does not necessarily care where literature ends and history, philosophy, or political theory begins. Yet each of these disciplines has its boundary markers, and those who crash through them do so at their peril. This book focuses mainly on works of literature, but it also invades the neighboring territories of political theory, philosophy, and politics. Dialogic freedom is a concept that must be situated among other theories of freedom, and these theories cross disciplinary boundaries.

This book also suggests that an idea once taken for granted but now dismissed as naive—that reading literature can help us better understand our lives—deserves revisiting in the twenty-first century. We live in a polarized world, dominated by a political discourse in which people with strong opinions construct echo chambers among the like-minded and dismiss dissenting voices. That even in this climate we still enjoy reading works of literature and thus entering into the worlds they create, shows that these works continue to awaken in us the ability and the desire to see things from the perspectives of others. I seek to show how the challenges of dialogic freedom, presented in literature from ancient Greece to contemporary America, unfold as dramatically as do the adventures of an epic hero. Better understanding this concept can enrich the ways we go about reading literature, as well as the ways we go about making decisions and taking action. I hope others will join in this examination of the problems and possibilities of coauthoring choice in a polarized world.

Sharon Schuman, Eugene, Oregon, 2013

## NOTE

1. Franz Kafka, "Letter to Oskar Baum, April, 1921," *Letters to Friends, Family, and Editors*, tr. Richard Winston and Clara Winston (New York: Schocken, 1977), 276.

*Chapter One*

# Introducing Dialogic Freedom

Throughout history people have died and killed for freedom, yet there are few words more slippery to pin down. Today's teenagers, politicians, refugees, artists, criminals, professors, priests, and parents view freedom from radically different perspectives. To a politician, freedom might suggest the right to vote; to a teacher, the ability to think; to a minister, openness to God; to a teenager, being left alone; to a car salesman, the open road—while Janis Joplin sings to us from the other world, "Freedom's just another word for nothing left to lose."[1] According to Isaiah Berlin, there are "two hundred senses of the word recorded by historians of ideas."[2] Perhaps this is why Hannah Arendt warned, "To raise the question, what is freedom? seems to be a hopeless enterprise."[3] Yet if something is important, chances are someone will praise it or condemn it in the name of freedom. That being the case, our ideas about freedom are embedded in our most significant decisions, in our sense of who we are, and in the polarizing debates that swirl around us. For example, the 2010 U.S. Health Care and Education Reconciliation Act (H.R. 4872), celebrated by supporters for protecting the right to health care, was condemned by opponents as a tyrannous government takeover. Before passing, the bill nearly derailed over the debate about a woman's freedom to choose to have an abortion. In the battles about these and other polarizing issues, from the death penalty to gun control, the ways in which opponents play out their opposition—in the media, in courtrooms, and in election booths—reflect and are driven by their views about freedom.

At this point, we need to reexamine the ideas about freedom that we cherish most, consider the roles they play in our polarized thinking, and formulate a new approach to freedom that helps us move beyond polarization. In the United States today, two ideas of freedom stand out: freedom as autonomy, enshrined by John Stuart Mill in *On Liberty*; and freedom as

1

enlightenment, enshrined by Plato in *The Republic*. These ideas, by no means mutually exclusive,[4] are nonpartisan in their ability to appeal to both right and left. Ironically, these shared views of freedom as autonomy and enlightenment, instead of establishing common ground, actually promote polarization. I argue that we need to think about freedom in a new way, according to which we become more free the better able we are to see from the perspectives of others and take action in a world codetermined by them.[5]

## FREEDOM AS AUTONOMY

According to the view of freedom as autonomy, we should all have the right to be left alone to do as we please, as long as we don't hurt anyone else. In his "Introduction" to *On Liberty*, John Stuart Mill argues, "The sole end for which mankind are warranted, individually or collectively, in interfering with the liberty of action of any of their number, is self-protection. . . . The only purpose for which power can be rightfully exercised over any member of a civilised community, against his will, is to prevent harm to others."[6] From Mill's perspective, the individual's autonomy, or "liberty of action," is at the heart of freedom and should be vigorously protected. Autonomy makes life worth living and should not be interfered with unless such interference is absolutely necessary to prevent harm to others. The choice of phrases like "sole end" and "only purpose" emphasizes how much Mill values thinking hard before we impose any limits on autonomy. It is not enough to argue that it would be good for us—make us happier, smarter, or better people—to limit our freedom to do as we please. Except for one circumstance, to "prevent harm to others," the individual must be the judge.

This caveat, which has come to be called the "harm principle," sets the only just limit, according to Mill, on freedom as autonomy. Isaiah Berlin classifies this concept of freedom as "negative liberty," not because it is wrong, or reflects a negative view of human nature, but because it focuses on the individual's right *not* to be interfered with. Berlin explains that according to this view, "the wider the area of non-interference the wider my freedom" (123). The idea of freedom as autonomy has appealed to generations of Americans and continues to be popular today. Yet the limits imposed on autonomy by the "harm principle" turn out to be highly debatable. Both in our personal lives and in a wider public context, we constantly debate what constitutes harm to others, and we struggle to determine who gets to decide that question. Pointing to Mill's recognition of the need to limit freedom to "prevent harm to others," Berlin adds, "it is assumed . . . that the area of men's free action must be limited by law" (124). With the law as the final arbiter, many of the debates about the proper limits to freedom as autonomy play out in today's legislatures and courtrooms.

In 2012, the citizens of Colorado and Washington tilted the balance between autonomy and harm toward autonomy when they concluded that the individual's freedom to consume marijuana outweighs the threat of harm adults pose to others by using specified amounts of that drug. The proper balance between autonomy and harm also was central to the debate about gun control in the aftermath of the massacre of twenty first-graders in Newtown, Connecticut. What should be the proper limit to an individual's freedom to own a gun? Some argued in favor of arming teachers and security guards at schools, others for reducing access to assault weapons and ammunition. In 2013, the state of New York tilted the balance toward preventing harm. It passed a bill to expand its ban on assault weapons, reduce the size of permissible gun magazines, and take other measures to reduce the likelihood of another massacre.[7]

Meanwhile, in the ongoing abortion debate, both sides once again formulate their positions in terms of the proper balance between autonomy and harm. They weigh a woman's freedom from interference in making decisions about her body against the potential harm to her unborn fetus. Opposite sides in this debate disagree with each other not because one favors autonomy and the other opposes it, but because each side draws the line between autonomy and harm in a different place. If from the moment of conception the fetus is a person, aborting it at any point harms a person. If the fetus is not a person until the moment of viability, aborting it in the first trimester does *not* harm a person. The fate of *Roe v. Wade* will hinge on whether or not future Supreme Court rulings shift the definition of "personhood" to include the fetus in earlier stages of gestation. In the United States today, whether the subject is abortion, the death penalty, immigration, gay marriage, gun control, or legalizing pot, arguments on both sides are couched in terms of just how free we should be to do as we please, as long as we do not harm anyone else.

You would think that such a widely shared reverence for freedom as autonomy, embraced by both right and left, would promote communication and cooperation. However, because both sides view freedom as the right to do as one pleases, as long as no one else gets hurt, and because such rights are limited or expanded by laws, the commitment to autonomy shared by both right and left encourages not cooperation but a raw struggle for the power to enact or overturn laws. This struggle plays out in the media, in courtrooms, in the chambers of legislatures, and in voting booths, where rights get advocated, protected, or trampled on, depending on your perspective. In an atmosphere of winner-take-all, freedom as autonomy nurtures polarization by encouraging us not to try to understand each other or to seek common ground, but to caricature and vilify each other as we dig in for the next fight.

## FREEDOM AS ENLIGHTENMENT

The other concept of freedom that is popular today is the idea that a person should be free to do what is right. According to this view of freedom as enlightenment, we all need to be emancipated from the illusions that enslave us. Depending on our personal, spiritual, political, or philosophical perspectives, the illusions in question might involve religious convictions, nationality, geography, race, gender, sexual orientation, or a host of other variables. In Book VII of *The Republic*, Plato creates his famous metaphor of the cave, which presents freedom as an escape from the illusions of the physical world of the senses to the philosophical enlightenment of the mind. Socrates says, "The world of our sight is like the habitation in prison," a place where what we see is like shadows on the wall of a cave. We have to escape the cave, and "the ascent and the view of the upper world is the rising of the soul into the world of the mind."[8] For Plato, freedom is something that exists only in "the world of the mind" and is achieved only by those few who can face the blinding light of truth. The rest of us carry out our lives enslaved by our inability to see things as they really are.

The concept of freedom as enlightenment has evolved throughout the centuries, embraced by adherents of various philosophical, political, or religious movements. Isaiah Berlin calls it "positive liberty," not because it is good, or because it reflects a positive view of human nature, but because in contrast to "negative liberty," which focuses on "non-interference" from outside influences, it focuses on emancipation from internal influences like illusion. From a perspective of positive liberty, explains Berlin, "freedom is not freedom to do what is irrational, or stupid, or wrong" (148). Many of the world's religions value emancipation from illusion as one of life's greatest potential achievements. In political terms, this concept of freedom as enlightenment crosses ideological divides, appealing to both right and left. Whether I denounce the death penalty, abortion, radical Islam, or homophobia, and whether I extol the value of salvation, medical marijuana, heterosexual marriage, or equality between the sexes, I am very likely to think that I have been emancipated from illusions that blind my opponents and that my enlightened views deserve to be shared by all. This conviction might lead me either to try to persuade you to agree with me or to shun you as unreachable. My commitment to the truth as I see it might lead either to a quiet confidence or to an effort to impose my views on you, even by force.

The concept of freedom as enlightenment exacerbates the polarized debates that dominate American society today. For example, in the aftermath of the massacre at Sandy Hook Elementary School in Newtown, Connecticut, the Associated Press reported that opposite sides in the gun control debate were so sure they were right that "communication has broken down." A gun rights advocate at a sporting goods store in Wexford, Pennsylvania, said of opponents, "You cannot communicate with them. . . . Their minds are set." A gun control advocate had the same complaint about his opponents: "I don't know that they would hear me."⁹ Both sides consider themselves custodians of a truth that is obvious, yet all but inaccessible to those who disagree, who either through rigidity or a kind of willful deafness cannot be reached. Both sides consider themselves liberated from the illusions that prevent their critics not only from seeing the truth but also from being open to the possibility of altering their views in any way. On the issue of gun control and so many others, the idea of freedom as enlightenment from illusion promotes polarization by encouraging adherents of one position or another to take refuge among true believers and dismiss critics.

## AUTONOMY AND ENLIGHTENMENT: A DOUBLE THREAT

These two approaches to freedom—as autonomy and enlightenment—are not mutually exclusive. Opposite sides may disagree vigorously about specific issues. They might disagree about how best to protect a person's right to be left alone, or about what an enlightened person should think, but they often agree that freedom involves being left alone or knowing what is right. This shared commitment to both autonomy and enlightenment intensifies polarization exponentially as each side retreats to echo chambers among the like-minded, leaving their safe havens only to engage in contests for power. As a result, more and more subjects have become almost impossible to discuss: gay marriage, the death penalty, embryonic stem-cell research, immigration, Islam, terrorism, torture—even what constitutes an acceptable school lunch. In our attempts to confront the hot-button issues of the day, all of us are constantly tempted to simplify the perspectives of others. The problem is not that we disagree, but that we disagree dismissively, satisfied that we already know the truth.

At this point in history, we need to venture beyond concepts of freedom as autonomy and enlightenment. We need to formulate a concept of freedom that reduces rather than promotes polarization. Yet thinking about freedom from a less polarizing perspective is fraught with challenges. Isaiah Berlin warned, "The meaning of this term [freedom] is so porous that there is little interpretation that it seems to resist" (121). His metaphor of seepage and leakage conjures well the nature of the problem—not that the word means too little, but that it means too much, or that its potential meanings fragment in too many directions. The centrifugal force of a daily reality filled with moments that can never be exactly repeated (and that therefore threaten chaos) resists our attempts to make sense of the word "freedom" as one unified concept. How, then, should we begin?

# DIALOGIC FREEDOM

I coin the term "dialogic freedom," but the concept has been recognized in bits and pieces by thinkers of all stripes. My formulation is inspired by the work of Mikhail Bakhtin, the Russian linguist, literary critic and philosopher who focused on the dialogic aspects of language, but its roots reach back to Aristotle's *Politics*, and its operations can be experienced in our daily lives. Dialogic freedom is not so much a new idea as a new recognition of an impulse that has driven our attempts at living among other human beings from the ancient world to the present. Just as speech is dialogue, always anticipating a response from someone who may be hostile, friendly, or indifferent, our choices are also dialogic. For example, if I ask you, "Will you marry me?," it matters very much whether you are a five-year-old, my college sweetheart, a total stranger, or another woman. Your perspective as listener—your encouragement, neutrality, confusion—codetermines what I say, what my words mean, and the range of actions you or I decide to take. The exact same words can mean different things and imply different choices, depending on our relationship. A five-year-old would probably know that I am playing a game and either go along with it because I am a favorite aunt or babysitter, or rebel. In either case, the child probably would have little idea what marriage means. My college sweetheart is a different story. He may be pleased, or surprised, or embarrassed, or alarmed, but unless I am laughing, he probably would not take my proposal as a joke. A total stranger might consider me deranged for asking such a question out of the blue. Another woman might react like my college sweetheart, or she might have concerns about the legality of same-sex marriage in our state. In any case, the expectations and reactions of my listener factor significantly into the meaning of my question and the choices it poses, even before that listener has an opportunity to say one word.

This dialogic aspect of communication and decision making is at the center of the concept of dialogic freedom. I extend Bakhtin's concept of the dialogic from language to freedom, evolving a definition of dialogic freedom not as autonomy or enlightenment but as *a two-sided act that involves deliberation from multiple perspectives, within a context of forces for unity and chaos.* Explaining and expanding this definition will take up the rest of this chapter. Then we will examine key moments in literature that invite us to reflect on various aspects of dialogic freedom. Literary worlds resemble our own, in that they are filled with people, places, and events, but unlike our realities they are contained within the pages of a book, where, in a sense, the evidence of decision making is presented for all to see. These fictional worlds serve up experiences that we as readers can react to and argue about. They give us a fictional landscape rich in possibilities and often more intense and revealing than "real" life. My claim is that reading for and with dialogic freedom not only enhances our understanding and enjoyment of literature, but it also strengthens our ability to navigate the troubled waters of contemporary political life. Hence my last chapter presents a practical application: rethinking the debate about abortion in terms of dialogic freedom. There we see how an idea extracted from literature, linguistics, political theory, and life can be applied to the most vexing issues of our day, to help us break through the polarization that currently divides us.

We begin by clarifying key components of dialogic freedom: the context of others; the two-sidedness of decisions; the forces for unity and chaos that shape our world; and the alien perspectives that are vital to our own freedom.

## THE CONTEXT OF OTHERS

In Book I of *Politics*, Aristotle presents his famous formulation of man as a *politikon zoion* [1253a, 1].[10] Benjamin Jowett translates this phrase as "Man is a political animal," which readers often interpret in a contemporary way, like, "Human beings are conniving, corrupt, power-hungry self-maximizers, out to get rich by abusing the prerogatives of public office." I favor Ernest Barker's translation: "Man is by nature an animal intended to live in a *polis*." By retaining the root word of the adjective *politikos*, which is the noun, *polis*, usually translated "city-state," Barker extricates us from the partisan associations of contemporary cynicism and asks us to imagine what Aristotle might have meant to suggest by using that word. Barker underscores Aristotle's view that from a teleological perspective, people are inherently incapable of developing properly unless they have the educational, cultural, military, and civic advantages gained by participating in life among others, available only in a *polis*. The presumption here is that mankind, if left alone, would not flourish (as John Stuart Mill argues). It would wither and die, just as the acorn, not planted in soil, and not watered, would fail to become an oak. To those who dismiss this way of thinking as deterministic, I argue that the acorn and oak metaphor so often associated with Aristotle, but not actually used by him, avoids both the Scylla of determinism and the Charybdis of license. First of all, we should not lose sight of the fact that it is a metaphor. A person is not finally a tree. Yes, the metaphorical soil of environment is beyond the control of individuals, thus in some sense deterministic. Yet the metaphorical oak must have the capacity to rule and be ruled in turn—to make decisions and take action—hence the capacity for freedom, and it is the unfolding of this capacity that is captured in the metaphor of the majestic tree. Aristotle's presumption is that this capacity to choose will not unfold automatically and will have to be nurtured, so that the environment, rather than determining the individual, creates the conditions that make the free individual possible, in all his or her argumentative glory. In *Politics*, Aristotle sets out to examine the many ways a citizen can develop and the many forms of government a *polis* can embrace, from monarchy, oligarchy, tyranny, and democracy, to polity.

For Aristotle, an essential given of human existence is that we live fully and meaningfully only among others. He chooses "polity" as the best form of government because in his judgment it does the best job of creating citizens capable of handling decisions. To him, there is no choice to be "apolitical." Rather, "the man who is isolated—who is unable to share in the benefits of political association, or has no need to share because he is already self-sufficient—is no part of the *polis*, and must therefore be a beast or a god" (I.ii.1253a). Here, Aristotle's contempt for isolation is not obvious until we consider the likelihood of any human being falling into the category of god. Given that gods lie beyond the material world, and human claims to being gods are by definition problematic, we see Aristotle's point that the isolated man is almost certainly a beast. He goes on to explain, "Man, when perfected is the best of animals; but if he be isolated from law and justice he is the worst of all." Here, Aristotle recognizes the physical reality of human existence, our animality, and he sees the institutions we create as forces that shape that human material into our best selves. He is not talking about law and justice in the abstract, but as the products of human deliberation and dialogue, "the determination of what is just," under circumstances created to facilitate these interchanges at the highest level. This context of others is crucial to the choices we make and hence is a key aspect of dialogic freedom.

## FREEDOM AS A TWO-SIDED ACT

Our choices are made not in a vacuum but among other people, both present and absent. Whether this context involves friends, relatives, colleagues, strangers, or enemies, our expectations about how they will react to something we say or do—even our fears of being ignored—codetermine decisions that we might otherwise consider highly individual. Take, for example, a simple decision about whether or not to go to a movie. Say I want to suggest to my husband that we do this. I might wait until he seems receptive to the idea. I might suggest a movie I know he wants to see, at a time he is likely to be free, with friends he enjoys. I might also wonder if he is happy with me for getting a new job, or angry with me for losing my wallet or spending too much time in front of the computer screen. As I anticipate his reception, he codetermines what I am about to say, even though he has not yet opened his mouth, and he may not even be aware of my desire to go out. My freedom to go to the movie reflects more than my capacity to do as I please. The decision is two-sided, and not just because my husband will eventually respond "Yes" or "No," but because I take into consideration his possible responses even as I formulate my invitation. He is an addressee who codetermines my choice, even if he is unaware of the role he plays.

The addressee varies from situation to situation: friend, enemy, boss, client, relative, stranger, etc. There may be complexities within the relationship, in that the addressee might be both relative and boss, both enemy and client. Or there may be several addressees at once, say, in a courtroom where the judge, jury, defendant, accusers, and supporters all listen to a lawyer's presentation. They all have different perspectives involving different assumptions. Observers in the courtroom can see the reactions of the defendant, jury, and judge to the lawyer's speech. The defendant probably sees an unfamiliar, and very likely distasteful, person refracted through the eyes of the prosecutor. Despite the complexities of these relationships within and among addressees, all of the people in the courtroom are present in the same time and place. In this sense, they meet on the same plane.

To Mikhail Bakhtin, there is also a third presence presupposed by the speaker, beyond the potential addressees listed above, which constitutes a *perfect* listener (real or imagined), by whom the speaker will be understood and even judged. The speaker feels answerable to this third presence, the superaddressee, as if to God, or to the political collectivity "the people," or to what God or the people create, "the law." The important thing here is not whether God exists, or whether "the people" or their laws are worth revering, but rather that from the speaker's perspective, God or "the people" or "the law" is invested with ultimate authority. The speaker has faith that this authority can perfectly understand and respond to what he or she is trying to say. If several people share the same superaddressee, so much the easier for them to come to a meeting of minds and take action together. There can be no argument, no polemic, no equality of give and take between addressee and superaddressee, only a ratification of a preexisting relationship through veneration or ritual worship, or conversely, a rejection of that relationship through rebellion, revolution, or heresy. As Bakhtin sees it, answerability to addressee and superaddressee is both a fact of language and a human need, for if we find ourselves in a situation in which we think we are not being heard, we despair. According to him, "For a human being there is nothing more terrible than a *lack of response.*"[11] Chapter 7 explores what happens when a human being, the Grand Inquisitor, attempts to have a conversation with his superaddressee, Christ. Though Christ never says a word, just by listening intently he constantly codetermines the Grand Inquisitor's efforts to force him to speak.

In *Marxism and the Philosophy of Language*, it is the importance of the context of others that is captured in the formulation "Word is a two-sided act." The authors explain, "It is determined equally by *whose* word it is and for whom it is meant. As word, it is precisely the *product of the reciprocal relationship between speaker and listener, addresser and addressee.*"[12] Extending this idea of a "two-sided act" from language to freedom, we can describe freedom as the product of a "reciprocal relationship between *chooser* and the one to whom the *choice* is addressed." In this case, not just "word" but "freedom" is determined equally by whose freedom it is and by whose "responsive presence" it is witnessed. When we factor in the additional category of superaddressee, we include a wide context for choices made and enacted. In this sense, not just the word I say, but the path I follow is determined both by me and by those I answer to. What I may think of as my own autonomous decision involves the coauthorship of many others, present and absent, acknowledged and unacknowledged. The dialogic relationships implied in the statement "Freedom is a two-sided act" can be myriad; thus "two-sided" becomes shorthand for "multi-sided."

In the hypothetical courtroom imagined above, a number of choices are being made. The defendant is choosing what to admit or deny, each lawyer is choosing what kind of narrative to weave about the defendant's guilt or innocence, the judge is deciding what evidence to permit, and the jury is deciding the question of guilt or innocence. In each of these decisions, logic plays a role as evidence is weighed, arguments evaluated, demeanors assessed. Cultural forces of history and ideology, psychological forces of personality, and the like also weigh in. From the perspective of dialogic freedom, these forces of logic, history, ideology, and psychology manifest themselves as orientations toward others in the act of choosing. The defending attorney might notice that the jury consists mostly of women, and his or her assumptions about what might prompt a woman to exonerate the defendant will help shape the choice of words for addressing the jury, not to mention the verdict sought. If counsel glances at an individual juror just as the summation begins, that juror's smile, frown, or fight to stay awake might call forth a different emphasis from that lawyer. Without saying a word, the juror codetermines the lawyer's decision to say one thing rather than another. Conversely, a juror might be waiting eagerly for the defending attorney to provide crucial evidence to exonerate the accused. If the evidence does not come, not just its absence, but the disappointed expectation—in which the lawyer, wittingly or unwittingly, plays a key role—makes the lawyer a coauthor of the juror's decision to convict. Both lawyer and juror might feel answerable to God and/or "the people," which will also influence the choices they make. For both the hypothetical lawyer and the hypothetical juror, the decisions they make, not just the words they say, are two-sided acts that are really multi-sided, within a context of addressees and superaddressees.

The concept of dialogic freedom here being described arises from Bakhtin's fundamental sense of social context as a given of life and language. "Two-sidedness" suggests that this context is more, however, than the presence of others who are seen as something like wallpaper, scenery in a play, or weather. On the contrary, these others coauthor freedom. Even the listener who says or does nothing can be someone whose approval is sought, dreaded, disdained, anticipated, or despaired of, and who in that sense coauthors actions thought of as free. This does not mean that all actions are "determined" by others, but rather that they are codetermined. Thus, our choices are as "two-sided" as are our words, and we can begin to define dialogic freedom as *a two-sided act*. Chapter 2 shows just how far back in history our fascination with this social aspect of dialogic freedom goes. There we examine the two-sidedness of key decisions at the climax of Homer's *Iliad*: King Priam's decision to risk his life in order to beg Achilles to give up Hector's corpse for burial and Achilles's decision to give the old man what he has come for. In both cases, not the ability to do as one pleases unless this action harms someone else, or the ability to see the truth, dominates the action. Rather, both men, caught up in a highly polarized war, codetermine each other's decisions to do the right thing.

## FORCES FOR UNITY AND CHAOS

The "two-sidedness" of dialogic freedom emphasizes the answerability of actions we call free and identifies those we answer to as coauthors of our chosen actions. This process of coauthorship is anything but neat and tidy, because many factors can destabilize the mutuality of our understanding. Whereas for the ancient Greeks of the *Iliad* meaning was a "given," expressed in the undisputed heroic ideal of Homer, which Bakhtin called "monologic"—the product of a stable, unified ideology—for us meaning is something we make and debate. For the ancient Greeks it was obvious that a hero should be physically strong, courageous, and admired for his leadership. Even enemies like Trojans and Achaeans could take for granted widely shared agreement about what constituted strength, courage, and leadership. Today, by contrast, any handful of Americans might completely disagree about the attributes of a hero.

The ancient Greek world that Bakhtin called "monologic," where meaning could be assumed as given, has been replaced by a polyphonic world of disputed values, where meaning gets made. Relativists might consider the process of meaning-making arbitrary, feminists might see it as a product of gender relations, Freudians might link it to the superego, Marxists might identify economic forces, and religious practitioners might invoke God. Adherents of these various perspectives might balance the forces for determinism or autonomy in different ways, but most share a general consensus that no all-embracing philosophy is capable of unifying and orienting all mankind, let alone explaining to what degree we are free. Those who believe in such an explanation tend to be considered fanatics, and those who impose such a vision on others, tyrants. Still, we do not like to let go of the thought that a particular idea can explain a great deal—hence the attractions of feminism, Marxism, Freudianism, various religions, political affiliations, and so on. Each of these orientations has the capacity to appeal to our desire to unify our understanding and find order in a daily reality that resists our attempts to order it. These two opposing forces Bakhtin refers to as centripetal (unifying) and centrifugal (fragmenting).

In "Authorizing Meaning in *The Merchant of Venice*," I discuss how "in 'Discourse in the Novel' Bakhtin explores the tension between centripetal forces of language that 'unite and centralize verbal-ideological thought' and centrifugal forces of language that carry on 'the uninterrupted process of decentralization and disunification.'"[13] To illustrate the tension between these two forces, I give the example of the word "tree." When I say "tree" I invoke the centripetal force of a stable, unified concept that for most people involves a trunk and branches. If my listener shares this conception he or she reinforces its unifying force:

> But in tension with this unifying effect is the centrifugal force of hundreds of types of trees, specific trees, specific experiences of trees (romantic interludes, childhood escapades, escapes, lynchings, crucifixions), metaphorical possibilities (the tree of life, family tree), slang ('up a tree'), and the listener's receptivity (hostile, agreeable, tuned out). The word "tree" carries with it at all times all these possibilities and many more, and while the centripetal force tends toward one meaning (or a particular meaning in a particular moment), the centrifugal force of the language tends to fracture meaning in many directions." (50)

When we think of language and life in this way, we see that at any given moment there will be not just one meaning, or conversely, many meanings, but a tendency to center on one among many meanings, in tension with a tendency to find this centering process unsatisfactory in the face of a richly textured prosaic reality. Meaning gets made collaboratively by speakers and listeners, within a complex field of forces that encourage both unity and chaos.

The tension between these two forces can be taken to the level of concept, ideology, political perspective, and so on, in that a feminist might privilege one particular theory to explain history, while a Marxist might privilege another. Each theoretical orientation attempts to center or unify thought in such a way as to provide coherent explanations for a reality that resists such explanations. Various schools of thought can thus be seen as competing to unify our thinking. Viewed in this light, our polarized political parties can also be seen as creators of competing narratives that seek to unify our thinking in one direction or another. The Republican narrative of prosperity for all through fiscal restraint, generational responsibility, and the free market competes with the Democratic narrative of opportunity for all through education, health care, and access to good jobs. In the process, both parties weave unified counternarratives that vilify each other. Democrats cast Republicans as heartless opportunists who seek to widen the gap between rich and poor. Republicans cast Democrats as heartless opportunists who seek to promote class warfare. Both parties broadcast narratives that present explanations for why it is the right party to lead, and the other party is not. The world that politicians, philosophers, professors, and priests seek to explain, however, refuses to be unified (or "finalized," as Bakhtin would put it) from any one perspective. Even as we create unified narratives, our daily lives, filled with an overwhelming amount of data, carry on the chaotic centrifugal work of fracturing meaning in many directions. In fact, the human effort toward meaning-making can be seen as authorizing one approach as more legitimate than the next, in a never-ending search for coherence.[14] Conversely, the variables of human life can be seen as the uncooperatively centrifugal material that never quite gets explained. Within this force field of unity and disunity, human beings engage in the two-sided act of choosing.[15]

When we talk about freedom, we are working with a word that has experienced centuries of centripetal efforts to unify its meaning as positive liberty, negative liberty, autonomy, free will, and so on. When Isaiah Berlin remarks that freedom has been given over two hundred different definitions by historians of ideas, his observation reflects both the unifying efforts of different perspectives that compete to define "freedom" once and for all (but together fracture meaning in many directions, hence acting centrifugally) and the more directly centrifugal forces of a chaotic reality that gives rise to so many theories. Each theory is an attempt to unify meaning and create coherence, while together the sheer number of theories is evidence that such unification is a hopeless task. For Bakhtin, the never-ending clash between unifying and chaotic forces in human activity is anything but simple. Whether their choices involve what person to love, what literary genre to create in, what topic to debate, what candidate to endorse, what profession or religion to follow, what community to embrace, or something more trivial, like what color of sofa to buy, human beings will always construct abstract ideas to help unify (or to confuse) their thinking processes, yet live experiences that both resist these unifying verities and demand actions for which there can be no alibi to excuse them from responsibility. With these complexities in mind, we can expand our definition of dialogic freedom: *a two-sided act, chosen within a field of unifying and fragmenting forces.*

## NAVIGATING THE PERSPECTIVES OF OTHERS

In *Marxism and the Philosophy of Language* Bakhtin/Voloshinov argue that in the two-sided act of speech every phrase is spoken from "a position" of some kind (a sociopolitical, ideological, cultural, relational, professional, or personal perspective) and addressed to a listener at his or her own position. To supply some examples, which Bakhtin/Voloshinov do not, this position might be as simple as the doctor's orientation toward a patient, the child's toward a friend, the clerk's toward a customer, or the prisoner's toward a guard. Or it could be more complex, like the husband's toward the wife who expected a present but didn't get one, yet had an affair and wonders if he knows; or the professor's toward the plumber, who he suspects considers him inadequate for not fixing his own faucet. The more complex the factors that enter into the relationship, or even the greater their number, the more centrifugal forces enter the picture to prevent the positions of the speaker and listener from being clear-cut and understood by both parties in the same way. These centrifugal tendencies multiply possibilities, so that at any given moment most people could inhabit dozens of different positions.

According to Bakhtin, we all inhabit many different arenas in life, all with their own language "genres." He lists "professional jargons, generic languages, languages of generations and age groups, tendentious languages, languages of the authorities, of various circles and of passing fashion, languages that serve the specific sociopolitical purposes of the day, even of the hour (each day has its own slogan, its own vocabulary, its own emphasis)" (DI, 263–64). This "heteroglossia" or "diversity of social speech" is a reflection of the many perspectives possible for people under diverse circumstances and in different relationships. To the extent that their positions are similar or overlap, they can share a generic language, which facilitates communication. Thus two doctors, two tile-setters, two mafiosi, two musicians, two depressed people, or two travelers might share a particular jargon, shorthand, or language.

Even so, other differences between them (age, race, gender, religion, nationality, geography, ideology) might get in the way of communication. The multiplication of possibilities inherent in human relationships and the abundance of "speech genres" generate enough centrifugal force to splinter meaning in many directions. These centrifugal forces carry significant implications for the possibility of freedom. Bakhtin scholars Katerina Clark and Michael Holquist explain, "Those who can not learn to exploit the capacity of words to mean different things in different epistemological layers of their cultural system are condemned to exist unfreely, within a very small number of such layers."[16] The implication here is that freedom involves a kind of mobility, a capacity to navigate among different ways of knowing, to see from multiple "positions," or "horizons," to be polyphonic rather than monophonic, to cultivate awareness of the dialogic potential of every moment. The more able a person is to see from the perspectives of others, the more that person is free.[17]

One way to imagine the mobility Bakhtin suggests, as well as its potential dangers, is to consider a hypothetical situation in which I face a friend who is suffering the loss of a child. We could say that my friend and I navigate the same ways of knowing the world in that we share mutual experiences and affections, but we navigate different ways of knowing in that, although I see that he is suffering and I empathize with the loss of his child, I cannot experience that loss as he does. Even if I, too, were to lose a child, it would not be *his* child felt as *his* loss. How can I navigate the epistemological layers of my suffering friend's experience? In both "Author and Hero in Aesthetic Activity" and *Toward a Philosophy of the Act,* Bakhtin examines the relationship between one who is suffering and another who observes this suffering. In "Author and Hero" he describes the suffering person as one who "does not see the agonizing tension of his own muscles, does not see the entire, plastically consummated posture of his body, or the expression of suffering on his own face. He does not see the clear blue sky against the background of which his suffering outward image is delineated for me."[18] Only the observer can see these things. Hence, only the observer can fulfill the unifying task of completing, consummating, or filling in the image of the sufferer. According to Bakhtin, my empathy calls on me to do even more, "to penetrate" my friend who has lost a child "and almost merge or become one with him from within."

Bakhtin warns, however, against remaining at this point, "experiencing another's suffering as one's own," which he calls "pathological"—"an infection with another's suffering, and nothing more." He presents this state of "pure empathizing" as a kind of emotional black hole that threatens to suck the observer into the helplessness of suffering itself. According to Bakhtin, such "a pure projection of myself into another" is "hardly possible" and "in any event, it is quite fruitless and senseless." The important thing is that I experience my friend's suffering "precisely as *his* suffering," so that my reaction is not "a cry of pain" but "a word of consolation or an act of assistance" (AH, 26). According to Bakhtin, this capacity, which in this essay he calls "sympathetic understanding," requires an all-important "*return into ourselves.*" He emphasizes how important it is for me to navigate the epistemological layers of my friend's suffering, contributing to the centripetal, unifying task of helping him piece together his experience, yet to resist the impulse to disappear into that suffering, or to relinquish my ability to navigate other perspectives on my friend's experience. By resisting the pull of complete identification with the sufferer, I can return to myself on the way to making choices about how to console or otherwise help him. Bakhtin distinguishes between this "sympathetic understanding," which he applauds, and "exact, passive mirroring or duplication of another's experience within myself," which he considers dangerous (AH, 102).

Throughout his career Bakhtin would explore the mobility required to navigate the perspectives of others.[19] In *Toward a Philosophy of the Act*, he makes similar points about suffering, once again warning against the dangers of taking empathy too far. He clarifies the distinction between "exact duplication" through "pure empathizing" (a bad idea) and "sympathetic understanding" through "active empathizing" (a good idea). Resorting to daunting jargon, he warns that "pure empathizing" is "the act of coinciding with another and losing one's own unique place in once-occurrent Being." With "active empathizing," on the other hand, "I empathize actively into an individuality and, consequently, I do not lose myself completely, nor my unique place outside it, even for a moment" (TPA, 15). Once again, the return to myself is an essential aspect of navigating the epistemological layers of my suffering friend's experience.[20]

Beyond the specific situation of empathizing with suffering, the more fundamental problem, according to Bakhtin, involves trying to duplicate another's experience, positive or negative. He calls this "being-possessed by Being," and it is this state that is at the core of his rejection of the "absurdity" of Nietzschean Dionysianism, which he considers an "irresponsible self-surrender" (TPA, 49). For Bakhtin, suffering is not the only state of mind that we can lose ourselves in. He encourages us to cultivate the mobility to see from the perspective of someone else, positive or negative, to navigate the ways of knowing that are part of another person's experience, while retaining the ability to avoid passively disappearing into that experience, so that we can return to ourselves and take responsibility for our actions (a process that he does not consider linear, since its elements can occur simultaneously). Chapter 3 explores how Dante presents the dangers of this mobility in the form of empathy for the exalted lover Francesca, as imagined in Canto V of the *Inferno*. Chapter 9 explores how in *Beloved,* Toni Morrison relentlessly untangles both the attractions and the life-threatening dangers of empathy. She makes us see just how dangerous it can be to risk disappearing into someone else's suffering perspective. In the situation presented in *Beloved*, the loss of freedom is nearly fatal for the novel's protagonist, Sethe.

If the ability to experience "participative thinking," "active empathizing," and "sympathetic understanding"—within limits—promotes freedom, the inability to navigate the perspectives of others undermines it. Barriers to navigating the perspectives of others appear as barriers to our own freedom. Beyond the logistics of time and place, the accidents of friendship and trauma, and the dangerous pathologies of "pure empathy," what prevents the kind of active empathizing that Bakhtin describes? If the observer is indifferent to the sufferer's predicament, or even hostile to it, seeing it, for example, as what the sufferer deserves, the observer will have little empathy. In that case (one that Bakhtin does not imagine in his discussions of suffering but glances at elsewhere),[21] an observer's centripetal ability to pass a final verdict on a sufferer, to label him or her not as one who grieves a loss but as a stranger, an enemy, or an unenlightened fool, carries significant implications not just for the sufferer's chances of getting help, but also for the observer's dialogic freedom. The more an observer's ability to see behind another's back, or to see the expression on his or her face, contributes not to a fuller image of that person, but to a reduced or distorted image, the more that observer reduces his or her own opportunities for navigating and returning from the ways of knowing entailed in that person's experience. The observer's dialogic freedom is circumscribed by the refractive horizons of his or her own indifference, prejudice, and fear. Chapter 4 examines the relations between Jews and Christians in *The Merchant of Venice* in terms of such failures of empathy that constitute a loss of freedom for them both. Chapter 6 focuses on how a resourceful slave in "Benito Cereno" can take advantage of such failures of empathy, manipulating the master's vision to promote the slave's quest for freedom.

In an essay in honor of Robert Louis Jackson, Caryl Emerson takes Bakhtin to task for "the overall benevolence" of his readings and for his blindness to the darker side of dialogue. She argues, "The possibility that dialogue might actually drain away value . . . is not a theoretically serious issue for Bakhtin."[22] According to her, "In his view responsible consciousness always moves outward into the world" (253). She asks, "What is it about chaos, pathology, and apocalypse that Bakhtin's benign vision of the polyphonic word cannot encompass?" (248). The discussion of the virtuosity of Milton's Satan in chapter 5 sketches the darker side of dialogic freedom. I argue that the ability to navigate the ways of knowing of another creature need not necessarily be employed for good ends. Dialogic freedom can be a source of liberation but also a potent weapon for manipulation. Thus, like positive and negative liberty, the concept of dialogic freedom calls for a critical understanding of both its dangers and its potential for good. It requires habits of mind that embrace the ongoing challenges of making choices among other human beings. These challenges, born of each new day's experiences, can never be overcome totally, or once and for all. Bakhtin would say that they can't be "finalized."[23] Hence, the development of our dialogic freedom becomes an ongoing and incomplete task.

At this point, we are ready to define dialogic freedom: *a two-sided act, chosen within a field of unifying and fragmenting forces along a continuum of minimal to maximal layers of knowing that are never final.* This definition is valuable both as a description of how dialogic freedom happens within a context of other people, and as a guide for evaluating degrees of freedom, with maximal ways of knowing (short of chaos) linked to the most meaningful freedom. This concept of dialogic freedom shares with Aristotle an appreciation for the formative power of life among other people. It shares with J. S. Mill an appreciation for the free and open encounter between truth and falsehood. It shares with Alexis de Tocqueville the idea that "feelings and opinions are recruited, the heart is enlarged, and the human mind is developed by no other means than by the reciprocal influence of men upon each other."[24] It shares with Hannah Arendt the conviction that "to *be* free and to act are the same" and also her vision of freedom as virtuosity. According to her, "the performing arts . . . have indeed a strong affinity with politics. Performing artists—dancers, play-actors, musicians, and the like—need an audience to show their virtuosity, just as acting men need the presence of others before whom they can appear; both need a publicly organized space for their 'work,' and both depend upon others for the performance itself."[25] It shares with Isaiah Berlin the warning that "one belief, more than any other, is responsible for the slaughter of individuals on the altars of the great historical ideals—justice or progress . . . or even liberty itself. . . .This is the belief that somewhere, in the past or in the future . . . there is a final solution."[26]

The concept of dialogic freedom discussed here is intended not to advance a particular political agenda, but to promote discussion of the enactment and problems of freedom. It focuses our attention not on encompassing explanations of, or solutions to, specific problems (though it acknowledges them as potent forces for unity in a fragmenting world), but rather on what Bakhtin calls the "eventness" of daily life as it unfolds moment by moment. It foregrounds the value of daily life as an arena for freedom. In *Narrative and Freedom*, Gary Saul Morson extols the virtues of these daily activities, where open, debatable, plural opinion resists the rigidity of oracular, utopian, or ideological conviction. This is a realm that is open rather than closed, where time becomes not a linear movement from point A to point B, but a "field of possibilities."[27] Morson invokes Tolstoy's idea that "our lives tend to no goal; neither are they destined to be shaped into a story. They are filled with chance events that nevertheless have lasting effects and are shaped by incidental causes that need not have happened" (78). Within this "universe of radical contingency what matters most is experience and alertness" (157). Morson explains that "the need for coherence leads us to transform contingency into necessity" (157). This necessity, however, is a product not of a determined condition of the world but of our unifying efforts to explain the world in deterministic terms. Far better, argues Morson, that we should direct our attention to our experiences in the daily world, as if we were all novelists, in order to "expand our own perspective by imagining how it appears from another perspective" (273), even the most alien consciousness (210). A person "might still maintain the rightness of his original position or he might be moved to change his judgment, but in any case his view is richer and more complex" (210).

Morson's call for a novelist's alertness toward imagining how one perspective appears from an alien one, which echoes elements of Bakhtin's concepts of "active empathizing," "sympathetic understanding," "participative thinking," and "willingness to listen," is at the heart of the concept of dialogic freedom. Dialogic freedom, with its invitation to navigate the perspectives of others, summons us to recognize the unrealized but real possibilities within a world among other people, and conversely, to recognize the chance events that contribute to a present that is not at all inevitable. It calls each of us to aspire to be one of those praised by Henry James as someone "upon whom nothing is lost."

## CONCLUSION

The story of dialogic freedom has been evolving for as long as human beings have attempted to communicate or make decisions. Its challenges pervade our daily lives and are presented in works of literature from authors as diverse as Homer, Dante, Shakespeare, Milton, Melville, Dostoevsky, Kafka, and Morrison. This book examines provocative moments in literature that explore how we coauthor dialogic freedom: Priam's request for his son's corpse from Achilles; Dante's swoon before the condemned Paolo and Francesca; Satan's manipulative virtuosity in *Paradise Lost*; Babo's ability to exploit the master's racism in "Benito Cereno"; the Grand Inquisitor's efforts to force Christ to speak; Kafka's provocations of readers of "In the Penal Colony"; and Toni Morrison's vision of freedom under impossible circumstances in *Beloved*. These works of literature help us understand the complexities of dialogic freedom, even as this concept gives us a new tool for reading such texts. The last chapter presents a discussion of contemporary implications of this concept for the debate about abortion.

With this introduction to dialogic freedom, I hope to clarify the foundations for a concept whose time has come to influence a conversation that for millennia has occupied philosophers, politicians, and citizens. Although, as Isaiah Berlin and Hannah Arendt both observe, "freedom" is a word that fractures centrifugally in hundreds of directions, every age and culture is called upon to refine, recharge, and reshape its definitions. I have sought to show that implicit in Bakhtin's ideas about language lurks a conception of freedom that is fundamentally political, in an Aristotelian sense. This is the idea of dialogic freedom as a two-sided act, chosen within a field of unifying and fragmenting forces along a continuum of minimal and maximal layers of knowing that are never final. I argue that this perspective on freedom can help us resist the Siren call of polarization in a world full of issues that we can no longer discuss except among like-minded friends. If instead of seeing ourselves as more free the more we are left alone to do as we please, or more free the better able we are to see the truth, we were to see ourselves as more free the better able we are to navigate the perspectives of others without losing ourselves in them, we would constantly seek to hear rather than dismiss our opponents. We would be more highly motivated to see things from their perspectives, even for a moment. The reward would be not just the satisfaction that comes from trying to be fair, but also the pleasure that comes from feeling more free. Listening for the common humanity that helps us make the decisions that really count, we might make headway on vexing issues like gun violence, immigration, terrorism, the death penalty, or a host of other issues. If we did, it would not be because someone finally won, but because we all more fully embraced the challenge of being free.

## NOTES

1. Janis Joplin, "Me and Bobby McGee," lyrics by Fred Foster and Kris Kristofferson, *Pearl* (New York: Columbia Records, 1971), used by permission of Sony, Inc., Hal Leonard Corporation.

2. Isaiah Berlin, "Two Concepts of Liberty," in *Four Essays on Liberty* (1958; repr., London: Oxford University Press, 1969), 121. Further citations of Berlin are to this edition and are given in the text.

3. Hannah Arendt, "What Is Freedom?," in *Between Past and Future: Eight Exercises in Political Thought* (1954; repr., New York: Viking Press, 1968), 143. Further citations of Arendt are to this edition and are given in the text.

4. 4 Autonomy and enlightenment are often viewed as opposing concepts of freedom. For example, David Spitz explains, "In the history of political thought, two conceptions of liberty have long been opposed to each other. These are the liberty to do as one wants versus the liberty to do as one should." "Freedom and Individuality: Mill's *Liberty* in Retrospect," in *On Liberty: John Stuart Mill*, ed. David Spitz (New York: Norton, 1974), 226. I will argue that autonomy (to do as one wants) and enlightenment (to do as one should), though often considered opposing ideas of freedom, are both embraced by both sides in our most polarizing debates today. Citations to *On Liberty* are to this edition.

5. 5 I do not argue that we should think about freedom *only* from a dialogic perspective, or that the concepts of freedom as autonomy or enlightenment should have no place in our thinking. These ideas of freedom have become deeply embedded in our values, because over the centuries they have served mankind well. I argue only that we need to recognize certain dangers posed by focusing too much on autonomy or on enlightenment, to the exclusion of other ways of thinking about freedom, especially the dialogic perspective I advocate.

6. John Stuart Mill, *On Liberty*, ed. David Spitz (New York: Norton, 1974), 10–11. *On Liberty* has been continuously in print since 1859, a source of inspiration to many and of frustration to others. Some attribute Mill's defense of individual freedom to his resentment of the established church, or to his unconventional relationship with Harriet Taylor, or to the tyrannizing effects of his unusual education at the hands of his father. Philosophical examinations of Mill's utilitarianism and his compatibilism (sometimes called "soft determinism," which holds that determinism and freedom, properly understood, are compatible; all events are caused by something, but we are morally responsible for what we choose) are beyond the scope of this discussion. I focus here on Mill's role as one of the clearest and most convincing advocates of freedom as autonomy.

7. Thomas Kaplan, "Sweeping Limits on Guns Become Law in New York," *New York Times*, January 15, 2013.

8. Plato, *Great Dialogues of Plato*, trans. W. H. D. Rouse (New York: New American Library, 1956), 315.

9. Associated Press, "Sides in Gun Debate Taciturn," *Eugene Register-Guard*, December 31, 2012.

10. Aristotle, *Politics*, ed. Gregory R. Crane, Perseus Digital Library Project, accessed February 1, 2009, http://www.perseus.tufts.edu. Translated "Man is by nature a political animal,"

by Benjamin Jowett in *Introduction to Aristotle*, ed. Richard McKeon (New York: Modern Library, 1947), I.ii.1253a, 556; and "Man is by nature an animal intended to live in a *polis*," by Ernest Barker in *The Politics of Aristotle* (London: Oxford University Press, 1958), I.ii.1253a, 9. Citations of Aristotle are to the Barker translation of *Politics* and are given in the text.

11. Mikhail Bakhtin, *Speech Genres and Other Late Essays*, ed. Caryl Emerson and Michael Holquist; trans. Vern McGee (Austin: University of Texas Press, 1986), 127. Citations of *Speech Genres* are to this edition, with the abbreviation SG, and will be given in the text. See also Bakhtin's "Appendix II: Toward a Reworking of the Dostoevsky Book" (1961), where he says: "To be means to communicate. Absolute death (non-being) is the state of being unheard, unrecognized, unremembered." *Problems of Dostoevsky's Poetics*, ed. and trans. Caryl Emerson (Minneapolis: University of Minnesota Press, 1984), 287. Citations of *Problems of Dostoevsky's Poetics* are to this edition, with the abbreviation PDP, and will be given in the text.

12. Bakhtin/Volosinov, *Marxism and the Philosophy of Language*, in *The Bakhtin Reader: Selected Writings of Bakhtin, Medvedev, Voloshinov*, ed. Pam Morris (London and New York: Arnold, 1994), 58. Texts published under the names of Ivan Ivanovich Kanaaev, Valentin Voloshinov, and Pavel Medvedev are attributed to Bakhtin by Michael Holquist and Katerina Clark in *Mikhail Bakhtin* (Cambridge, MA: Harvard University Press, 1984), 146–70. Gary Saul Morson and Caryl Emerson dispute this claim with regard to Voloshinov and Medvedev in their introduction to *Rethinking Bakhtin: Extensions and Challenges* (Evanston, IL: Northwestern University Press, 1989), 31–49. I steer clear of the dispute by referring to the disputed works as jointly or ambiguously authored, in this case by Bakhtin/Volosinov. Citations to *Marxism and the Philosophy of Language* are to this edition, with the abbreviation MPL, and will be given in the text.

13. Sharon Schuman, "Authorizing Meaning in *The Merchant of Venice*," *Text and Performance Quarterly* 22, no. 1 (2002): 47–62.

14. For a more complete discussion of the idea of "authorizing meaning," see my essay, "Authorizing Meaning in *The Merchant of Venice*."

15. The tensions between centripetal and centrifugal forces occupied Bakhtin throughout his career, from his early philosophical writings to his later preoccupation with genres, and the complexities of this distinction for him can only be suggested here. Many are familiar with statements like the one in "From the Prehistory of Novelistic Discourse," where Bakhtin explains, "Every concrete utterance of a speaking subject serves as a point where centrifugal as well as centripetal forces are brought to bear." *The Dialogic Imagination: Four Essays by M. M. Bakhtin*, ed. Michael Holquist; trans. Caryl Emerson and Michael Holquist (Austin: University of Texas Press, 1981), 272. Citations to *The Dialogic Imagination*, with the abbreviation DI, are to this work and given in the text. In this passage, Bakhtin focuses on specific literary genres, which he sees as tending in one direction or the other, the poetic genres (especially the epic) toward the centripetal, the novel toward the centrifugal. Even in his earliest known sustained work, written between 1919 and 1921, Bakhtin notes the tensions between the centripetal and centrifugal forces in our lives, without specifically using those terms. He explains, "An act of our activity, of our actual experiencing, is like a two-faced Janus. It looks in two opposite directions: it looks at the objective unity of a domain of culture and at the never-repeatable uniqueness of actually lived and experienced life." *Toward a Philosophy of the Act*, ed. Vadim Liapunov and Michael Holquist; trans. Vadim Liapunov (Austin: University of Texas, 1993), 2. Here, we see Bakhtin's characteristic focus on experience not just as action, but rather as action from a particular perspective ("it looks"). In this case, the glance moves in two opposite directions, one centripetal, the other centrifugal. The "domain of culture" represents centripetal "unity," while the "never repeatable" activity of life represents the centrifugal pull of the unique. Citations to *Toward a Philosophy of the Act* are to this work, with the abbreviation TPA, and will be given in the text.

16. Holquist and Clark, *Mikhail Bakhtin*, 227.

17. Advocates of "positive liberty" might see in Holquist and Clark's observations about navigating epistemological layers of meaning a validation of the idea of freedom as "enlightenment," or "learning what to want"—in this case learning to cultivate the ability to "exploit the capacity of words to mean different things in different epistemological layers." The linked concepts of "heteroglossia" and "epistemological layers," however, resist recruitment into the

positive liberty agenda. To begin with, the "positions" from which speakers operate, their very identities, and the two-sided act of speaking, all acknowledge potent centrifugal forces that resist the utopian unities of positive liberty. Furthermore, reconceiving enlightenment as the ability to operate among the greatest number of "epistemological layers" short of chaos, tilts the scale toward the pluralism Isaiah Berlin advocates. In his introduction to *The Dialogic Imagination*, Michael Holquist recognizes this tendency when he explains that for Bakhtin, "true freedom" consists in "extraordinary sensitivity to the immense plurality of experience" (xx). Yet it would also be a mistake to equate this pluralist tendency with pluralism. Berlin's focus on "the ideal of freedom to choose ends without claiming eternal validity for them, and the pluralism of values connected with this" is different from Bakhtin's focus on the intersubjectivity of meaning-making within a field of unifying and fragmenting forces. True, Berlin's "ends" acknowledge the unifying forces for coherence and ideology, while the phrase "without claiming eternal validity" acknowledges the centrifugal forces of a complex world of competing ideologies and chaos. Yet, for Berlin, the focus is on competing ideologies, rather than on how meaning gets made and how action gets taken within a social, political, and historical context that is always "two-sided."

18. Mikhail Bakhtin, "Author and Hero in Aesthetic Activity," in *Art and Answerability: Early Philosophical Essays by M. M. Bakhtin*, ed. Michael Holquist and Vadim Liapunov, trans. Vadim Liapunov (Austin: University of Texas Press, 1990), 26. Citations to "Author and Hero in Aesthetic Activity" are to this work, with the abbreviation AH, and are given in the text. Citations to other chapters from *Art and Answerability*, with the abbreviation AA, will be given in the text.

19. In *Toward a Philosophy of the Act*, Bakhtin describes this mobility as "participative (unindifferent) thinking," which he considers essential to being "an answerable participant from within oneself, to affirm one's compellant, actual non-alibi in Being" (TPA, 49). He is at great pains to emphasize the inadequacy of relying on abstractions like "the good" or "the beautiful" to constitute the values by which we live. The ethical imperative comes not so much from these abstractions (which, after all, we create) as from our obligation to take responsibility for ourselves in a world of other people. He explains, "To live from within oneself does not mean to live for oneself, but means to be an answerable participant from within oneself" (TPA, 49). To him "all these emotional-volitional tones" are possible "only in relation to the existence of another" (AH, 105). There is no mention here of dialogism, speech genres, addressees, or superaddresses. That would come later. With words like "answerable," "non-alibi," "participative," and "another," however, there is a strong sense in these early texts that our orientation toward others in the world is an essential aspect of a life lived fully. Whatever gets in the way of "participative thinking" gets in the way of life itself. Later in his career, when he was revising the Dostoevsky book, Bakhtin did not leave behind these key relationships. There he would come to explain the importance of "not merging with another, but preserving one's own position of *extralocality* and the *surplus* of vision and understanding connected with it . . . simply an active (not a duplicating) understanding, a willingness to listen." There he concludes, "The most important aspect of this surplus is love" (PDP, 299).

20. An interesting thing about Bakhtin's change in thinking between the early philosophical fragments, where "consummation" is devoutly to be wished, and his later literary texts, where "finalization" is to be avoided at all costs, is that in the early writings his emphasis is on the centripetal dangers to the author (who runs the risk of losing himself in the hero's suffering), whereas in the later texts the danger is to the hero (who runs the risk of being trapped in a predetermined plot). The shift here is not just in how finalization is regarded but in whose fate winds up front and center. When did Bakhtin start worrying more about the hero than the author?

21. See *Speech Genres*, 127, for Bakhtin's discussion of "lack of response."

22. Caryl Emerson, "Word and Image in Dostoevsky's Worlds," in *Freedom and Responsibility in Russian Literature: Essays in Honor of Robert Louis Jackson*, ed. Elizabeth Cheresh Allen and Gary Saul Morson (Evanston, IL: Northwestern University Press, 1995), 253–54.

23. Bakhtin proclaims, "Man is not a final and defined quantity upon which firm calculations can be made; man is free, and can therefore violate any regulating norms which might be

thrust upon him" (PDP, 297). Here, he presents the centripetal force of meaning-making, of unifying and finalizing, as a threat to freedom.

24. Alexis de Tocqueville, *Democracy in America*, trans. Henry Reeve (New York: Schocken Books, 1974), 2:131.

25. Arendt, "What Is Freedom?," 153–54.

26. Berlin, "Two Concepts of Liberty," 167.

27. Gary Saul Morson, *Narrative and Freedom: The Shadows of Time* (New Haven, CT: Yale University Press, 1994), 119.

## Chapter Two

# A Father Begs for His Son's Corpse in the *Iliad*

Dialogic freedom: *a two-sided act*, chosen within a field of unifying and fragmenting forces along a continuum of minimal to maximal layers of knowing that are never final.

Homer's *Iliad* allows us to examine a central feature of dialogic freedom—its two-sidedness—as it is presented in one of the earliest texts of the Western tradition.[1] In doing so, we should note that Bakhtin himself did not identify two-sidedness with the epic. On the contrary, he called Homer's world[2] monologic, dominated by a "valorized epic past" and the "sacrosanct tradition" of the classical Greek heroic vision.[3] In "Epic and Novel," distinguishing this epic vision from the polyphonic world of the novel, Bakhtin described the epic with unappetizing adjectives like "congealed" (14), "ossified" (7), "stilted" (10), or "half-moribund" (14). In "Discourse in the Novel," he described it as "static," "dead" (342), "narrow," "cramped" (266), and "naïve" (334).[4] To him, it was the genre of closedness, by implication the last place we would look for dialogic freedom. True, he left us a loophole in "Discourse in the Novel," where he allowed that "heteroglossia[5] . . . spills over even into the high poetic genres" (383), and I intend to squeeze through this loophole. But we need to respect Bakhtin's apparently dismissive words as an indication of just how strongly he might disagree with the argument I am about to make.

For Bakhtin, epic traditions focused on "heroizing," which he saw as representing the "pre-packaged and unchanging nature of their heroes" (EN, 10). To him the epic hero was closed off from us in a remote world of "peak times," where "everything is finished, already over" (EN, 16). Though Bakhtin meant to provoke idolizing readers who genuflect before the Homeric

25

bard and fail to appreciate the unique accomplishments of modern novels, he loved reading the *Iliad* and *Odyssey,* and he was far from the first to notice that the heroes that populate them, whether Trojan or Greek, all seem to be part of a distant world, larger than life, saturated with shared traditional values of courage, honor, friendship, fame, family, oaths, obligation, and reverence for elders. Compared with the diversity of orientations in Bakhtin's time or today, this archaic world, which was distant even from Homer (who described it centuries after it had disappeared), seems much more unified and stabilized by the centripetal force of shared values. If Bakhtin saw in the epic one singular belief system, so have many others. This does not mean, however, that we need to agree with him that the genre is "ossified" or that "there is no place in the epic for any openendedness, indecision, indeterminacy" (EN, 16). Nor do we need to agree that in terms of ideology "naïve conflictlessness . . . characterizes the epic" (DN, 335). The scene we are about to examine is filled with "openendedness" and is anything but "ossified," as two characters struggle in each other's presence to negotiate internal conflicts within some of their deepest shared values.

The *Iliad* presents a violent world, where warriors routinely kill each other in the name of their shared values. The role of dialogic freedom in this bloody process could be examined scene by scene throughout the work, but one scene in particular throws into relief most clearly the two-sidedness of choice: the encounter between Achilles and Priam, in which the Trojan king begs for the corpse of his son Hector. This scene appears almost at the end of the story, after Hector has been killed in battle by Achilles. Against everyone's advice, King Priam decides to risk the perilous journey behind enemy lines to confront the man who has killed his son and to beg him to release the corpse. This meeting between Priam and Achilles, which is the climax of the *Iliad,* seems at first like a letdown. It presents not a battle between heroes or even a fortress in flames, but negotiations for a funeral. Only when we see what it takes to make this funeral happen do we realize that this negotiation requires the most intense confrontation in the epic. Nicholas Richardson calls it "not the most obvious ending," yet also "the most dramatic moment in the whole of the *Iliad*."[6] For ten years Hector had led the effort to repel the Greek assault on Troy. Only days earlier he was cut down by Achilles, who now spends a good part of his time dragging Hector's body by its heels round and round the tomb of Patroclus, killed in battle by the Trojan prince. The theme of the *Iliad,* the anger of Achilles, is vividly on display , with Hector's head bouncing in the dust behind Achilles' chariot, as Achilles takes his revenge on a corpse. Into this volatile situation comes Hector's father Priam, unarmed, in the dead of night, across enemy lines, past sentries, with a wagonload of treasure to ransom the body of his son. Priam has been urged not to attempt such a feat, because it is highly unlikely that an unguarded man far beyond his warrior years could make it through the encampments of thousands of soldiers, to reach and return from an enemy whose main object is to destroy him.

Yet this is exactly what happens. Chalk it up to the intervention of the gods if you like, since Zeus sends Achilles's mother, the nymph Thetis, to urge her son to accept the ransom and return the body, while Apollo protects the corpse from being shredded as Achilles drags it around, day after day. Zeus also sends his messenger Iris to tell Priam to embark on this mission, and he sends Hermes to accompany and protect the old man—shrouding him in mist when needed, or drugging a sentry. Faced with such blatant interventions, readers often blame fate and the gods for the confrontation between Priam and Achilles and other critical events in the *Iliad*, as if it does not really matter what the human beings in the story want, say, or choose. In the introduction to his translation, Richmond Lattimore suggests another possibility: "We simply do not know how seriously Homer took his Olympian gods, to what extent they are his divinities, or those of his tradition, or those of his audience. . . . But one thing the gods-as-persons of Homer do not do: they do not change human nature. . . . The choices are human; and in the end, despite all divine interferences, the *Iliad* is a story of people."[7] Here, Lattimore emphasizes the importance of human choice, despite the interventions of the gods. In his introduction to the Robert Fagles translation, Bernard Knox elaborates: "These gods. . . are figures symbolic of those aspects of our lives that seem incomprehensible and uncontrollable."[8] If it is passion that sweeps Helen and Paris away, blame Aphrodite; if it is anger, blame Ares; if it is a hurricane, blame Zeus. According to Knox, the Greek deities can be understood literally, metaphorically, or psychologically. The point is that, however we interpret their role, there is still room for human responsibility, which is at the center of the encounter between Achilles and Priam, when the old man begs for his son's corpse.

It is significant that what matters most here is not the personalities of Priam and Achilles but their situations: Achilles's role as the Achaian military leader, whose best friend has been killed by the son of the Trojan king; and Priam's role as the Trojan king whose son led the city's defenses until Achilles killed him. Unlike a novel that opens a door on the personality and psychology of a character—Elizabeth Bennet's irony, Dimitri Karamazov's anxiety, or Humbert Humbert's obsession—the *Iliad* presents characters in terms of their roles: king, lover, warrior, wife, prisoner, father, guest, or host. There are differences between the wily Odysseus and the angry Achilles, but both warriors share the same heroic vision. In fact, all the characters in the *Iliad*, whether Greek or Trojan, make sacrifices to the same gods, speak the same language, and share the same customs about fighting, feasting, and burying the dead. What characters in the *Iliad* say and do arises more from their situations than from their personalities. To put it differently, though living people surely have personalities, the only traces in the *Iliad* of the personalities of the people who are supposed to have lived in the twelfth century BCE are the outlines of a few key decisions and actions, passed from one rhapsode to another and eventually written down, revised, translated, and read by us several millennia later.

Thus it is that we can look at the encounter between Priam and Achilles not in terms of their personalities but in terms of the roles they occupy at the moment they meet. Achilles is the chief Greek warrior, the only son of a mortal and a deity, a friend to Patroclus, a host to Priam, and an angry, dangerous man. Priam is the Trojan king, a father, a husband, a guest, a suppliant, and an old man who was once a great warrior. The meeting between them is a function of the intersection between the perspectives entailed in the various roles they occupy. Whether the roles are public (king, chief warrior), private (father, son), or emotional (a grieving man, or an angry one), the characters in the *Iliad* are presented to us in terms of the perspectives on the world these roles invite. Whereas a hero in a Dostoevsky novel might do something out of character, capricious, or entirely unexpected, Homer's characters make their choices within the range of possibilities suggested by the values in their culture and their roles within it. Achilles can choose to return Hector's body or not to return it, but not according to whim.[9]

## BEING HEARD

Twelve days after Hector's death, Priam draws his wagonload of treasures through the Greek defenses, to the tent of Achilles, where he throws himself at the feet of his enemy:

> The majestic king of Troy slipped past the rest
> and kneeling down beside Achilles, clasped his knees
> and kissed his hands, those terrible, man-killing hands
> that had slaughtered Priam's many sons in battle.[10]

Here, Priam is the "majestic king," with the public function of representing the people of Troy to Achilles, who also has a public role as the preeminent Greek warrior. Whatever else this encounter will be, it will be a confrontation between leaders with well-established public identities, who speak from the perspectives of those public roles. Priam does not enter with a king's ceremony, however. Instead, he assumes the traditional posture of suppliant, kneeling at his enemy's feet, clasping his knees. Throughout the *Iliad,* people in this pose are routinely decapitated and only occasionally spared.[11] It would be as easy as snapping a twig for Achilles to break the old man's neck. Simone Weil registers the full force of the danger in this encounter, between one who has the power to snuff out the other's life, and the other, who must fear at every moment that it might be his last. She talks about the power of might "to transform man into a thing" and calls this power "double . . . it cuts both ways; it petrifies differently but equally the souls of those who suffer it, and those who wield it."[12] Here, Priam must make a heroic effort, not just to influence Achilles, who might be turned to stone by the power of a young warrior over his elderly guest, but to master his own petrifying fear, moment by moment. Norman Postelthwaite calls Priam's kiss "the supreme act of forgiveness and reconciliation,"[13] but it is much more. Focusing on the darker possibilities, Michael Lynn-George speaks of "the ambivalent complexities of reconciliation and repudiation" in this scene, as well as the paradox of "the separation of shared grief as each mourns the losses which bring them together and keep them apart."[14]

We need to examine these complexities. Kneeling before Achilles, Priam asks him to remember his own father, Peleus, no doubt plagued by the warlords around him, defenseless, while his warrior son, his only child, spends a decade laying siege to a distant city. As desperate as Peleus must be, at least he can rejoice to hear from time to time that his son is alive. Priam explains that he can never again rejoice in this way, but he can hope to take his son's body home to bury. He asks Achilles to remember his own father, pity Priam as a father, and release Hector's body. Priam goes so far as to kiss Achilles' hands, saying, "I have endured what no one on earth has ever done before—/ I put my lips to the hands of the man who killed my son."[15] In this act we see not only that Homer has given Priam a gesture to perform that he has given no other suppliant in the *Iliad* or *Odyssey*, but also that Priam is presented as aware that his action is unique. He is aware that Achilles will register it as unique, though within the context of the traditional suppliant who grasps his knees. Priam carefully balances the traditional with the unnerving. The effect on Achilles is immediate:

> Those words stirred within Achilles a deep desire
> to grieve for his own father. Taking the old man's hand
> he gently moved him back. And overpowered by memory
> both men gave way to their grief. (XXIV, 592–95)

In this volatile situation, when the sudden appearance of the enemy king could lead to carnage, Priam is able to touch Achilles with the shared value of the bond between father and son, which, as Weil has noted, for the moment trumps violence. They weep together, and when "Achilles had had his fill of tears" (XXIV, 600), he invites Priam to rise and sit in a chair, while Achilles laments their mutual sorrows. The anger of a warrior is held at bay by the grief of a son sympathizing with his own father, which allows Achilles to empathize with Priam in his loss of a son. The tears of Achilles are also for Patroclus, whose death he now registers, perhaps for the first time, as a cause for grief, rather than anger.

Yet, the balance of empathy is delicate, the anger of Achilles never far from the surface. Emboldened by his host's shared tears, Priam insists on the point of his mission:

> Don't make me sit on a chair, Achilles, Prince,
> not while Hector lies uncared-for in your camp!
> Give him back to me, now, no more delay—
> I must see my son with my eyes.
> Accept the ransom I bring you, a king's ransom!
> Enjoy it, all of it—return to your native land,
> safe and sound . . . since now you've spared my life. (648–54)

Priam's insistence awakens the wrath of his host, who struggles with himself and warns his guest:

> No more, old man, don't tempt my wrath, not now!
> My own mind's made up to give you back your son. . . .
> So don't anger me now. Don't stir my raging heart still more.
> Or under my own roof I may not spare your life, old man—
> suppliant that you are—may break the laws of Zeus! (656–57, 667–69)

Achilles is internally at war with himself; the forces for piety—respecting a father's grief, fulfilling the host's role, obeying the gods' laws—chafe against the warrior's desire for revenge and his capacity to enact it in the blink of an eye.

There is also the darker, more chaotic force of rage itself, which lies within us all, and threatens to obliterate all sense of order and self-control. Rage is Achilles' special nemesis. The more Priam calls Achilles' attention to the identity of this particular corpse, the more Achilles wants to hook it back up to his chariot, drag it by the heels, and watch its head bounce. At this moment he feels the tenuousness of his commitment to follow "the laws of Zeus," the god of hospitality, who calls on the host to protect his guest, on the son to respect the grief of a father, and on the powerful to heed the plea of a supplicant. One flash of anger could crush Priam. Homer makes us feel the intensity and fragility of this highly charged equilibrium. Achilles is aware of the problem himself, as he frets about Priam seeing the corpse of his son before it has been properly prepared:

> He feared that, overwhelmed by the sight of Hector,
> wild with grief, Priam might let his anger flare
> and Achilles might fly into fresh rage himself,
> cut the old man down and break the laws of Zeus. (684–87)

So Achilles convinces Priam to wait until morning to leave, and he feasts him and beds him down outside his tent, where the other Greek soldiers are less likely to discover him. Before dawn, the old man slips away with his son's royally dressed body and the pledge of a twelve-day truce, which will allow time for Hector's funeral ceremonies before the Trojan War resumes.

Who is responsible for the success of this mission? The retrieval of the body, up in the air until the final moment, is coauthored by Zeus, who has forged the laws of hospitality and piety and has sent several gods to intervene between Priam and Achilles; by Achilles, who must make the hard choices to break or follow "the laws of Zeus"; and by Priam, who must establish the father-son connection with Achilles, then insist on it, though not enough to unleash his host's rage. The challenge here for Priam is to extricate the body of Hector, pack it up, and cart it home, without reminding Achilles too much that Hector is the warrior who killed the man Achilles loved. Both men are acutely aware of the dangerousness of the situation and the difficulty of their roles as they speak with each other, anticipating what each other will think, or say, or do. The words they coauthor respond to the gods and the traditions that are their superaddressees, anticipate the receptions they expect from each other, respond to the receptions they get from each other, and create the action they take together, returning Hector's body for burial.

## DIALOGIC FREEDOM IN THE *ILIAD*

This encounter between Priam and Achilles, besides thrilling readers, offers us a window into understanding the nature of dialogic freedom as a two-sided act, chosen within a field of forces for unity and chaos. To begin with, the conversation between Priam and Achilles is the two-sided act of two public leaders. Priam is not merely transmitting a message to Achilles, communicating information from inside his own mind to another's. The receptivity of Achilles is an equal factor in Priam's act of speech. This is why the Trojan king begins with the traditional posture of the suppliant, kneeling at the foot of the preeminent warrior, embracing his knees, begging for mercy. In a Greek epic, it is bad form not to hear out a suppliant, whether or not his or her request is granted. Any Greek hero who fails to heed "the gods" or "the laws of the gods"—a superaddressee that demands respect for the suppliant—is asking for trouble. If Priam could not expect that the shared values of the culture would incline Achilles to listen to the kneeling suppliant, he would not have used the suppliant's posture to preface his plea. But he knows that he and Achilles are both answerable to the gods. He chooses to begin by kneeling and embracing Achilles's knees, under the expectation that Achilles will listen. Thus before anyone says one word, Achilles and the gods coauthor Priam's first freely chosen act.

Once Priam speaks, he begs for mercy not for himself but for the corpse of his son. Achilles will listen to what Priam has to say only if Priam can get

Achilles to think about his own father, Peleus, in far-off Phthia. Once again, they have a shared superaddressee, this time in the form of familial piety. Priam must make Achilles imagine the anxiety of old Peleus, waiting ten years for every shred of news that his warrior son is still alive, and the indignities the man must be suffering at the hands of neighboring warlords who take advantage of his frailty in the absence of this only child. Because Priam is so focused on how Achilles will be listening to his words, he is able to come up with this powerful approach, which Achilles coauthors by being receptive to it. Priam thus adds an epistemological layer to the suppliant role by getting Achilles to remember his own father, then draw the connection to Priam as a suffering father (rather than enemy king).

There is no guarantee, however, that this approach will work, because there is a competing perspective that draws the attention of Achilles and threatens to undermine Priam's project. As much as Achilles is a loving son, he is also a warrior and an angry man. At any moment, he might take revenge on the father of the enemy who killed his best friend. Priam is aware of the warrior perspective, not to mention the deep reservoirs of rage, both of which compete in Achilles with empathy for a grieving father. He also knows that Achilles shares this awareness of conflicting perspectives, as well as a sense of his own anger. The challenge will be to trump killer with father: to get Achilles to see his killer role (which cannot be erased from his consciousness) as secondary to a more benign father/son relationship. To do this, Priam must take the risk of drawing Achilles's attention to the killer in himself, even as Priam asks him to show mercy. Thus it is that Priam says, "I put my lips to the hands of the man who killed my son." The killer role gets reframed from the position of the vulnerable old father who loves his son so much that he is willing even to kiss the hands of the man who killed that son. The father/son and killer perspectives merge, but the former takes precedence. Priam makes Achilles register just how hard it is for the father to kiss the hands of his son's killer. This gesture expresses a love worth respecting, worth deferring to, in spite of a warrior role that would turn the enemy's father into just another corpse. Within Achilles, these two entirely different centripetal perspectives compete to unify his thinking. Priam's job is to keep Achilles focused not on the concept of warrior as avenger, but on the concept of father—the young warrior's own father in particular, and Priam as a father—thereby helping him succumb not to anger but to grief. As Priam does this, the response anticipated or received from Achilles coauthors his every move. Achilles and Priam speak and act freely, but always in response to, or anticipating, a response from each other.

As they negotiate the terms of the release—the corpse will be cleaned and dressed in fine robes, Priam will have twelve days to bury it and return to war, Achilles will keep the treasure brought as ransom—they reach mutual agreements that benefit both sides. The effects will be global, with consequences for all the people of Troy, as well as their Greek attackers. The Trojans will be able to bury their most noble hero, while the Greeks will gain wealth and see their main warrior liberated from an obsession. This negotiation would not have been possible if both Priam and Achilles had not been able to navigate the the most subtle layers of each other's perspectives. It also would not have been possible if both leaders had not respected the enormous destructive potential of the anger of Achilles, a force for chaos that threatens all centripetal attempts at order, even within the world of war. Destruction is limitless chaos, but the warrior's destruction is limited by, confined to, war and the rules of engagement. The anger of Achilles is useful in war when unleashed on the enemy, but it is also a threat to the warrior life precisely because it challenges the discipline of war. Anger can lead either to the warrior withdrawing from battle (which dominates the first half of the *Iliad*), or to the warrior being trapped in a repetitive ritual of revenge (dragging the corpse behind his chariot). In either case, anger undermines the forces for order in war. By getting Achilles to imagine war from a father's perspective and release the corpse, Priam not only succeeds in retrieving his son's body but also helps Achilles cope with the chaotic force of his own anger, so that he can be free to return to the battlefield.

Thus, the moment when Achilles releases Hector's body to Priam for burial is one in which Achilles and Priam coauthor each other's choices. Both in words and in deeds their freedom is dialogic, in that it is a two-sided act, chosen within a field of unifying and chaotic forces along a continuum of perspectives within the ancient Greek heroic world. Its two-sidedness encompasses not just Priam and Achilles, who coauthor the release of Hector's body, but also Zeus and the gods, who are superaddressees for both heroes as they seek to make hard choices. In this process, filial piety is the centripetal force that prevails against the competing ideal of warrior aggression and against the more directly centrifugal force of rage. That Priam has the flexibility to imagine Achilles's love for his father, and uses this epistemological mobility to help Achilles see things from Priam's fatherly perspective, is a significant element of Priam's success. Adopting the terminology of Bakhtin's early philosophical manuscripts, we could say that Priam in this encounter is able to see behind Achilles well enough to help him fill out and "consummate" an identity that is more loving son than angry warrior (AH, 23). Priam uses the "excess" of his seeing to "render the other complete precisely in those respects in which he cannot complete himself by himself" (24). In the process, Priam must "empathize or project" himself "into this other human being, see his world . . . as he sees this world . . . and then, after returning to" his "own place, 'fill in' the hero's 'horizon'" (25). This "consummation" is quite precarious, however, as both men understand. Priam "authors" Achilles as "hero" just long enough to retrieve Hector's body. In this encounter, both Priam and Achilles engage in "active empathizing"[16] and "sympathetic understanding" (AH, 102), which I discuss in chapter 1, running no risk, however, of the "pure empathizing" (TPA 15–16) that Bakhtin rejected as "fruitless and senseless" (AH, 26), and that could have caused them to lose themselves in each other's perspectives.

The complexity of the two-sided coauthorship of dialogic freedom presented at the climax of the *Iliad* challenges Bakhtin's centripetal conclusion that "there is no place in the epic for any openendedness, indecision, indeterminacy" (EN, 16). In a brilliant reading of this scene, Michael Lynn-George sees it as part of the "contested closure" of the poem (244), whose last line Lattimore translates: "Such was their burial of Hektor, breaker of horses." According to Lynn-George, "the fiction of closure breaks apart once more in frictions which keep the text open" (248). When Achilles attempts to console Priam for the loss of his son, "the speech is also a recognition of the inconsolable" (250). In the end, they bury Hector, but "the text does not stage a final, full revelation of meaning" (252). Rather, it "combines a sense of finality with the awareness of what is still to come" (255), of what is not included in the *Iliad*: the death of Achilles and the destruction of Troy. Just how open-ended the scene between Priam and Achilles is, in terms of the possibilities that each participant weighed, considered, anticipated, feared, and responded to, becomes horrifyingly clear when we consider the creative reception and reading this encounter got from Virgil centuries later.

## A DIFFERENT OUTCOME

At every moment in this encounter between Priam and Achilles, Homer makes us register that the outcome could be far different, that in the shadow of Achilles's decision to send Hector's body home with Priam, lay another, darker alternative. This thought was not lost on Virgil when he decided to write an epic for his own time, in Latin instead of Greek, to glorify Rome. Based on the *Iliad* and the *Odyssey*, the *Aeneid* imitates Homer both in subject matter and in form. Far from being an oral composition-in-performance, though, it was painstakingly written out first in prose, then in poetry, a project that was not quite complete when Virgil died in 19 BCE. Unlike Homer, who shuns presenting the fall of Troy at the end of the *Iliad* in favor of a funeral, Virgil describes in detail the fire that destroyed the city and the bloodbath that finished it off. Troy's demise is told by the Trojan hero Aeneas, who has fled the flames, carrying his father and his household gods, in order to fulfill his destiny to establish Rome. His audience, which listens to the horrors of the final collapse, includes the Carthaginian queen Dido, who is in the process of falling in love with him, largely because of his ability to tell this story.

Aeneas explains that after the Greek warriors burst from the bowels of the Trojan horse to lay waste to the city, fires rage and the Trojans themselves pull down the walls of their palaces to crush their attackers. When it becomes apparent that the ten-year war is about to end with the destruction of Troy, Priam takes refuge with his family in the upper reaches of his palace, where the household gods are kept on the altar stone. The king is in the process of throwing on his armor, "long unused,/ across his shoulders, tottering with age,"[17] when his wife Hecuba dissuades him:

> This is no time for such defense and help,
> not even were my Hector here himself.
> Come near and pray: this altar shall yet save
> us all, or you shall die together with us. (II, 701–4)

Whereas in the *Iliad* Priam persisted in his quest, despite Hecuba's pleas to desist, here he bows to her wishes. He joins her "upon the sacred seat" just in time to see their son Polites enter the chamber, frantically fleeing the son of Achilles, Neoptolemus (also called Pyrrhus). Achilles is now dead, struck down by an arrow from the bow of Priam's son Paris, who hit Achilles in the vulnerable spot above his heel. His goddess mother had held him by the heels as a babe, when she dipped him headfirst in the waters of immortality, leaving that spot untouched by the waters. This detail of the story was widely known among Greeks and Romans, though only obliquely referred to by either Homer or Virgil. At any rate, in the *Aeneid*, Pyrrhus is now intent on avenging his father's death by killing as many of Priam's offspring as possible, and, if the occasion arises, Priam himself.

Aeneas's narrative of what follows not only seduces Dido, but it allows Virgil to suggest why a Trojan prince who is Hector's cousin would choose not to martyr himself in Troy, but rather to round up his father, wife, and child, and flee. With the breathlessness of an eyewitness,[18] Aeneas puts us in the middle of the action:

> But then Polites, one of Priam's sons
> who had escaped from Pyrrhus' slaughter, down
> long porticoes, past enemies and arrows,
> races, wounded, across the empty courts.
> But after him, and hot to thrust, is Pyrrhus;
> now, even now he clutches, closing in;
> he presses with his shaft until at last
> Polites falls before his parents' eyes,
> within their presence; he pours out his life
> in streams of blood. Though in the fist of death,
> at this, Priam does not spare voice or wrath;
> "If there is any goodness in the heavens
> to oversee such acts, for this offense
> and outrage may you find your fitting thanks
> and proper payment from the gods, for you

have made me see the murder of my son,
defiled a father's face with death. Achilles—
you lie to call him father—never dealt
with Priam so—and I, his enemy;
for he had shame before the claims and trust
that are a suppliant's. He handed back
for burial the bloodless corpse of Hector
and sent me off in safety to my kingdom."
The old man spoke; his feeble spear flew off—
harmless; the hoarse bronze beat it back at once;
it dangled, useless now, from the shield's boss.
And Pyrrhus: "Carry off these tidings; go
and bring this message to my father, son
of Peleus; and remember, let him know
my sorry doings, how degenerate
is Neoptolemus. Now die." This said,
he dragged him to the very altar stone,
with Priam shuddering and slipping in
the blood that streamed from his own son. And Pyrrhus
with his left hand clutched tight the hair of Priam;
His right hand drew the glistening blade, and then
he buried it hilt-high in the king's side. (707–43)

On display here are the same Homeric values that were shared by the Greeks and Trojans: respect for the gods, family, father/son relationships and obligations of the powerful to the suppliant. These are the very values that Aeneas will transport with him when he escapes the flames of Troy to found a new civilization. Once again, Priam is also the suppliant before a wrathful enemy. But where the old king was able to gain a hearing from Achilles in the *Iliad*, here (weeks later in the story, centuries later in the telling of it) Pyrrhus is deaf to his pleas. The impieties pile up as the son of Achilles kills a child before his parents' eyes, then drags the father through his son's blood to slaughter him on the altar of the gods.

Why is it that the son's treatment of Priam is so different from his father's? To begin with, the situation has changed dramatically. Whereas in the *Iliad* Priam made his way into Achilles's camp during a lull in the action, this encounter between Priam and Pyrrhus comes in the heat of battle, with the ten-year assault on Troy on the threshold of success. Pyrrhus has every reason to want to be the warrior to clinch the victory. Also, although Priam can be presumed to have witnessed Hector's death from the parapets of Troy, as Hector and Achilles fought before the city gates, he had time after that death to plan an approach to Achilles before actually encountering him in his tent. The present slaughter of Polites, only a few feet away, within the most sacred chamber of the palace, leaves no time for any planning, and it unleashes in Priam not a suppliant's plea but a father's curse as he calls down upon Pyrrhus "proper payment from the gods." He also invokes the father's shame of a dead Achilles. Polites's death elicits not a kiss for the killing hands, a unique and arresting gesture, but the feeble flight of a harmless spear, which must seem to Pyrrhus almost laughable. Priam has faced an unspeakable outrage, and his anger does nothing to deflect Pyrrhus from his murderous intent.

It is as if Virgil has Homer's text open before him, where Achilles ponders what might happen if Priam were to be overwhelmed by the sight of his dead son, flare with anger, and unleash the rage of the Greek warrior:

> . . . overwhelmed by the sight of Hector,
> wild with grief, Priam might let his anger flare
> and Achilles might fly into fresh rage himself,
> cut the old man down and break the laws of Zeus. (*Iliad*, XXIV, 684–87)

Centuries later, Virgil gives a local habitation and a name to the thoughts of Achilles, as his own son dares to do what he hesitated to imagine. As Priam's anger feeds the anger of Achilles's son, Virgil shows that anger, as well as grief, is a two-sided act. He also shows that in the openendedness of conflict, the tension between two competing perspectives—respect for a father and thirst for revenge—can resolve itself in the direction of revenge. Even as Priam tries to remind Pyrrhus of the earlier encounter with his father, which led to the "burial of the bloodless corpse of Hector," Pyrrhus readies himself to drag a father through his son's blood. Pyrrhus glories in this defilement, hurling at the soon-to-be-dead Priam a sarcastic message for the shadow of Achilles in the underworld: "let him know/ my sorry doings, how degenerate." Just before the slaughter of Priam, Pyrrhus shows contempt for the underworld, the dead, the gods, the family, and the decency that spares the suppliant. These are the superaddressees which Priam and Achilles shared, to which Achilles felt answerable. These are the superaddresees that Priam knew he could rely on Achilles taking into account as he weighed the relative merits of hearing Priam out or snapping his neck.

Pyrrhus is not unaware of these invisible presences. He has just chosen to disregard or even defy them. They are not *his* superaddressees. This complete breakdown of values is registered in the deafness of Pyrrhus to Priam's call for him to honor the "the claims and trust/ that are a suppliant's." This lack of receptivity, on vivid display, convinces Priam in advance that any plea for mercy will not be heard. Thus Priam curses Pyrrhus instead of kissing his hands, fanning his anger rather than quelling it. Their exchange is still a two-sided act, yet dysfunctional. It shows how dialogic freedom breaks down when the speaker and listener are deaf to each other's words, when they refuse to see things from each other's perspectives, and when speaking becomes not an effort to communicate but an announcement of the end of communication. If the enemy does not register the humanity of the opponent, dialogue, to the extent that it takes place, only reinforces hostilities, promotes violence, and signals domination.

Pyrrhus is free in the sense that he exerts his will over Priam. He turns his back, however, on the kind of dialogic freedom coauthored by Priam and Achilles in the *Iliad*. He embodies instead the destructive might that Simone Weil describes when she says, "He who possesses strength moves in an atmosphere which offers him no resistance. Nothing in the human element surrounding him is of a nature to induce, between the intention and the act, that brief interval where thought may lodge" (163). Weil draws our attention to the dialogic deafness of the warrior who feels no need to anticipate, listen to, or respond to any voice that might offer resistance. Pyrrhus hardens himself in the midst of the "human element surrounding him." To the extent that his encounter with Priam is dialogic, Priam coauthors Pyrrhus's rage by insulting him; but the encounter really is not very dialogic at all, because Pyrrhus, unlike his father in the *Iliad*, appears to give only perfunctory thought to what Priam is saying. Pyrrhus refuses to listen not only to Priam's call to live up to the memory of Achilles, but also to the superaddressees of tradition and the gods that are part of his culture and that Priam is trying to invoke.

For Aeneas, the point of this story is not the death of Priam, or even the destruction of Troy, but the necessity to avoid the breakdown of civilization personified by Pyrrhus, who has become a force only for destruction. Seeing this carnage, which he is powerless to prevent, Aeneas bolts for his father's palace, where he will rescue him and his household gods, to found a civilization beyond the burning walls of Troy. His decision to flee is a response to the encounter between Pyrrhus and Priam and hence is coauthored by them. Where Homer gave us dialogic freedom under explosive circumstances, Virgil emphasizes the fragility of that freedom. He emphasizes the extent to which it depends both on people's efforts to articulate, acknowledge, and respect shared values, and on their ability to empathize enough to anticipate, respond to, and coauthor each other's choices. If dialogic freedom is a two-sided act that involves deliberation from multiple perspectives, within a field of forces for unity and chaos, Homer emphasizes the unity forged through shared values, while Virgil, in his creative reception to Homer's story, and in his meticulous reading and retelling of it, emphasizes the chaos those values hold at bay. When all efforts to coauthor choice break down, the alternatives reduce to destroying a way of life, illustrated by the death of Priam and the fall of Troy, or embracing a vocation to establish a new civilization, illustrated by the flight of Aeneas from Troy. For both Homer and Virgil, dialogic freedom is a matter of life and death.

# PROTOCOLS FOR READING

The discussion above reflects my attempt to read one scene from the *Iliad* for and with dialogic freedom. I read *for* dialogic freedom in the sense that I am on the lookout for situations that present the complexities of the process of coauthoring choice experienced by speakers in relationship both to each other and to the superaddressees they answer to. This chapter is intended to be evidence of how one might begin to do that by focusing on a key element of the definition of dialogic freedom as a two-sided act in the encounter between Priam and Achilles as they negotiate the conditions of burial for Hector's corpse. I read *with* dialogic freedom in the sense that, at every moment in my reading I make choices that are coauthored by the responses I anticipate from editors, readers, students, colleagues, and so on. My choices are also coauthored by the theoretical traditions that have shaped me as a reader (originally new criticism, then political theory, Bakhtinian analysis, and certain elements of cultural analysis, new historicism, deconstruction, feminism, etc.). In this process I am also answerable to superaddressees like honesty and "making a contribution." Just as characters in an epic experience the push and pull of a complex array of unifying and chaotic forces in the decision-making process, so do readers.

In *Protocols of Reading*, Robert Scholes describes some of these forces. He quotes Jacques Derrida in *Positions*, where he argues that "reading is transformational. . . . But this transformation cannot be executed however one wishes. It requires protocols of reading."[19] Here, we see the tension for Derrida between the centrifugal force of reading "however one wishes" and the centripetal force of "protocols of reading," which limit one's choices. Derrida concluded, "I have not yet found any [protocols] that satisfy me," suggesting that the search for the right methods is not easy. Listing dozens of phrases from Derrida's *Speech and Phenomena*, *Grammatology*, and *Positions*, all of which contain the word "rigor," Scholes nevertheless tries to identify one of Derrida's protocols of reading. Scholes argues that "rigor is Derrida's talisman against relativism and historicism" (86). The centripetal force of "rigor" resists the centrifugal force of "anything goes" or "it all depends." According to Scholes, for Derrida reading also involves a tension between the centripetal force of "doubling commentary," which seeks to "recapitulate the meaning that is already given in a text," and the centrifugal force of a "critical reading" that "produces a new signifying structure." It is a real balancing act, because the rigorous critical reading includes the respectful "doubling commentary" as a "guardrail" (77).

In his own search for protocols of reading, Scholes focuses on the distinction between centripetal and centrifugal forces: "Centripetal reading conceives of a text in terms of an original intention located at the center of that text. . . . Centrifugal reading, on the other hand, sees the life of a text as occurring along its circumference, which is consistently expanding, encompassing new possibilities of meaning" (8). He goes on to say that "our notion of reading depends upon some irreducible minimum of recuperation or centripetality in the process of generating meaning" (60) and that "we have no choice but to read both rigorously and exhorbitantly, centripetally and centrifugally at the same time" (88). Applying these distinctions to my readings above of the *Iliad* and the *Aeneid*, we might say that a reading of the *Iliad* that focuses on Priam as the successful suppliant of Achilles (a reading shared by virtually all commentaries on the *Iliad*) cannot be repeated as is once we read Virgil's creative reception and reading of the scene. Rereading this scene from the *Iliad* under the influence of Virgil, we feel an increased sense of dread in the face of the potential explosiveness of Achilles's wrath. We also gain a new respect for Achilles's effort at self-control, which allowed Priam to retrieve his son's corpse. We also imagine the ways in which this story, with a different, more bloody outcome, contributes to Virgil's agenda for heroizing Rome and its mythic founder. In any case, reading Virgil's reading of Homer makes us into different readers of the *Iliad*, as it expands the work for us as a text, "encompassing new possibilities of meaning."

Reading with dialogic freedom encompasses both the centripetal force of a particular theme, story line, or intention, and the centrifugal force of various competing theoretical orientations, each with its own internal centripetal forces. Reading in this way also involves taking into consideration the centrifugal forces of the different circumstances of different readers, of the endless rereadings possible for a single reader under changing circumstances, and of approaches to reading that can themselves be centrifugal. Within this force field of centripetal and centrifugal forces, a reader must choose how to read.

Under these circumstances, reading for and with dialogic freedom becomes a protocol for reading that we can test throughout this book. Just as dialogic freedom ultimately calls for the ability to navigate diverse epistemological layers of meaning in the perspectives of others, so reading with dialogic freedom requires cultivating the ability to navigate the veritable sea of diverse theoretical approaches to reading currently available. It also requires that we hold on to whatever "guardrails" we can find to give us the bearings we need to be the kind of reader Kafka imagines "crouching in the corner." Scholes quotes T. S. Eliot's letter to Stephen Spender in 1935, in which he says, "You have to give yourself up, and then recover yourself, and the third moment is having something to say, before you have wholly forgotten both surrender and recovery" (78). Here, Eliot enters into a dialogue with Bakhtin's distinction between "author" and "hero." The "author" must empathize, but not too much, with the "hero," entering into the hero's perspective, then returning from it to represent it. Reading for and with dialogic freedom, we seek to enter the field of centripetal and centrifugal forces that circulate about and through a work of literature, but not travel too far into it, so that we can return to ourselves with something to say.

## NOTES

1. Among the questions not directly addressed in my discussion will be whether there was a single Homeric bard (or later, a single writer), who was responsible for an authoritative version of the *Iliad* (the position of the "Unitarians"), or whether "fifty or more Hellenic bards over five hundred years on two continents perhaps composed this epic," as Donald Lateiner suggests in "The *Iliad*: An Unpredictable Classic," in *The Cambridge Companion to Homer*, ed. Robert Fowler (London: Cambridge University Press, 2004), 13. John Miles Foley express-es a position shared by many "Analysts" when he argues, "We would do better to understand Homer as an anthropomorphisation of the epic tradition, a name for the art and practice of epic poetry." "Epic as Genre," in *Cambridge Companion*, 186. Gregory Nagy argues that the *Iliad* belongs to an oral tradition that called for "composition-in-performance." *Homeric Questions* (Austin: University of Texas Press, 1996), 33. This tradition was the subject of Milman Parry's revolutionary *The Making of Homeric Verse* (1967). According to Nagy, through a process that began orally in the eighth century BCE, involving "text-fixation" during the Panathenaic games of 550–450 BCE (40) and then "'standardization'. . . after around 150 BCE," as a consequence of the emerging Athenian book trade (97), more-or-less uniform manuscripts emerged that would become the basis for all modern versions of the *Iliad* (42). According to him, "what we have really admired all along is not the author, about whom we never did really know anything historical, but the Homeric poems themselves" (111). According to John Peradotto, more recent approaches to reading the *Iliad* regard both "Unitarians" and "Analysts" as "backward-facing," because they "look to recover original truth or original authorial intent or original audience response as governing protocols that will yield readings more or less impervious to change," as opposed to "forward-facing" approaches, which affirm "the large part played by the reader in the production of meaning" and harbor "an abiding skepticism about immutable meanings." John Peradotto, "Modern Theoretical Approaches to Homer," in *A New Companion to Homer*, ed. Ian Morris and Barry Powell (New York: Brill, 1997), 382. For "forward-facing" readers like Peradotto, the "Homeric question" takes a back seat to the receptions of the *Iliad* over time and in time. Without attempting to take a position in this debate, and recognizing that the word "Homer" might refer to a person, many people, or a whole tradition, for the sake of brevity and convenience I will refer to Homer as if he were the creator of the *Iliad* and *Odyssey*.

2. See note 1. Gregory Nagy in *Homeric Questions* is particularly annoyed by people who refer to "Homer's world," as if there were one Homer, or one such world. This practice "risks the flattening out of the process of oral poetic creation" (20). Bakhtin did just this.

3. Mikhail Bakhtin, "Epic and Novel," in *The Dialogic Imagination: Four Essays by M. M. Bakhtin*, ed. Michael Holquist; trans. Caryl Emerson and Michael Holquist (Austin: University of Texas Press, 1981), 16–17. Citations to "Epic and Novel" are to this text, with the abbrevia-tion EN.

4. Mikhail Bakhtin, "Discourse in the Novel," in *The Dialogic Imagination*. Citations to "Discourse in the Novel" are to this text, with the abbreviation DN.

5. Bakhtin defines "heteroglossia" as "specific points of view on the world" (DN, 291).

6. Nicholas Richardson, *The Iliad: A Commentary*, vol. 6, Books 21–24 (Cambridge, UK: Cambridge University Press, 1993), 272, 323.

7. Homer, *The Iliad,* trans. Richmond Lattimore (Chicago: University of Chicago Press, 1951), 54.

8. Bernard Knox, "Introduction," in *The Iliad*, trans. Robert Fagles (New York: Penguin, 1990), 42.

9. Here my dispute with Bakhtin, or in a sense his dispute with himself, about whether or not the epic is an "ossified" genre, is clearest. In "Author and Hero in Aesthetic Activity," Bakhtin discusses the "classical hero" as a function of the roles he plays, and he goes on to

conclude that these roles totally determine him. "His entire life is given, given in the sense of what it might ultimately achieve." He is "motivated not by his moral free will, but by his determinate being." In *Art and Answerability: Early Philosophical Essays by M. M. Bakhtin*, ed. Michael Holquist and Vadim Liapunov; trans. Vadim Liapunov (Austin: University of Texas Press, 1990), 176. Further citations to "Author and Hero" are to this text with the abbreviation AH. This characterization of the "classical hero" as unfree is for Bakhtin an aesthetic issue, involving the already finished nature of people described as classical heroes, from the perspective of the author. From the internal perspective of the hero himself, his life is not yet finished, and from this perspective "an ethical determination defines a given human being from the standpoint of what-is-yet-to-be accomplished" (AH, 226). The hero can feel himself to be free with regard to decisions not yet made, while the author, looking back on history (or on an oral tradition), presumably knows what those decisions will be. My discussion focuses on Homer's presentation in this scene of "what-is-yet-to-be accomplished" from the characters' perspectives, which is an open question, depending on a host of variables that must be delicately balanced by both Priam and Achilles. The outcome that from the perspective of centuries later seems inevitable (since it *did* happen) might not have happened. Homer implies that in the "sideshadow"—a term coined by Gary Saul Morson in *Narrative and Freedom: The Shadows of Time* (New Haven, CT: Yale University Press, 1994)—of the decision to send Hector's body home with Priam, lies the corpse of Priam in the dust beside his son.

10. Homer, *Iliad*, trans. Lattimore, XXIV, 559–62.

11. Nicholas Richardson points out that although the pose of suppliant is common in the *Iliad*, this is the only place in the Homeric epics where the suppliant kisses the hands of the person in addition to grasping his knees. The line is sometimes translated instead, "to reach with my hand to the mouth of my son's killer." Nicholas Richardson, *The Iliad*, 326–27.

12. Simone Weil, "The *Iliad*, Poem of Might," in *The Simone Weil Reader*, ed. George A. Panichas (New York: David McKay Company, 1977), 173–207.

13. Norman Postelthwaite, *Homer's Iliad: A Commentary on the Translation of Richmond Lattimore* (Exeter, UK: University of Exeter Press, 2000), 302.

14. Michael Lynn-George, *Epos: Word, Narrative, and the Iliad* (Atlantic Highlands, NJ: Humanities Press International, 1988), 237, 243–44.

15. Homer, *Iliad*, trans. Fagles, XXIV, 590–91. Further citations of the *Iliad* are to this text.

16. Mikhail Bakhtin, *Toward a Philosophy of the Act*, ed. Vadim Liapunov and Michael Holquist; trans. Vadim Liapunov (Austin: University of Texas, 1993), 15. Citations to *Toward a Philosophy of the Act* are to this edition, with the abbreviation TPA.

17. Virgil, *The Aeneid of Virgil*, trans. Allen Mandelbaum (New York: Bantam, 1971), II, 684–685. Citations to *The Aeneid* are to this text.

18. Here Aeneas fills the role not of warrior but of rhapsode or epic singer, except that instead of doing what Demodocus is praised by Odysseus for doing in the Fagles translation of the *Odyssey* (singing "as if you were there yourself or heard from one who was"), he sings as one who really was "there himself" (though presumably not in a position to help Priam). Homer, *The Odyssey*, trans. Robert Fagles (New York: Penguin, 1996), I, 374–76. Andrew Ford describes the "distinctive rhetorical stance of the poet toward the audience" as that of one who has "eyewitness knowledge from the Muses." "Epic as Genre," in *A New Companion to Homer*, ed. Ian Morris and Barry Powell (New York: Brill, 1997), 409, 406. In the case of Aeneas, no Muses were needed.

19. Robert Scholes, *Protocols of Reading* (New Haven, CT: Yale University Press, 1991), 78.

*Chapter Three*

# Passion and Freedom in Dante's *Inferno*

Dialogic freedom: *a two-sided act*, chosen within a field of unifying and fragmenting forces along a continuum of minimal to maximal layers of knowing that are never final.

Canto V of Dante's *Inferno* allows us to examine in greater depth the coauthorship of dialogic freedom as a two-sided act. Here, Dante the pilgrim[1] encounters the loquacious lover Francesca and coauthors her decision to speak by being receptive to what she has to say. The occasion for her death—murder by her enraged husband—was adultery, a decision Francesca had coauthored with her husband's brother, Paolo. In presenting her story, Dante the poet coauthors the responses of readers, by having them witness Dante the pilgrim's empathetic swoon at the plight of these lovers, while at the same time readers observe the poet's punishment of them in the second circle of Hell. In this canto, Dante explores the expansion and contraction of dialogic freedom, as well as the dialogic ambiguities of deliberating from multiple perspectives. In the process he suggests that empathy, like romantic passion, may be a moral snare.

## LIFE IN HELL

In Virgil's *Aeneid*, the woman who falls in love with Aeneas as he describes the destruction of Troy does not get to live happily ever after with her charismatic refugee, whom she has aided and come to see as her husband. He is on a mission to be the founder of Rome, and reluctant as he is to leave behind Dido and the city she has founded, he must. Her very success at creating ramparts, palaces, markets, and a whole way of life secure enough to offer hospitality to the stranded Trojans is a constant reminder of the vocation that Aeneas fails to accomplish every day that he lingers in Carthage. Yet a queen cannot be expected to desert the city she has established and now rules, just so that she can be with the man she loves. There is no place for Dido outside Carthage. Aeneas winds up sneaking off in the night. Unable to survive his abandonment, as her last civic project Dido constructs her own funeral pyre, climbs onto it, and stabs herself. Her suffering body clings to life, but the gods take pity on her. They send "Iris down to free the struggling spirit/ from her entwining limbs," because Dido's death "was not merited or fated,/ but miserable and before her time/ and spurred by sudden frenzy."[2] As his ship leaves the harbor Aeneas is just able to make out the glow of the flames from Dido's pyre. Virgil's description of the "sudden frenzy" that causes her to take her own life is important, because he follows Homer and all classical thinkers in regarding passion as a force that clouds reason and enslaves the mind. Not until eleventh-century Provence did writers begin to present romantic passion as a good idea.[3] Thus, to Virgil, Dido's love for Aeneas was a destabilizing force that undermined her ability to do her job as queen and led to her suicide. Yet Virgil's heart still goes out to Dido in her misery. He describes her efforts to die: "She breathes; the deep wound in/ her chest is loud and hoarse. . . . / Three times with wandering eyes she tried to find/ high heaven's light, and when she found it, sighed" (IV, 949–54). In an Olympian nod toward death with dignity, Juno sends Iris to cut the lock and free Dido's spirit from her body.

So it is that by the time Dante calls on Virgil to be his guide through the underworld of the *Inferno*, he cannot bear to consign Dido to the seventh circle of Hell, where suicides are punished. Those who took their own lives must spend eternity in a barren woods, imprisoned inside the branches of thorn bushes, while ferocious Harpies feed on the foliage, creating "Pain, and an outlet for the pain as well."[4] There they wait for the Apocalypse, when the bodies they once destroyed will be reunited with them, each body draped over the appropriate thorn bush, before the gates of Hell are sealed shut. This is not Dido's fate. Dante has placed her instead in the second circle of Hell (the first, hence mildest, circle of actual punishment), among the lovers whose reason was mastered by desire. There "she who died/ By her own hand for love" (V, 52–53) joins other lovers buffeted about by the hot hurricane winds that are their *contrapasso*, or fitting punishment, for being swept away in life by the heat of passion. Lives that once included many aspects and roles are here reduced to the one way of knowing that eclipsed all others as they came to be dominated and imprisoned by their passion. The winds that blow them about, as beyond their control as unpredictable weather, reflect the centrifugal force of the passion that blew away the centripetal limitations of family ties and marriage vows.

It is here among the shades of Dido, Helen, and Paris that Dante finds
Francesca. Her body is fused with her lover Paolo's, but he cannot talk, so
she speaks for both. She does not need to tell Dante her whole story, because
the double murder was still big news in Italy and beyond when he was
writing his poem between 1308 and 1314. The real-life Francesca had married Paolo's older brother around 1275, and when he discovered them in the
act, he killed them both.[5] Today's tourists in Rimini can visit the very bed-
room in the palace where it is supposed to have happened. According to
Francesca, it was all about a book. She and Paolo were reading the love story
of Launcelot and Guinevere, "Alone, suspecting nothing, at our leisure" (V,
114):

> Sometimes at what we read our glances joined,
>> Looking from the book each to other's eyes,
>> And then the color in our faces drained.
> But one particular moment alone it was
>> Defeated us: the longed-for smile, it said,
>> Was kissed by that most noble lover: at this,
> This one, who now will never leave my side,
>> Kissed my mouth, trembling. (V, 115–22)

In one of the great understatements of X-rated art, Dante has Francesca add,
"that day we read/ No further" (V, 123–24).

As Mark Musa and others have observed, there are two Dantes listening
to this tale: Dante the pilgrim, who is going through a journey through Hell,
with Virgil as his guide; and Dante the poet, who is imagining and telling the
story. The pilgrim Dante is filled with sympathy toward the lovers. He says
to his guide, "Alas—that sweet conceptions and passion so deep/ Should
bring them here!" (V, 101–2). He says to the sinner, "Francesca, your suffering makes me weep/ For sorrow and pity" (V, 103–4). At the end of her
story, the pilgrim is so moved that "Swooning as in death, I fell like a dying
body" (V, 127). He can bear to hear no more, and he faints. At the beginning
of the next canto, Dante explains that his mind has returned from being
closed in the presence of his pity for Paolo and Francesca: "Al tornar de la
mente, che si chiuse/ dinanzi a la pieta' d'i due cognati," (VI, 1–2), which
Robert Pinsky translates, "Upon my mind's return from swooning shut/ At
hearing the piteous tale of those two kin."[6] These words hint at what Dante
the poet must have been thinking while his pilgrim self was fainting in
empathy. The poet, after all, has consigned these two lovers to the second
circle of Hell, hurled there by the monster Minos, where they suffer the
torment of never being able to choose where they drift, never being able to
leave each other's side, wind-tossed through the malignant air. We are told at
the beginning of Canto VI that when Dante the pilgrim fainted with empathy,

he was confused, his mind somehow closed. Dante the poet wants us to think about this. How could empathy close our minds?

Part of the intellectual challenge of reading the *Inferno* is to register Dante's double perspective as he presents the underworld simultaneously as the pilgrim sees it, moment by moment, and as a poet reflects on it. This challenge leads us to reexamine Francesca's words. She tells Dante the pilgrim that love "seized" Paolo and also made her own heart burn for him. The story they were reading at the moment, "suspecting nothing," was about Launcelot, "by love constrained." The pattern established by words like "seized" and "constrained" is consistent. Lovers are not responsible for what they do, because their passion takes control of them and makes them burn. It enslaves them, obliterating their freedom. They are passive victims of forces beyond their control. This is the same idea we saw in Virgil's portrait of the suffering Dido, enslaved by her passion for Aeneas. It is also the explanation Homer gives for the abduction of Helen by Paris in the *Iliad*. Various characters in that epic blame Aphrodite, the goddess of love. Even today we talk about people being swept away by passion, as if they had no control over what they were doing. The centripetal impulse to focus the meaning of passion on one idea, enslavement, pervades Francesca's logic, even as the centrifugal force of passion itself pervades her consciousness, undermining the restraints imposed by marriage, honesty, and self-control. Yet, just as characters in the *Iliad* can blame both the gods and Paris for spiriting away Helen, recognizing the simultaneous presence of forces beyond people's control (gods, fate) and human responsibility (violation of the guest-host relationship) for choices people make—readers of the *Inferno* do not need to try hard to imagine that if Paolo and Francesca took the trouble to find a secluded spot to read a steamy book, they were pretty far from being "sanza alcun sospetto," or "suspecting nothing." Dante wants us to think critically about Francesca's tendency to blame it all on Love, Paolo, her husband, and a book.

Dante's Catholicism did not require that people lead lust-free lives to reach salvation. It did, however, require that they take responsibility for their decisions. From a Christian perspective, admitting responsibility was the first step toward repentance, vital for entry into Purgatory, let alone Heaven. Francesca is not willing to take that first step. She blames everyone but herself. Thus, she winds up among the multitudes who have "abandoned all hope." The inscription above the gate to Dante's Hell is usually translated "Abandon all hope, you who enter here!" (III, 7). What Dante actually said was, "Lasciate ogne speranza, voi ch'intrate" (III, 9). Every translation puts this inscription in the imperative mood, as a command: "Abandon all hope!" Yet in Italian the second person plural ending, *-ate*, is the same for both the imperative and the present.

A consequence of this linguistic quirk is that the phrase in question can just as accurately be translated, "You who are entering are abandoning all hope." This double possibility is significant, because even as the inscription emphasizes the eternal hopelessness of the Christian Hell, it emphasizes that it is the responsibility of every person to decide to accept or reject the hope of salvation. The sinner who chooses to abandon the whole process of repentance, which leads to forgiveness and salvation, abandons the hope of finding God's forgiveness. More importantly, the sinner who decides that his or her situation is hopeless is actually denying that the Christian God has the freedom and power to forgive. Thus the hopeless sinner denies God's omnipotence and commits the deadliest sin of all, pride. Without repentance there is no hope for redemption, not because the Christian God is powerless to help, but because he insists that humans be free to choose to let him choose to forgive. Redemption is coauthored by God and man. Those who abandon hope have chosen to abandon God. When we read, "Lasciate ogne speranza, voi ch'intrate," we see that in Francesca's case its double meaning is especially clear. She abandoned all hope when she entered Hell, but she also continues to abandon hope by showing no sign of taking responsibility for what she has done, which would have been the first step toward repentance.

Far from acknowledging this process, Francesca frames her situation as God's abandonment and lack of love for her and Paolo:

> . . . if heaven's King bore affection
> For such as we are, suffering in this wind,
>> Then we would pray to Him to grant you peace
>> For pitying us in this, our evil end. (V, 81–84)

On the surface, Francesca seems to be wishing she could call upon God to bless Dante's pilgrimage through Hell. What she is really saying, though, is that the Christian God, who is supposed to be perfect and to embody love, is not and does not. What she doesn't say is that she can't pray to God at all, having refused to take responsibility for, or be sorry for, her sin. She is sorry she got caught. She is sorry she got killed. She is sorry she is spending eternity blown about by hot, hurricane winds. But she is not sorry for what she has done, because she does not even consider herself responsible for the actions that have led to her death and punishment. If while she lived she were at any point sorry to have committed adultery, she would not be in Hell. Readers can be certain that even now Francesca does not look back on her adultery as anything but wonderful. She says, "Nessun maggior dolore/ che ricordarsi del tempo felice ne la miseria" (V, 121–23), or "There is no greater pain than to remember a happy time in the midst of misery." She would not still be referring to her adultery as "a happy time" if she were capable of regretting the decisions that it represents. To her, it is a matter of God's whim whether he has affection for some and not for others, so he joins the list of those she blames for her fate.

Dante does not explain any of this. Rather, he leaves it for readers to figure out that Francesca is reasoning from the position of one who "has lost the good of intellect" (III, 15), whose despair causes her to join the other damned to curse "the human race,/ God and their parents" (III, 84–85). That she is so persuasive is a mark of Dante the poet's art, which calls on us to share the pilgrim's empathy, yet to see through Francesca's self-absorbed rhetoric that has caused the mind of Dante the pilgrim temporarily to swoon shut. In this process, we are meant to vigorously exercise the intellectual powers that are our only defense against a passion as strong as Paolo and Francesca's. In so doing we are not expected to reach obvious, clear-cut conclusions—rejecting Francesca and embracing reason—but rather to strengthen our minds, as going to the gym strengthens our bodies, so that should we confront a similar temptation we will not share her fate.

In Dante's mind, the whole geography of Hell depends upon freedom. Without people being capable of exercising moral freedom, there would be no justification for Dante's Hell. Why punish someone for something he or she is not responsible for? For Dante, choosing to act one way or another is important, and a sinner cannot wind up in Hell at all without having made one choice to sin and another choice not to repent. When it comes to the problem of romantic passion, he describes the carnal sinners, "i peccator carnali/ che la ragion sommettono al talento" (III, 39). These are "the carnal sinners who submit reason to desire." Notice that it is not merely a question of being swept away by passion, as the problem was presented by Homer and Virgil. The emphasis here is not on desire's ability to overwhelm lovers and enslave them, which is Francesca's self-defense. The emphasis is on the choice that lovers make to submit reason to desire. The verb "sommettono" (submit) has as its subject not passion but "i peccator carnali," carnal sinners. They are the ones who choose to submit reason to desire—to disregard reason's role as guide, in favor of passion.[7] For Dante, the power of passion is an extenuating circumstance, but it does not absolve the sinner of responsibility, as Francesca would have it. Thus Dante the poet puts Francesca in Hell, because he holds her responsible for her sin; but, in homage to Virgil and Homer and in his own humanity, he softens the blow by putting her in the least punitive circle of punishment.

Dante divides his Hell into two parts. In upper hell, the first five circles, sins of appetite (lust, gluttony, greed, wastefulness, anger, and laziness) are punished, but not nearly as severely as are the sins of malice in the four circles of lower hell. In these depths, we find sinners who choose to inflict pain on themselves or others, who sow discord, and who violate the trust of the most vulnerable—their family, country, guests, and benefactors—suffering an array of tortures that reflect the nature of their crimes. Thus, while

Paolo and Francesca are blown about by wind in upper Hell, Judas, Brutus, and Cassius are each munched on by one of the three mouths of Satan, who is trapped at the bottom of Hell, encased up to his shoulders not in fire but in ice. This division into upper and lower Hell, into sins of appetite and sins of malice, emphasizes that although even the sinners who indulge their appetites are responsible for their behavior, they are less culpable than the sinners who coldly, deliberately, commit fraud. The subprime lenders who duped people into taking on mortgages that stranded them under water would not fare well in Dante's Inferno. True, their victims lusted to own homes they could not afford, but their sins of appetite were not as great as the sins of those who manipulated them. Dante presents the sins of appetite as gateway sins that can lead to lower Hell only if sinners decide to intentionally harm others. Greed, punished in circle 4, might lead a banker to violate the trust of clients and commit fraud, punished in circle 9. Similarly, wrath, in circle 5, the deepest part of upper Hell, if acted out, will land a sinner in lower Hell, among the murderers of circle 7. If the victims are relatives, as in the case of Paolo and Francesca, the wrathful can wind up as low as the ninth circle, in Caina (named for the murderer of Abel), among those who commit fraud against kindred, stuck for eternity in ice up to their genitals. This is where Francesca wants her husband to land: "Caina awaits the one who took our lives" (V, 96). Since he was still alive at the time that Dante wrote the *Inferno*, we never find out whether the vindictive Francesca gets her way.

## DIALOGIC FREEDOM IN HELL

Freedom is essential to Dante's design, in that the more willful the sin, the lower the sinner falls in Hell. In the case of Paolo and Francesca, they are less guilty than the fraudulent, who are hurled to the bottom of Hell, but they are nonetheless responsible for their acts. Dialogic freedom enters the picture with Francesca's description of their experience reading together, which is itself a two-sided act. We know from recent scholarship on medieval reading practices that Dante probably would have imagined Paolo and Francesca as reading to each other out loud.[8] A person can read aloud to someone else who is indifferent, hostile, or receptive. An indifferent or hostile response might inspire a reader to try harder to gain or keep the listener's attention, or to give up and close the book. Paolo and Francesca are far from indifferent listeners. Both are receptive to the story of adultery between Launcelot and Guinevere. As they read, their meaningful glances encourage each other's responsiveness, and that responsiveness gives them both a way to express their mutual attraction, without directly saying a word to each other, beyond the reading of the book:

> Sometimes at what we read our glances joined,
> Looking from the book each to other's eyes,
> And then the color in our faces drained. (V, 115–17)

Thus, they coauthor each other's reading of the book. They also coinscribe each other into its narrative as lovers in the pattern of Launcelot and Guinevere. Together, or taking turns, they read of the kiss between the literary lovers; then, "that day we read/ No further." Their decision to fall into each other's arms is coauthored, just as their reading of the book and of each other has been, without one word of conversation in the usual sense.

Dialogic freedom is a significant aspect of every conversation between a sinner in the *Inferno* and Dante the pilgrim. In Francesca's case, it is the "animal grazioso e benigno" (V, 88), the "gracious, benign soul" she hears in Dante's voice, which makes her want to speak to him after he calls against the wind, "O wearied souls! If Another does not forbid,/ Come speak with us" (V, 71–72). Francesca can have no idea just how receptive Dante will be to her story. She does not know, for example, that he spent a large part of his early adulthood writing the kind of love poetry that idealizes passion.[9] What she does know is that "his loving call" indicates that he will be receptive to her tale. When the pilgrim calls out to them for the first time, "O anime affannate" (V, 80), Musa, Pinsky, and Sinclair all translate these words as "O wearied souls." The word "affannate" actually means "breathless" or "panting," however, both of which are more evocative of being blown about by winds and of the sin that led to this *contrapasso*. However you translate it, Dante's address, prefaced by "O," which intensifies the emotional effect, shows that he registers with sympathy their weariness or breathlessness, even before they speak. The effect is so strong that Paolo and Francesca cannot resist responding. Thus, just as they were highly receptive to each other reading a book, now they are highly receptive to the gracious, benign soul apparent in Dante's loving call to them. His receptivity is the precondition for Francesca's willingness to speak.

This receptivity encourages Francesca not just to speak to Dante but to justify herself to him. Thus, she constructs a self-presentation that would appeal to someone who is already sympathetic to lovers. Many readers have noticed how much she herself sounds like a medieval love poet of the *dolce stil novo* (sweet new style) when she begins three very formal and formulaic stanzas with the word "Love" and even repeats the word three times in one line, "Amor, ch'a nullo amato amar perdona" (V, 103). We can translate this line literally, "Love, which to nothing loved pardons loving." In addition to presenting a central piety of love poetry (love is so powerful that it cannot be resisted by either the lover or the loved), Francesca has the audacity to use the very idea of not being pardoned (a dangerous metaphor for someone in Hell) to defend her adultery. No one who is loved can be pardoned from the responsibility to respond to love with love, she argues, as if to say, "In this situation there is no alibi, no excuse not to love." She inscribes herself within the poetic tradition that she sees as justifying her passion, even demanding it, and this performance is called forth and hence coauthored by Dante's receptivity to this poetry as well as to her.[10] Thus Dante the pilgrim coauthors the two-sided act of her self-presentation. The pilgrim's receptiveness never falters, as, hearing her story, he weeps for sorrow and pity, and at the end, faints like a dying body. Seeing her story from Francesca's perspective enables Dante the pilgrim to coauthor it by encouraging her to tell it to someone who is moved by it. It also allows Dante the poet to ensnare the reader in the same empathy felt by the pilgrim. What better way for the poet to emphasize the attractions of passion? If sin were repulsive, if it were simple to avoid, how easy it would be for everyone to take the moral path!

## PROTOCOLS OF READING DANTE FOR AND WITH DIALOGIC FREEDOM

Just as Paolo and Francesca coauthor each other's decision by reading a book together, and Dante the pilgrim coauthors Francesca's decision to tell her story by being receptive to it, Dante the poet coauthors his reader's judgment of the situation by inviting that reader first to share the pilgrim's empathy, then to rethink the wisdom of that perspective.[11] Empathy is a good thing, Dante seems to be telling us. It humanizes us. He presents the pilgrim going through the experience of empathy, inviting us, too, to empathize with Paolo and Francesca. Yet Dante the poet also gives a reader reasons to question this empathy. For example, even before Dante the pilgrim encounters Paolo and Francesca being blown about by the winds, he has already reacted to seeing Helen of Troy, Dido, and more than a thousand other lovers, by being overcome by pity. The Italian, "pieta' mi giunse, e fui quasi smarrito" (V, 72) is translated by John Sinclair, "Pity came upon me and I was as one bewildered" (V, 77); by Robert Pinsky, "Pity overwhelmed me. Half-lost in its coils" (V, 63); and by Mark Musa, "Pity confused my senses, and I was dazed" (V, 72). All three translators focus on the word "pity," which will be vital to Dante's receptivity of Francesca, and on its disabling effects (bewildered, overwhelmed, half-lost, confused, dazed). My attempt at a most literal translation is "Pity reached me, and I was almost lost."

The word *smarrito* (lost) echoes the very opening of Canto I, where Dante described himself waking up terrified in a dark wood, where "la diritta via era smarrita," or "the right road was lost." The word appears again in Canto II, when Beatrice urges Virgil to help Dante, saying, "temo che non sia gia' si smarrito" (II, 64), "I fear he may already be lost." That Dante should choose the same word (*smarrito*, lost) to describe his reaction to seeing over a thousand condemned lovers, even before he encounters Paolo and Francesca, is significant. It shows not only that he is predisposed to take pity on them, because he has already taken pity on other lovers, but that this pity will be dangerous, threatening a relapse into some version of the lostness that he experienced in the dark wood of Canto I, which inspired Beatrice to appeal to Virgil for help.

In the terminology of Bakhtin, which I discussed in chapter 1, empathy calls on us "to penetrate" the sufferer and "almost merge or become one with him from within."[12] The word "almost" is an extremely important qualifier here, in that according to Bakhtin, "pure empathizing" would be "fruitless," "senseless," and "pathological." In his mind "pure empathizing" is also "hardly possible," since this act of "coinciding with another" would be disastrous for the sympathizer, who would lose himself in someone else's suffering. The important thing, according to Bakhtin, is that we experience another's suffering "precisely as *his* suffering," so that our reaction is not a "cry of pain" but "a word of consolation or an act of assistance." This capacity for "sympathetic understanding," which, unlike "pure empathizing," Bakhtin sees as a good thing, requires a "*return* into ourselves." He explains, "I empathize actively into an individuality and, consequently, I do not lose myself completely, nor my unique place outside it, even for a moment." Even at our most empathetic, Bakhtin argues, we must retain a sense of outsideness that keeps us from losing ourselves in the suffering of another.

It is fascinating to ponder Dante's empathy for Francesca from this Bakhtinian perspective. The pilgrim's swoon at the end of Canto V not only becomes evidence of an empathy veering perilously close to the "pathological," but it also becomes evidence of the body's ultimate resistance to continuing in a state of consciousness that threatens Dante with a loss of himself. Mark Musa argues that Francesca "attempts to identify the pilgrim with her and Paolo to such an extent as to usurp his identity."[13] Call it evidence of usurpation, loss, or feelings too intense to sustain, but Dante the pilgrim's swoon at the end of Canto V, "come corpo morto cadde" (like a dead body falls), is described in menacing language that seems to imply that the empathy he is experiencing goes too far and risks too much, in some sense becoming deadly.

Just before the pilgrim faints, we learn for the first time that Paolo, who has been there all along, fused with Francesca, unable to leave her side, has been weeping the whole time she has been speaking. The shock of this revelation emphasizes not only the loss of speech and autonomy that has been the price of passion for Paolo, but the self-absorption of Francesca, not to mention the fascination of the poet, both of whom seem to ignore Paolo's tears while she tells her story. This revelation of Paolo's tears right at the end of the scene is timed by the poet to awaken readers to Paolo's pain and Francesca's vanity, just before the pilgrim swoons. Robin Kirkpatrick observes of the weeping Paolo and the swooning Dante, "Both are reduced to a condition of utter inactivity by Francesca."[14] Contrasting this inactivity with "the activity required of the reader in Canto 5," Kirkpatrick argues that "the reading it requires may be contrasted directly with the way in which Francesca and Paolo read the romance of Lancelot and Guinevere, allowing themselves to be drawn, by an increasingly urgent bond of shared suggestions and gesture, into obliviousness."[15] The implication here is that we as readers must resist the force of an empathy that could sweep us, too, into oblivion.

The first line of the next canto, "Al tornar de la mente che si chiuse," which I translate, "At the return of the mind that closed itself," emphasizes Dante the pilgrim's recovery as a return to himself and an opening of his mind, implying that whatever it was that made him faint in the presence of Paolo and Francesca threatened to alienate him from himself and close his mind. The poet seems to suggest that empathy, wrongly experienced, has the power to close down our minds. The emotional experience of empathy can open us up, but it can also confuse us and cloud our judgment, even to the point of threatening us with a loss of identity, responsibility, and freedom. Dante the poet invites us to think about the dangers of empathizing so well with another person's perspective that we suspend our own critical thinking skills and somehow disappear into that empathy. He also invites us to rethink the self-serving logic of Francesca, as she constructs a unifying narrative that blames her fate on everyone but herself, and as she rejects Christian forgiveness in favor of a vengeful call for her husband to land far deeper in Hell than she has landed, in the midst of the most gruesome punishments. Lanfranco Caretti calls this moment of spite toward her homicidal husband—which is the opposite of the empathy she seeks and gains from the pilgrim—a kind of contamination of the thread of her elegant discourse. For him, it is an eruption of her "autentico volto" (her authentic face), which is revealed in her "verso gelido" (gelid verse): "Caina attende," (Caina, the region where Abel's murderer lies, in the ninth and most punitive circle of Dante's Hell, is waiting for him).[16] Francesca's "authentic face" is every bit as passionate in hating her husband as it is in justifying her love for Paolo. For Dante the poet, though, reason is the superaddressee that trumps passion, just as for Homer, a father's love is the superaddressee that trumps revenge. Thus, at the beginning of Canto VI, Dante's mind returns from being closed down by Francesca's appeal.

Readers of the *Inferno* often find it hard to embrace such a moralistic agenda, as they witness the attractions of Francesca and her effect on Dante the pilgrim. Mark Musa, who translated the poem into English in 1971, points out that "dozens of critics, unaware of the wiles of sin, have also been seduced by her charm and the grace of her speech."[17] John Freccero, who wrote the introduction to Robert Pinsky's 1994 translation, notes ironically that although this episode presents Francesca as a "deluded victim of medieval romance," it also creates her as "one more heroine in love's canon. It is therefore just as seductive as the literature against which it warns."[18] Freccero suggests that without Dante's portrait, Francesca would have been just another object of titillating but forgettable gossip. Thanks to Canto V of the *Inferno*, however, she rivals Helen of Troy and Dido of Carthage. John Sinclair, who translated the poem into English in 1939, considers Dante's ambivalence toward Francesca to be at the heart of the appeal of her story. Sinclair points out that there is not even a hint of reproach from either Dante the pilgrim or Virgil the guide in their responses to her words. This lack of reproach creates a tremendous tension for readers, between Dante's "profound human sympathy" and his "unflinching moral realism."[19]

The point here is not that Dante fails to make us judge Francesca as harshly as he himself appears to when he opens Canto VI by describing his own empathetic mind as shut. The point is that Dante makes us experience the tension between passionate attraction and rational judgment, and he forces us to find this tension difficult to resolve. If dialogic freedom is a two-sided act that involves deliberation from multiple perspectives, within a field of forces for unity and chaos, we as readers also experience this freedom. We constantly make choices about the text that we are reading, and those choices are codetermined by a host of factors, including but not limited to the exegetical tradition of Dante scholarship (see note 11), our educational and theoretical backgrounds, our personal experiences, our friends, our moods, our prejudices, and so on. Confronting the tension between admiring and condemning Francesca, a reader's temptation will be to resolve it by focusing on one force or another (passion or reason), to the exclusion of the messy terrain in between. Dante invites readers to experience first one perspective, the pilgrim's empathy (which is both centripetal in that it unifies the pilgrim's response, and centrifugal in that it threatens chaos), then another perspective, the poet's judgment (which is both centripetal in that it condemns Francesca to a definite circle of Hell, and centrifugal in that it deconstructs itself in the multiple directions discussed above). Francesca's self-justifying rhetoric—which inscribes her as a heroine in a narrative of medieval love poetry, and which has appealed so much to Dante the pilgrim—and the moral judgment provided by Dante the poet, constitute competing centripetalities within a field of forces that include other unifying perspectives. These centripetal forces include Christian values, medieval gender stereotypes, revenge patterns, and literary images of lovers from epics and romances. There is also the centrifugal force of Dante's own diverse personal experiences and all the daily events—paths taken and not taken by Paolo, Francesca, and her husband, moment by moment—that led up to the opportunity for adultery and murder.

Within this field of forces for unity and chaos, instead of insisting that readers make a clear-cut choice, Dante invites readers to inhabit a liminal territory that resists simplification but also avoids the moral relativism that would let us off the hook. From Dante's perspective, our freedom depends on cultivating the ability to see through specious logic and self-serving attempts to deflect blame onto others. In this challenge, empathy can ensnare us as effectively as romantic passion can. To be free we must let the experience of empathy happen, yet retain the ability to "return to ourselves" and judge this empathy and the grounds upon which we feel it. We must try to navigate the many perspectives listed above, without giving in to the temptation to reduce meaning to any one perspective, because that would trap us in one narrow epistemological layer, as Francesca is ultimately trapped. We must also resist the temptation to give up trying to judge the situation at all, even though together all these perspectives seem overwhelming. The imperative of dialogic freedom, as Dante sees it, is to register as fully as possible the complexity of life's moral terrain, then choose the best possible path within this field of forces for unity and chaos.

At the heart the *Inferno* is Dante's intense relationship with his imagined reader. Dante Alighieri was a civic leader, banished from his native Florence in 1301, on trumped-up charges, with a death sentence hanging over his head. He wrote letter after letter, begging for permission to safely return, all of which fell on deaf ears. Meanwhile the Black and White Guelphs lost themselves in decades of civil war that threatened to destroy the city. No longer able to address his fellow citizens in person, Dante could reach out to them only with the three volumes of his *Commedia*, in the hope that they would choose a different path—personally, spiritually, and politically. The *Inferno* is a kind of conversation with Florence, every word written with an imagined audience of Florentines in mind. This imagined audience coauthors Dante's text. As we read it centuries later, we still experience the urgency of Dante's call to rethink life from within its midst and to confront our choices before it is too late. Dialogic freedom is at the heart of this process, not just because our decisions among others are two-sided acts, but because our ability to make good decisions requires us to experience our centripetal need to make meaning, within a context of competing centripetalities and amid the more directly centrifugal forces of daily life, which include passion and war. To consider who it is we answer to—family, friends, lovers, community members, laws, divinities, principles of rationality and compassion—we need to cultivate the flexibility to navigate among the perspectives within which these voices can be heard. Only then can we sort out how these addressees coauthor the actions we call free. If multiple, and often conflicting, voices become too loud, too centrifugal, too chaotic, we are tempted to simplify things by shutting some of them out. Indeed, it is sometimes essential to simplify things in order to take action. Dante's warning to us in the *Inferno* is that in the quest to choose well it is a matter of life and death that we not shut out the wrong voices. He calls on us to strengthen our understanding of the different voices we answer to, to strengthen our ability to balance their various demands, to decide what is most important, so that "Nel mezzo del cammin di nostra vita" (in the middle of the journey of our life), each one of us can choose the right path through the forest. Dialogic freedom, as Dante presents it, is a continuous challenge rather than a reachable goal.

## NOTES

1. Mark Musa explains, "A reader must be careful from the beginning to distinguish between two uses of the first person singular in the *Commedia*: one designating Dante the Pilgrim, the other Dante the Poet. The first is a character in the story created by the second." *Dante Alighieri's Divine Comedy: Verse Translation and Commentary*, trans. Mark Musa (Bloomington: Indiana University Press, 1996), 2:3. Musa gives as an example of the two Dantes: "How I entered there I cannot truly say."

2. Virgil, *The Aeneid of Virgil*, trans. Allen Mandelbaum (New York: Bantam, 1971), IV, 957–61.

3. C. S. Lewis, *The Allegory of Love* (New York: Oxford University Press, 1958), 3.

4. Dante Alighieri, *The Inferno of Dante*, trans. Robert Pinsky (New York: Noonday, 1994), XIII, 95. Unless otherwise indicated, citations to Dante's *Inferno* are to this edition.

5. Boccaccio's version of events is slightly different from Dante's. Musa explains in his commentary that according to Boccaccio, Francesca, required for political reasons to marry into the Malatesta family, "was tricked into thinking that she would be married to Gianciotto's handsome younger brother Paolo." When Gianciotto discovered the affair between his wife and his brother, he "killed them both, although according to Boccaccio's perhaps romantic account, he meant to kill only Paolo—Francesca lost her life by running between the two men just as Gianciotto's sword was about to strike" (73).

6. John D. Sinclair translates these lines, "With the return of my mind that was shut off before the piteous state of the two kinsfolk," in *Dante's Inferno*, trans. John D. Sinclair (New York: Oxford University Press, 1961), 87. I translate these lines literally, "At the return of the mind that closed in the presence of the pity of the two relatives." Citations to the *Inferno* in Italian are to the Sinclair edition. Translations in my text from Italian to English not otherwise attributed to Pinsky or others are by me.

7. For Dante, passion in and of itself is not a bad thing, as long as passion serves reason, and not the other way around.

8. John Ahearn explains that "Medieval literacy was by and large 'recitative literacy.' Texts were often thought of as a function of oral performance." "Singing the Book: Orality in the Reception of Dante's *Comedy*," in *Dante: Contemporary Perspectives*, ed. Amilcare Fannucci (Toronto: University of Toronto Press, 1997), 217. Giuseppe Mazzotta includes in his volume of essays about Dante one of Petrarch's "Letters on Familiar Matters," where Petrarch observes that Dante "is extremely popular" in "taverns and marketplaces," where "the noble face of his poetry is befouled and beslabbered," presumably because it is being routinely mangled in oral performance by bards with less than perfect memories. *Critical Essays on Dante* (Boston: Hall, 1991), 35, 36.

9. *La Vita Nuova* was one of Dante's earliest works, a collection of love poems to Beatrice, with a running commentary about the poems and the occasions that prompted Dante to write them. See *The Portable Dante*, ed. Mark Musa (New York: Penguin, 1995), 587–649.

10. Robin Kirkpatrick makes the case that this canto constitutes a kind of "retrospective self-criticism" of Dante's earlier interest in the love poetry of *La Vita Nuova*, but not a palinode, or retraction, of that interest. *Dante's Inferno: Difficulty and Dead Poetry* (Cambridge, UK: Cambridge University Press, 1987), 9.

11. How we should read Dante is a major and unresolved question of Dante criticism. Almost as soon as Dante's ink was dry an extensive exegetical tradition arose. This tradition has been refracted through late twentieth- and early twenty-first-century theoretical perspec-

tives. According to Amilcare Fannucci, "By the end of the 14th century the *Commedia* had produced more commentary than Virgil's *Aeneid* had throughout the whole of the Middle Ages." *Dante: Contemporary Perspectives*, ed. Amilcare Fannucci (Toronto: University of Toronto Press, 1997), ix. Deborah Parker adds that "by 1400 twelve commentaries had appeared." "Interpreting the Commentary Tradition to the *Comedy*," *Contemporary Perspectives*, 241. The Darmouth Dante Project continues this exegetical tradition by providing a computerized database online, with over seventy commentaries. Many editions of the *Inferno* read today by Italian schoolchildren present only a few lines of text on each page, with the rest of the space devoted to commentary from this tradition. Perhaps this exegetical approach, which seeks to recapture contexts no longer accessible to a modern reader, is what led T. S. Eliot to complain, "The effect of many books about Dante is to give the impression that it is more necessary to read about him than to read what he has written." T. S. Eliot, "Vita Nuova," in *Selected Essays* (New York: Harcourt, 1950), 26. Dante himself must bear part of the blame, however, for his letter to Cangrande soon after the *Inferno* appeared, in which he explains, "The meaning of this work is not of one kind only; rather, the work may be described as 'polysemous,' that is, having several meanings; for the first meaning is that which is conveyed by the letter, and the next is that which is conveyed by what the letter signifies; the former which is called literal, while the latter is called allegorical, or mystical." This letter supplies an example from the Bible and explains its literal, allegorical, moral, and anagogical levels, all of which can in a general sense be termed "allegorical, inasmuch as they are different (*diversi*) from the literal or historical." *The Letters of Dante*, ed. and trans. Paget Toynbee (Oxford: Clarendon Press, 1920), 195–96. With such a complex scheme described by the author, is it any wonder that commentaries have proliferated?

More recently, Giuseppe Mazzotta, again asking how we should read the *Comedy*, has recommended that we focus on "the vast heteroglossia of the *Divine Comedy*." For him, its many voices, including Francesca's, draw us to a new appreciation for the "enigmatic other and alternate world of infinite resonances, dark riddles, and polysemous allegories." Recognizing the limitations of the exegetical tradition, despite its vastness, he argues that "poetic texts . . . have no *a priori* self-identical fixity of meaning but are part and parcel of the temporal mobility we claim for ourselves or Dante claims for himself in the *Divine Comedy*." "Why did Dante write the Comedy? Why and How Do We Read It? The Poet and the Critics," in *Dante Now: Current Trends in Dante Studies*, ed. Theodore J. Cachey (Notre Dame, IN: University of Notre Dame Press, 1995), 64–65. According to Mazzotta, we need to submit "to the challenge of the text's otherness in relation to ourselves" in our "love of the contingent, unique corporality of every word" (67). Robert Scholes, in *Protocols of Reading* (discussed above in chapter 2), would include the exegetical tradition of Dante studies as part of the "doubling commentary" acknowledged by Derrida as a "guardrail" in the "critical reading" that "produces a new signifying structure." Robert Scholes, *Protocols of Reading* (New Haven, CT: Yale University Press, 1991). I agree with Scholes that as readers we perform a kind of balancing act between recovering lost contexts for reading Dante and creating new ways to receive the *Inferno* into our contemporary worlds. Perhaps this is why Daniel Halperin was able to publish an edition of the *Inferno* in which its thirty-four cantos are translated into English by a total of twenty twentieth-century poets, testimony to the *Inferno*'s ongoing intervention in our lives. *Dante's Inferno: Translations by Twenty Contemporary Poets*, ed. Daniel Halperin (Hopewell, NJ: The Ecco Press, 1993).

12. See chapter 1.

13. Musa, *Commentary*, 77.

14. Kirkpatrick, *Difficulty and Dead Poetry*, 82.

15. Ibid., 85.

16. Lanfranco Caretti, "Canto V: Il canto di Francesca," in *Dante Alighieri: Cultura, Politica, Poesia: Antologia della critica dantesca*, ed. Tommaso Di Salvo (Florence: La Nuova Italia Editrice, 1987), 336–37.

17. *The Divine Comedy I: The Inferno*, trans. Mark Musa (Middlesex, UK: Penguin, 1971), 120.

18. John Freccero, "Notes on Canto V," in *The Inferno of Dante*, tr. Robert Pinsky (New York: Noonday, 1994), 313.

19. John Sinclair, trans., "Notes on Canto V," in *Dante's Inferno* (New York: Oxford University Press, 1961), 82.

## Chapter Four

# Deaf to Shylock in *The Merchant of Venice*

Dialogic freedom: a two-sided act, chosen within a field of unifying and fragmenting forces along a continuum of minimal to maximal *layers of knowing*
that are never final.

In *The Merchant of Venice*, Shakespeare explores the importance of navigating different ways of knowing the world as we coauthor freedom. The meaning of Portia's famous speech on mercy, and the actions it calls for, change
radically, depending upon whether the listener is Shylock or one of Portia's
Christian friends. The same words that call to the Christians with a reminder
to forgive, call to Shylock with an invitation to seek revenge. Portia and
Shylock are largely deaf to each other, incapable of knowing the world from
each other's perspectives, incapable of navigating epistemological layers that
are alien. This chapter explores the tensions between dialogic receptivity and
dialogic deafness. It examines how receptivity to kindred voices, which promotes dialogic freedom, can also be destructive to it, precisely because it can
encourage willful deafness to the excluded other. The destructiveness of
dialogic deafness undermines the freedom not just of those who are not
heard, but of those who do not hear.

In *Marxism and the Philosophy of Language*, Volosinov/Bakhtin explain,
"To understand another person's utterance means to orient oneself with respect to it, to find the proper place for it in the corresponding context. For
each word of the utterance . . . we, as it were, lay down a set of our own
answering words. The greater their number and weight, the deeper and more
substantial our understanding will be. . . . *Any true understanding is dialogic
in nature.*"[1] According to Volosinov/Bakhtin, we never listen to the words of
another in a neutral way. We always bring some kind of orientation in which

we "lay down a set of answering words." How we orient ourselves can either promote or impede "true" understanding, which is enhanced the greater "the number and weight" of our answering words. Volosinov/Bakhtin suggest an ideal mode of understanding in which the listener responds not just in one way, or not at all, but in myriad ways, which somehow carry "weight." In the discussion below of Portia's appeal to Shylock to show mercy, and of Shylock's reception of this speech, I hope to show how they both go about understanding or failing to understand each other by orienting themselves with answering words which undermine, rather than deepen, their mutual understanding, and which diminish, rather than enhance, their dialogic freedom.

## ADVOCATING MERCY

Thousands of high school students every year memorize Portia's famous speech about mercy:

> The quality of mercy is not strained,
> It droppeth as the gentle rain from heaven
> Upon the place beneath. It is twice blest;
> It blesseth him that gives and him that takes.
> 'Tis mightiest in the mightiest; it becomes
> The throned monarch better than his crown.
> His scepter shows the force of temporal power,
> The attribute to awe and majesty,
> Wherein doth sit the dread and fear of kings,
> But mercy is above that sceptered sway;
> It is enthroned in the hearts of kings,
> It is an attribute to God himself,
> And earthly power doth then show likest God's
> When mercy seasons justice. Therefore, Jew,
> Though justice be thy plea, consider this:
> That, in the course of justice, none of us
> Should see salvation. [2]

These words celebrate a central tenet of Christianity, the call to temper justice with mercy, indeed to elevate mercy above justice as the quality in humans that brings them closest to God. Portia has just appealed to Shylock to give up his murderous quest for a pound of Antonio's flesh, and he has responded with a question, "On what compulsion must I [be merciful]?" (4.1.178). He sees the situation in terms of autonomy, a question of the difference between what he is free to do, and what he can be compelled not to do. Portia replies that mercy is not something that can be compelled at all. It must be voluntary. It is a free decision that is as natural as rain, and it blesses both the merciful and the person granted mercy. It is also a powerful choice, more powerful than a king's decrees, because it is an attribute man shares with God. If God were not merciful to us, if he relied only on justice and we got only what we deserved, none of us would ever reach heaven.

This message would have resonated well with Dante in the *Inferno*. Because God takes mercy on Dante the pilgrim in the dark woods of Canto I, he is able to break free of his nearly suicidal mid-life crisis and embark on his journey toward salvation. It is because of God's mercy that Virgil arrives to guide the pilgrim through Hell, then Beatrice arrives to guide him through Purgatory to Paradise. The message of Portia's speech resonates well with her Christian audience in the hearing room where Antonio is to forfeit his bond, as well as with theater audiences, who never fail to experience the power of her rhetoric. Her words seem timeless and wise, evidence for regarding Shakespeare as a prophet of universal truths.[3] All the power a king has to make things happen is not as important, Portia says, as the capacity we each have in our hearts to choose to act mercifully. Remembering that we all answer to God, and that God calls on us to be merciful, we know that when we choose to respond to that call we are our best selves, most like God. It is a sermonic message, and it is not surprising that, lifted from the play, like a jewel from its setting, it finds its way into the pulpit as well as the classroom. Readers disagree about whether the Portia who delivers this sermon to Shylock is someone to be admired or doubted—whether she is a fairy-tale princess and ideal Christian, or a decadent Venetian who fails to extend the very mercy she advocates. They disagree about whether Portia is reaching out to Shylock with one last opportunity to abandon his revenge, or luring him into a false sense of security, so that she can trap him with her quibbles about drops of blood. Yet everyone agrees that this speech is a powerful statement of the Christian ideal.

## LISTENING TO A SPEECH ABOUT MERCY

When we look at Portia's speech from a dialogic perspective, focusing on it as a two-sided act (which is really multi-sided), coauthored by whoever is listening, we see how its meaning pulls centrifugally in several directions, even as various characters and audiences seek to unify its meaning centripetally as one coherent message. Portia's listeners include Shylock and the Christians who pack the room, as well her superaddressee, the Christian God, to whom she refers. In the fictional world of the play, she is aware of these listeners. Her words are codetermined by their presence and by her desire to please, influence, placate, ignore, or offend. Portia's listeners also include readers and playgoers who overhear what she says. These people do not directly codetermine her words, in that by convention she is unaware of them, but to the extent that Shakespeare anticipated their favorable, neutral, or unfavorable reactions, they codetermine his creation of her words.[4] Furthermore, listeners and readers over hundreds of years of historical change, inhabiting diverse "interpretive communities," have brought their own cultural assumptions and personal experiences to the play, as have actors and directors. These people, too, have a role in coauthoring the meanings of this speech. Behind the universal sermon that Portia's speech about mercy seems to be, then, lie a number of coauthoring forces with the potential to destabilize its presumed universal meaning. In fact, beneath its surface lie mutually exclusive possibilities that call on audiences and readers to impose their own coherence on the chaotic forces unleashed by it.

For her Christian listeners on stage, Portia's words about mercy reinforce everything they have ever heard about grace and forgiveness. They know Portia's centripetal, unifying message even before she opens her mouth, and we can just imagine them nodding along as she describes "the gentle rain from heaven" and the "attribute to God himself." Their God is the God of salvation, who confronts the sins of mankind with a love so great that it mitigates the just punishments that we all deserve and allows us to "see salvation." Portia's receptive Christian audience encourages her to express these central tenets of their religion. She can take for granted that they understand and agree with her message, which she regards as self-evidently, universally true. Many readers react to the speech in much the same way as Portia's Venetian listeners do, seeing it as an invitation to Shylock to abandon his murderous revenge before it is too late. Trying to persuade him, rather than force him, to spare Antonio's life, Portia leaves the choice in his hands, for better or worse, and many readers applaud her for that.

The speech means something entirely different to Shylock. Although it is ostensibly directed to him, since it answers his question "Why must I be merciful?," it paradoxically answers him without being answerable to him.[5] The very words that appeal so much to Portia's Venetian listeners exclude him from the conversation. As much as she can count on the Venetians to respond with enthusiasm, she can count on Shylock to bristle. As a captive listener turns a deaf ear to a tedious sermon, he can be expected to tune out much of what she has to say. What he does register is likely to offend. As an outsider to a religion and a cultural majority that has systematically excluded him—a majority he has no desire to join—he is not likely to react favorably to a speech that focuses on the central figure (Christ) and central tenet (mercy) of that hostile faith. The very words that register with his Christian listeners as eloquent, holy, and wise register with him as insulting and crude. The mercy that Portia trumpets as "above this scept'red sway, . . . enthroned in the hearts of kings" resonates for Christians with all the force of an uncontested absolute. These same words resonate for Shylock with centuries of expulsion and confiscation. Portia's speech, which carries a centripetal, unifying force for her Christian listeners, carries an equivalent centripetal, unifying force for Shylock, one that confirms him in his experience of exclusion and injustice.

If Portia had wanted to build bridges to Shylock, she could have chosen to speak of goodness, uprightness, generosity, the Ten Commandments—any number of values shared by Christians and Jews. She could have cultivated receptivity, common ground, or a face-saving way for Shylock to find "answering words" that would orient him to give up his designs on Antonio's life. She chooses instead the one value that celebrates the most revolutionary detail in Christianity, the existence of a Messiah who has come to earth, a Messiah whose legitimacy is not recognized by Jews. For her Christian audience every syllable Portia utters reminds them of their shared faith, just as in the *Iliad* Priam reminds Achilles of their shared reverence for a father's pain. For Shylock, however, Portia's words carry an equal but opposite valence, reminding him that he is not a member of their community. Thus, even as the Christians warm to her sermon, ever more receptive to the "gentle rain" and the "hearts of kings," these phrases make Shylock wince. Stephen Greenblatt observes that "Portia's plea for tolerance and compassion might seem to rest on universal premises, but it in fact neatly excludes the Jew from Portia's apparently inclusive 'we'" in "We do pray for mercy."[6]

The words that conclude Portia's sermon on mercy also register differently for Shylock than they do for the Christians:

> I have spoke thus much
> To mitigate the justice of thy plea;
> Which if thou follow, this strict court of Venice
> Must needs give sentence 'gainst the merchant there. (4.1.202–5)

The Christians hear: "Let mercy outweigh justice, because justice alone is not true justice." Shylock, however, hears: "If you were one of us, you would let go the idea that the Messiah has not yet appeared, and you would embrace our Messiah and everything he stands for, especially mercy. But this is beyond you. All we expect you to do is adhere to the strict laws of Venice, which allow you not only to proceed in your claim, but to triumph." Those who view Portia positively argue that here she gives Shylock a chance either to save himself by embracing Christian mercy, or to condemn himself by rejecting it. It could also be argued, though, that here she not only gives Shylock spiritual rope but uses it to trip him. Although she appears to be inviting him to listen to his better angels, first she alienates him with her mercy talk, and then she directs his hostility toward revenge. She reminds him that the Venetian laws of commerce—strictly enforced to protect the trade that is the city's lifeblood—will let him get away with murder. This she does without risk, since she knows all along that she is about to spring on him the Alien Law that she could have invoked earlier if she had wanted to. According to this law, which Shylock appears not to be aware of, anyone who seeks the life of a citizen of Venice will have half his wealth confiscated by the intended victim, the other half by the state, and will also face the death penalty, unless the Duke of Venice chooses to intervene. The Duke spares Shylock's life, and Antonio spares him half the fine, so we could say that Shylock receives mercy. The condition for this mercy that Antonio adds, though, is Shylock's forced conversion to Christianity. Is mercy, under these circumstances, still dropping "as the gentle rain from heaven?"

Some readers justify this treatment as a genuine attempt to save Shylock's soul. Others excuse it as characteristic of Shakespeare's anti-Semitic London, where Judaism could not be openly practiced and where the few Jews who remained after the expulsions of 1290 were compelled by law to worship as Christians. These explanations notwithstanding, both readers and theater audiences find it difficult to view Shylock's forced conversion as an act of mercy. When Portia asks, "Art thou contented, Jew?," they are made uncomfortable by Shylock's answer: "I am content" (1.4.390–91). They see this answer as given under duress to a Duke who has just threatened to "recant/ The pardon that I late pronounced" (1.4.388–89) and to a Portia who rubs in his humiliation by addressing him not by name but by the designation he is here being forced to relinquish.

The irony of a speech about mercy leading to this treatment is not lost on modern audiences, who, as listeners to Portia's speech on mercy, coauthor it. What audiences see and hear as the words of Shakespeare's character is, of course, not a single, unitary thing. It is a constellation of possibilities mediated by texts, actors, and directors, and influenced also by their own cultural assumptions, their attitudes toward history, the treatment of Jews, and the role of anti-Semitism in the world. Thus, there is no unified perspective on the speech about mercy, coauthored by all audience members, as is the case with the Venetian Christians or Shylock. Audiences and readers do have a unique orientation, however, in that they get to see Portia and Shylock both as they see themselves and as they see each other. In Bakhtinian terms you could say that while Portia sees behind Shylock's back, and Shylock sees behind Portia's back, only the other characters on stage and the patrons in the theater can see behind both their backs, not only taking in what Portia and Shylock fail to see, but watching them fail to understand each other. The other Christians on stage share Portia's views so completely that they cannot step back from them and benefit from this opportunity. The hostilities that make Portia and Shylock unable to share each other's perspectives are on display, however, for audiences to ponder. In the process the play invites us to break free from the limitations of the perspectives of either Portia or Shylock.

A key provocation for audiences is the irony in hearing a sermon about mercy, then seeing mercy enacted through legal tricks, death threats, confiscations, and a forced conversion. It makes us rethink the whole sermon that has made a case for why we should be merciful. We have been presuming that this argument is being made only for Shylock's benefit, because everyone else knows mercy's unquestioned value. What if this is not the case? Katerina Clark and Michael Holquist argue that "when a value judgment ceases to be automatic, when it needs to be explained or rationalized, its basis in society has already started to crumble."[7] From this perspective, Portia's most famous speech can be seen as a rationalization that would not be needed if the value it proclaims were not already beginning to crumble. From this perspective, Shylock is not the only one who requires an explanation. The Christians also need Portia's sermon as a centripetal reminder of what they profess to believe. Given the mercantile conditions that make Shakespeare's Venice possible as an international trading port, that make Antonio possible as a merchant, that make Shylock possible as a moneylender, and that make Elizabethan playhouses profitable, Portia's mercy speech works to stave off the centrifugal force of the modern commercial world. As she advocates central tenets of her faith, with a sense that God, to whom she is answerable, witnesses and in that sense coauthors her remarks, she is also expressing them before an audience that has trouble putting these tenets into practice.

Her efforts to stave off the force of the modern commercial world infiltrate her vocabulary. She aligns mercy not with the commercial language of ships, spices, and silks, but with the medieval language of scepters, crowns, and thrones (on earth), rain (in nature), and salvation (in heaven). By contrast, she presents justice as a disembodied abstraction, or she aligns it with "this strict court of Venice" that must "give sentence." Justice is linked most visibly not to Shylock and his Jewishness, but to the commercial world of Venice. According to the ideology that permeates this commercial context, human relationships are governed not by Christian mercy but by the joint decisions of strangers engaged in international trade. Antonio himself, the merchant of Venice, articulates this view:

> The Duke cannot deny the course of law;
> For the commodity that strangers have
> With us in Venice, if it be denied,
> Will much impeach the justice of the state,
> Since that the trade and profit of the city
> Consisteth of all nations. (3.3.26–31)

No talk here of scepters, crowns, thrones, and the medieval kingdoms they call to mind. Instead, we are given city, state, nation, and the modern commercial world of "trade and profit." This world is not viable without some way to handle communications and disputes between people from widely different backgrounds, people who might have absolutely nothing to say to each other, except out of commercial necessity. From this perspective, individuals are viewed not as members of families, tribes, or kingdoms, but as self-maximizers who enter into temporary agreements, not to seek salvation but to accumulate wealth. These agreements reward compliance and penalize default, all in terms mutually acceptable to the parties involved. The solution to the absence of personal, hierarchical, or cultural ties is the law of contract that makes Shakespeare's Venice and the modern commercial world possible.

It is not surprising that Portia, whose vast wealth "droppeth as a gentle rain" from a dead father who does not appear to have needed the commercial world to accumulate it, expresses her appeal for mercy in the language of medieval fantasy. She inscribes herself and her values within a medieval narrative that absolutely charms her Christian listeners. Nor is it surprising that this same Portia connects justice and penalty to commercial Venice, presenting them as the negative alternative to Christian mercy. While she unifies her speech by focusing on mercy, however, the centrifugal force of the commercial world of Venice threatens the unity of that idea. Just how precarious mercy is becomes evident in the way Portia finally wins. She says to Shylock:

> Tarry a little. There is something else.
> This bond doth give thee here no jot of blood.
> The words expressly are "a pound of flesh."
> Take then thy bond. Take thou thy pound of flesh.
> But in the cutting of it, if thou dost shed
> One drop of Christian blood, thy lands and goods
> Are by the laws of Venice confiscate
> Unto the state of Venice. (4.1.300–307)

Her legalistic sophistry about the drop of blood is authorized by a literal reading made possible not just by Shylock, who has insisted on the letter of the law, but by a city that owes its existence to strictly enforced contracts. If the hearing scene is the site of a contest between ways of succeeding in the world—medieval Christian vs. modern commercial—the latter prevails. Being able to function within the modern perspective makes Portia successful, but it also undermines her message as the spokesmodel of mercy.

The more we, as readers or members of a theater audience, think about how Portia succeeds against Shylock and the nature of the mercy he ultimately receives, the more we see that the ideal of mercy she advocates may be beyond the grasp, not just of Shylock, but of everyone in the room. We can imagine thoughts lurking beneath the surface of Portia's sermon: "Let me call up a Christian value we ought to share, because it is so true and so fundamental to everything we consider important. I can describe it just as it was presented to me by my father, and to him by his father, and I stand here to swear before God that this value is more important than any political power or earthly justice. I want this to be true, for myself, for my friends, and for Venice, even if the winds of change are blowing, and we live by other principles that Shylock now seeks to invoke to his own advantage and that I must use to beat him at his own game." By registering the complexity of the conditions under which it is delivered, both in the hearing room on stage and in the modern commercial world that they inhabit, the audience in a theater (or reading the play) joins Portia's more immediate Christian listeners, her God, and Shylock, as coauthors of her mercy speech.

## DIALOGIC DEAFNESS

Thus, Portia's speech on mercy is coauthored by her various listeners to mean different things. Though the words remain the same, their meaning changes radically depending on the listener's perspective. To the Venetian Christians, the speech articulates a revered value, mercy. To Shylock, the speech reenacts his exclusion from their world and that mercy. To audiences and readers, the speech carries overtones that are often confusing and ironic, depending on the historical context of a given performance. The choices that Shakespeare's characters make—to extend or not to extend mercy, or to seek revenge—are similarly coauthored. To the Christians, their willingness not to impose the death penalty and not to confiscate all of Shylock's estate are evidence of their decision to be merciful. Yet, faced with this decision, Shylock can only say, "you take my life/ When you do take the means whereby I live" (4.1.371–72). He does not experience the confiscation of his wealth as mercy. Conversely, for Shylock, the pound of flesh from Antonio would be a just penalty for years of spitting on him on the Rialto. For the Christians, however, it would be a monstrous crime. There is no meeting of the minds between how the Christians and the Jew view the choices they make. Thus, they coauthor action, but the action they coauthor is not mutually understood. They are in fact deaf to each other's most important concerns.

In "The Problem of the Text," Bakhtin explains that the word "always wants to be *heard*, always seeks responsive understanding. . . . For the word (and, consequently, for a human being) there is nothing more terrible than a *lack of response*."[8] Everything we say, according to him, is pitched toward the expectation of some kind of response. That response could be favorable, or it could be neutral, indifferent, bored, impatient, hostile, or even a total mystery. The one thing that we are not prepared for, according to Bahktin— which would in fact drive us to despair, because "there is nothing more terrible"—is the complete absence of response. When the bond agreement between Shylock and Antonio is made in the first place, it happens already within a context of a "lack of response." With currents of ethnic hostility circulating throughout the scene, there is anxiety on both sides about not being heard. Bassanio asks Shylock, "Do you hear?" (1.3.47), while Shylock takes care to correct being misheard: "No, no, no, no, My meaning in saying he is a good man is to have you understand me that he is sufficient" (1.3.13–14).

Both sides sense that whatever it is they say or want, they may well not be heard, or, if they are heard, they may be misunderstood. Hence, both sides take steps to remedy misunderstandings just well enough to agree to the conditions of the loan. This lack of response is an early warning of things to come. It only intensifies in the hearing scene, where Portia's plea for mercy falls on deaf ears, as far as Shylock is concerned, and Shylock's plea for justice backfires. Ultimately the Venetian Christians have each other and their God to save them from the fate of not being heard. That Shylock is deaf to their values is never much of a threat. But the newly minted Christian Shylock who leaves the stage saying "I am content" (4.1.391) has been stripped not just of his wealth and way of life, but of his last, best opportunity for being heard. He has been stripped of his superaddressee, the Jewish God, "whose absolutely just responsive understanding is presumed" (SG, 126). Bakhtin describes the "absolute absence" of the superaddressee, the "absolute *lack of being heard*" as akin to "the understanding of the Fascist torture chamber or hell" (SG, 126). Shylock has been condemned to and by a world that is deaf to him.

If dialogic freedom involves deliberation from multiple perspectives, the ability to see from multiple perspectives and make decisions among others is an important aspect of that freedom. Because Priam can see both from his own perspective as a grieving father and from Achilles's perspective as a grieving warrior and friend, he is able to persuade Achilles to release Hector's body. Because Dante can see from both the poet's and the pilgrim's perspectives, he can present the love of Paolo and Francesca as simultaneously moving and misguided. By contrast, Shylock and the Christians are deaf to each other's words and blind to each other's perspectives. Thus they are all less dialogically free than they would be if they could orient themselves to register each other's viewpoints by laying down a set of their own answering words, with weight and depth. Imprisoned in the narrowness of their orientations, they disqualify each other from humanity. Paradoxically, they abandon any effort to communicate, even as they exchange words. Antonio does not hesitate to admit to Shylock that he spat upon him in the past, and he brags that he would be pleased to do so again. Shylock, in turn, does not hesitate to respond to Portia's mercy speech by saying, "I crave the law,/ The penalty and forfeit of my bond" (4.1.201–2). Each views the other only in terms of winning, losing, and inflicting pain. This is the language of freedom seen as the power to impose one's will (to spit, to inflict pain), but it is not the language of dialogic freedom.

## PROTOCOLS OF READING *THE MERCHANT OF VENICE* FOR AND WITH DIALOGIC FREEDOM

The dialogic deafness of Shylock and the Christians creates both problems and opportunities for Shakespeare's audiences. You could say that generations of readers have reproduced this deafness, siding with either the Christians or Shylock. But the play also calls upon us to transcend the limitations of their perspectives. Though always popular, *The Merchant of Venice* has been one of Shakespeare's most controversial plays and one of his most difficult to perform. Directors often modify it to simplify the problem of multiple perspectives. Thus, the play has been successfully performed in venues as different as eighteenth-century London, Nazi Germany, and contemporary Israel. But it has been a very different play in each setting. The heavily edited eighteenth-century-London version presented Shylock as a comic caricature.[9] German Nazis witnessed an ethnically cleansed production that erased the intermarriage between Shylock's daughter and a Christian.[10] Israeli audiences in 1980 were spared Shylock's conversion to Christianity.[11] Some performances have also been spectacular failures, as was the 1994 Goodman Theatre production that included a projected image of the Rodney King beating in Los Angeles. Most evenings more than half the audience left at intermission.[12] Other performances have been more effective collaborations between actors, directors, and audiences. Patrick Stewart reported that in his 1979 Royal Shakespeare Company production, the director, John Barton, wanted him to play Shylock as a monster, but he was able to work out a portrait that changed from scene to scene and presented Shylock as a "small, complex, real, and recognizable human being, part of us all."[13] Stewart describes Shylock's insistence on his pound of flesh as "the brave, insane solitary act of a man who will defer no more, compromise no more" (19). This is much the spirit of Al Pacino's Shylock in the 2005 film of the play. In an Italian production in 2008, directed by Luca De Fusco, Eros Pagni's Shylock greeted Bassanio and Antonio with the expansive warmth of a host who has learned to pretend not to notice insults.[14] By the time they all reached the hearing room, this demeanor had been peeled away to reveal the hurt man who seizes his opportunity to take revenge.

All these performances struggled with the plasticity of the play and the problems it presents for a director who would like to avoid simplifying *The Merchant of Venice* by presenting it from either Portia's perspective or Shylock's, which are mutually exclusive and mutually incoherent. Though neither character is capable of navigating the epistemological layers of the other's ways of knowing the world, the audience is in a different position. An audience member or a reader can witness both Shylock's and Portia's perspectives, as we have been doing here with the mercy speech. Under these circumstances, the experience of dialogic freedom belongs more to the audience than to the characters in the play. It could be that Shakespeare is simultaneously acknowledging that people can hate each other so much that they must be deaf to each other's words and worth, and that those witnessing this hate can attempt to register both of these antagonistic perspectives. What this means is that although Portia and Shylock will never experience the freedom of looking at mercy from mutually exclusive perspectives, we can. Doing so may enable us to cultivate the ability to "lay down a set of our own answering words," in order to understand and converse with an enemy in ways that Portia and Shylock cannot and to navigate ways of knowing that they are deaf to. Thus, we ready ourselves to begin the conversation that could lead to mutual action which is not violence: something closer to Priam's exchange with Achilles than his slaughter at the hands of Achilles's son.

Shakespeare and Dante both call upon readers to engage in strenuous intellectual activity that they consider an essential precondition for freedom. In Shylock's experience at the end of *The Merchant of Venice,* Shakespeare dramatizes the depressing position of a person not being heard but capable of seeking an insane revenge. If mercy blesses both "him that gives, and him that takes," deafness to another's cry to be heard and understood must damn both "him that is deaf, and him that is not heard." For the Christians it matters only briefly that Shylock is deaf to them, because he is an enemy who can be crushed. For Shylock it matters more, because the Christians' deafness to him, at the center of his humiliation and his despair, wins the day. For both Shylock and the Christians, though, this deafness undermines dialogic freedom. Shakespeare seems to be implying that the world will always contain hateful people who are deaf to their enemies. Our hope lies in the bystanders who register the perspectives being demonized. This does not mean that we must embrace the enemy's perspective. Shakespeare does not present Shylock's revenge as an outcome to be endorsed. Productions that have made Shylock the hero have veered wide of the mark. Dante would see Shylock as someone who has abandoned "the good of intellect," swept away by his passion for revenge. What Shakespeare seems to be suggesting is that for us to be dialogically free we must humanize the enemy enough to coauthor a conversation that can take us beyond violence. To do this, we must cultivate the ability to see things from different perspectives, even uncomfortably different perspectives, rather than take refuge in stereotypes invoked by patriotism and prejudice. This is not an easy thing to do, because the very receptivity that makes us comfortable with and open to our friends makes us deaf to our enemies.

In the face of Shylock's humiliations, the behavior of Bassanio's friend, Gratiano, serves to warn us of the excesses inspired by receptivity to a friend. As Portia's trap is sprung, Gratiano becomes a receptive choral voice to her, mocking Shylock by calling out from the gallery: "O upright judge!" (4.1.310) and "O learned judge" (4.1.314). He echoes Shylock's earlier enthusiasm for revenge when he had praised Portia, "O wise young judge, how I do honor thee!" (4.1.221). Once Shylock has been condemned and his wealth confiscated, Portia commands him to "beg mercy of the Duke," and Gratiano rubs salt in the wound:

> Beg that thou mayst have leave to hang thyself—
> And yet, thy wealth being forfeit to the state,
> Thou hast not left the value of a cord.
> Therefore thou must be hanged at the state's charge. (4.1.359–62)

Gratiano's malicious joke is ignored by the Duke, who proceeds to pardon Shylock's life. It is as if Gratiano has become a bit of an embarrassment. In the absence of any textual response in the form of dialogue assigned by Shakespeare to other characters, a director of this scene must decide whether or not to have the people around Gratiano laugh while the sober Duke goes about his job of dispensing justice. When Portia asks, "What mercy can you render him, Antonio?" Gratiano blurts out, "A halter gratis" (4.1.376). He labors the joke about the newly impoverished Shylock not being able to afford a piece of rope to hang himself. The hangman can give him a noose for free! Once again his words are ignored as Antonio explains the condition of Shylock's mercy: conversion to Christianity.

We have already examined the audience's discomfort at Shylock's treatment by Portia, the court, and Antonio. Now, this bullying and gloating from Gratiano, replete with crude humor that is ignored by the speaking characters, registers with the audience as evidence of the receptivity Gratiano takes for granted from his friends. He is receptive to them, and they to him. He thinks he is being funny, and he expects them to share the joke. In the opening of the play, when everyone is trying to cheer up Antonio, who is inexplicably sad, Gratiano says:

> Let me play the fool.
> With mirth and laughter let old wrinkles come,
> And let my liver rather heat with wine
> Than my heart cool with mortifying groans. (1.1.79–82)

Gratiano gladly plays the fool, a role that he enjoys and others applaud. He would rather laugh than groan, and so he is the one to make jokes as Shylock is being dispensed with. This behavior would not surprise his friends. Only Shakespeare goes to some trouble to not have the speaking characters on stage react to Gratiano's jokes—jokes that reflect not just the choice of laughter over pain, but the choice to laugh while inflicting pain.

By presenting the Duke, Portia, and Antonio *not* reacting to Gratiano, Shakespeare makes us think twice about the very receptivity that has conditioned Gratiano to behave this way. Being heard is a very good thing, in that the listener's anticipated response coauthors our words and actions by giving us the courage to speak up or to act. Yet, being heard can also reinforce the prejudices that make us deaf to the suffering we inflict on others. Earlier patterns of receptivity have encouraged Gratiano's present behavior toward Shylock, enabling his cruelty, even as his friends stand by in silence. The Italian production of *Il Mercante di Venezia* in 2008 was especially revealing in this regard. While the characters on stage made no response to Gratiano's remarks, the audience in Perugia's Teatro Morlacchi erupted with laughter the first time he interrupted with "O upright judge! Mark, Jew. O learned judge!" (4.1.310).[15] Shylock had been hoist upon his own petard. Five lines later, when Gratiano repeated the line almost exactly, they laughed again. With the third iteration of the same joke five lines later, the laughter was less robust. Ten lines later Gratiano could not resist repeating, "A second Daniel, a Daniel, Jew!" (4.1.330). The chuckles in the audience were scattered, sounding a little self-conscious. By the time Gratiano called for "A halter gratis!" (4.1.376), there was complete silence in the hall. No one told the audience not to laugh, but together they experienced a diminishing response, moment by moment, to Gratiano's outbursts. Was it that they were tired of the repetition of the joke? Were they increasingly self-conscious about piling on? Had Shakespeare built in this response as a predictable consequence of eight interruptions? Was it a consequence of our "politically correct" times? Whatever the explanation, the lack of a response from the audience in Teatro Morlacchi was as audible as their earlier laughter. They had mimicked Gratiano's Christian friends in encouraging his behavior, but they gradually withdrew their complicity and eventually marginalized him with silence.

Whatever else it is, *The Merchant of Venice* is an invitation to readers and viewers to ponder this paradox: the very receptivity to others that is essential to dialogic freedom is potentially destructive to it, not just in the ways Dante experienced with Francesca, but because this receptivity can lead to dialogic deafness toward the excluded "other." This message is lost on the characters within *The Merchant of Venice*, who do not seem to register the mutually exclusive perspectives of Portia and Shylock. They lack the capacity to navigate the layers of knowing represented by these perspectives on mercy, justice, and revenge, and to orient themselves by laying down a weighty set of their own answering words. It remains for audiences and readers to try to succeed where these characters fail, not just within the imaginary world of a Shakespeare play, but in the world beyond the theater.

## NOTES

1. V. N. Volosinov, *Marxism and the Philosophy of Language*, trans. Ladislaw Matejka and I. R. Titunik (New York and London: Seminar Press, 1973), 102. Citations to *Marxism and the Philosophy of Language* are to this edition with the abbreviation MPL. I refer to the author of this work as Volosinov/Bakhtin, to acknowledge controversies about authorship, discussed above in chapter 1, note 12.

2. William Shakespeare, *The Merchant of Venice*, in *The Norton Shakespeare*, ed. Stephen Greenblatt (New York: Norton, 1997), 4.1.179–95.

3. This was the view held by Ben Jonson, who said of Shakespeare that "He was not of an age, but for all time!" William Shakespeare, *First Folio of Shakespeare Facsimile* (New York: Norton, 1968), 10. Many others have agreed. The critical tradition over several centuries is summarized by David Bevington in *The Necessary Shakespeare* (New York: Longman, 2002), lxxx–xcii. He explains that in the nineteenth century the tendency was to "exalt Shakespeare as a poet and a philosopher rather than as a playwright" (lxxxii). In the twentieth century, readers reacted to this "universal" Shakespeare by seeking "a better understanding of his historical milieu" (lxxxiii). They emphasized "artifice or convention in the construction of a play" (lxxxiii). The "New" Criticism valued "close reading," with a focus on imagery and "a whole vision of the play" (lxxxv). Deconstruction, in reaction to the formalism of this approach, noted the instability of Shakespeare's texts, while reader response criticism focused on the process of performance and the reception of Shakespeare by various "interpretive communities." Bevington calls the world of Shakespeare criticism today "one of consolidation" (xci). According to him, "Postmodernism and indeterminism have changed the critical landscape for better and for worse. . . . What the contemporary critical scene does best is to free critics to be who they are and to write without paying dues to any particular affiliation. The results are refreshingly diverse" (xcii). An array of those approaches, from New Criticism to Postcolonial Perspectives can be found in *Shakespeare: An Anthology of Criticism and Theory, 1945–2000*, ed. Russ McDonald (Malden, MA: Blackwell, 2004). In this volume René Girard's psychoanalytic "To Entrap the Wisest" (353–64) presents a provocative double reading of Shylock as scapegoat. For an approach to the play that seeks to recapture lost cultural contexts, see *The Merchant of Venice*, Longman Cultural Edition, ed. Lawrence Danson (New York: Longman, 2005). My approach combines what I hope is the best of the exegetical tradition (as a "guiderail") with new ways of responding to problems of indeterminacy, contradiction, and performance. My discussion is conditioned by and extends the protocols of reading for and with dialogic freedom discussed above in chapters 2 and 3.

4. Referencing books rather than plays, but making a point that applies to the Shakespeare who knew that audiences would be watching his plays, and that many in them would be reading quartos circulating in London, Volosinov/Bakhtin argue that "A book, i. e., *a verbal performance in print*, . . . is calculated for active perception, involving attentive reading and inner responsiveness, and organized *printed* reaction. . . . It responds to something, objects to something, affirms something, anticipates possible responses and objections, seeks support, and so on" (MPL, 95).

5. The analysis of *The Merchant of Venice* in this chapter repeats, with permission, some material from my article, "Authorizing Meaning in *The Merchant of Venice*," *Text and Performance Quarterly* 22, no. 1 (2002): 47–62.

6. Stephen Greenblatt, "Introduction" to *The Merchant of Venice*, in William Shakespeare, *The Norton Shakespeare*, 1087.

7. Michael Holquist and Katerina Clark, *Mikhail Bakhtin* (Cambridge, MA: Harvard University Press, 1984), 207.

8. Mikhail Bakhtin, "The Problem of the Text," in *Speech Genres and Other Late Essays*, ed. Caryl Emerson and Michael Holquist; trans. Vern McGee (Austin: University of Texas Press, 1986), 127. Citations to *Speech Genres* are to this text, with the abbreviation SG.

9. James Bulman, *The Merchant of Venice: Shakespeare in Performance* (New York: Manchester University Press, 1991), 23.

10. John Gross, *Shylock: A Legend and its Legacy* (New York: Simon & Schuster, 1992), 320.

11. James Shapiro, *Shakespeare and the Jews* (New York: Columbia University Press, 1996),
228–29.

12. W. B. Worthen, *Shakespeare and the Authority of Performance* (New York: Cambridge University Press, 1997), 77.

13. Patrick Stewart, "Performing Shylock," in *Players of Shakespeare: Essays in Shakespearean Performance by Twelve Players with the Royal Shakespeare Company*, ed. Philip Brockbank (Cambridge, UK: Cambridge University Press, 1985), 27.

14. William Shakespeare, *Il Mercante di Venezia*, performance at Teatro Morlacchi, Perugia, Italy, *Estate Teatrale Veronese*, April 6, 2008.

15. I give the English here, even though the Perugian production was in Italian. The point is not the exact words that Graziano used, which reflected a fairly literal translation into Italian, but rather, the audience's laughter.

## Chapter Five

# The Virtuosity of Satan in *Paradise Lost*

Dialogic freedom: a two-sided act, chosen within a field of unifying and fragmenting forces along *a continuum of minimal to maximal layers of knowing*
that are never final.

Milton's *Paradise Lost* is periodically reinvented by its readers. When a
casebook of critical essays was published on the cusp of the twenty-first
century, its editor boldly claimed: "The reading of *Paradise Lost* has been
transformed by contemporary criticism."[1] Several decades earlier, A. J. A.
Waldock had announced with similar conviction, "One of the most notable
events of contemporary criticism has been the rediscovery of *Paradise
Lost*."[2] In both cases, the word "contemporary" valorized a transformative
present presumed to penetrate more deeply than ever into how Milton's epic
should be read. Each generation boasts of greater clarity, only to be corrected
by the next. Although this kind of revisionism shapes the reception of all
texts, *Paradise Lost* seems to inspire in its readers an unusually strong desire
to rectify the mistakes of the past.[3] Hence, we hear William Empson say,
"The poem, if read with understanding," (*Milton's God*, 25), or John Runrich, "When we look closely enough at *Paradise Lost*" (*Milton Unbound*,
118), as if the answer is lying in wait for just the right reader. Even the
current fascination with the poem's indeterminacy rests on the assumption
that if we read it carefully enough we can come to appreciate just how
indeterminate it is. Thus, when in 2005 Peter Herman noted that "paradigms
governing Milton studies are shifting" with the recent emergence of "guerilla
Miltonists" who combat a "tendency toward theoretical conservatism," we
get the impression that we are once again on the verge of discovering just the

proper set of corrective lenses that will let us finally see the poem for what it is.

John Dryden, one of the first to correct how *Paradise Lost* should be read, "was among those who thought that the Devil had been Milton's 'hero, instead of Adam.'"[4] This idea appealed to the Romantic poets, including William Blake, who claimed that Milton was "of the Devil's party without knowing it."[5] In the twentieth century, Empson went so far as to conclude that "the poem, if read with understanding, must be read with growing horror unless you decide to reject its God."[6] For our purposes, it is not necessary to resolve this controversy about who is Milton's hero, because our interest lies in Satan's dialogic ability to coauthor choices, not with his heroism or infamy. We face a different and not altogether unrelated problem, however. When Bakhtin and his collaborators imagined the dialogic nature of communication, they imagined people like you and me speaking with each other, not gods, or demons, or the prelapsarian Adam and Eve. To the extent that God was a participant in human dialogue, Bakhtin described him as a "superaddressee" that the speaker felt answerable to—an unquestioned perfect being from a realm of unified values above and beyond the human—not an equal participant. As superaddressee, God, though a powerful force in human decision and action, could never participate as an equal in codetermining thoughts, words, or deeds. Milton's God is by definition a superaddressee, and in his perfection monologic, or one-dimensional. His nemesis Satan is similarly one-dimensional from a theological perspective, since he represents pure evil. Milton's Adam and Eve are also monologic before the Fall, because they are at that point perfect. Hence, strictly speaking, we cannot examine dialogic relationships between the major characters of Milton's *Paradise Lost* before the Fall. These characters are all beings who are not part of human experience as we know it.

Yet, when Milton set about to "justify the ways of God to man" in his Christian epic, he took it upon himself to turn God, Christ, and Satan into dramatic characters with anthropomorphic qualities, and he took it upon himself to present the unfallen Adam and Eve as like you and me in their desire for love, companionship, meaningful work, and understanding. This translation of indescribable, monologic deities, demons, and unfallen humans, into multi-faceted characters created many problems for Milton's epic. The Affable Archangel Raphael, sent by God to answer Adam and Eve's questions and to warn them about Satan, ponders the challenge, when he asks, "How shall I relate/ To human sense th'invisible exploits/ Of warring spirits?" (IV, 564–66).[7] His solution is to attempt to use metaphor and allegory to translate the fundamentally incomprehensible supernatural world into something humans can grasp: "What surmounts the reach/ Of human sense I shall delineate so/ By lik'ning spiritual to corporal forms/ As may express them best" (571–74). As many have noted, Milton uses Raphael to pose—

and to suggest a solution to—a problem that he himself faces when he decides to present demons, deities, and unfallen humans in dramatic situations in which they interact.

Through allegory, metaphor, and projected psychological identities, Milton makes these biblical beings into characters who are comprehensible in a human way; but such comparisons can only be approximate, and they run the risk of misleading, confusing, or frustrating readers. When he presents supernatural characters, as well as the perfect Adam and Eve, with human attributes, these humanized characters invite readers to judge them from their own human perspectives. Psychologizing Satan's rebellion runs the risk of inviting readers to see him as a noble rebel challenging a tyrant God, instead of as the Author of Evil. Psychologizing Adam's decision to join Eve in the Fall runs the risk of presenting him not as the First Disobedient Man, but as a noble self-sacrificing husband, willing to die with his wife rather than replace her with a better model. Psychologizing God runs the risk of presenting him as an irritable "School Divine," instead of as the perfect Creator of All.

These psychologized characters are at the heart of the various controversies about how Milton's epic should be read, and they provide evidence for its indeterminacy. When these characters interact, they also invite a dialogic reading of the poem, even though from a traditional theological perspective they are by definition incapable of the give and take essential to Bakhtin's concept of the dialogic. With this caveat—that the very qualities that identify Satan as capable of interacting with others (his heroic rhetoric, his rebellious resolve, his self-doubting exploration of options), render him theologically problematic (anthropomorphic rather than supernatural)—we can examine Satan as a case study in dialogic virtuosity. Whatever the doctrinal, political, and aesthetic problems Milton brought on himself when he made Satan sound like a human being, Milton's anthropomorphic Satan is a virtuoso when it comes to grasping the unifying, centripetal forces at the root of his listeners' perspectives and navigating the ways of knowing inhabited by others. He rises to an astonishing array of challenges in his encounters with fallen angels, his children, the anarch of Chaos, the Sharpest-Sighted Spirit (Uriel), and Eve, demonstrating that dialogic freedom, though a potent force for good, can also be used to accomplish evil. When Satan first imagines Eve's perspective, her innocence almost derails his project to undermine man's allegiance to God. Ultimately, his capacity to see things more innocently for a moment only deepens his misery as he rededicates himself to his decision to destroy goodness. The dialogic virtuosity of Milton's Satan impresses upon readers the need to strenuously exercise our intellects and hearts to understand the attractions of as many perspectives as possible, especially Satan's.

## MILTON'S FASCINATION WITH FREEDOM

Long before he published *Paradise Lost* in 1667, John Milton was already fascinated by freedom. He had almost landed in an Italian jail in 1639, "because the English Jesuits of Rome had taken offense at his habit of free speech, wherever he went, on the subject of religion."[8] In 1643 he sent shock waves through London by publishing a pamphlet justifying divorce, without bothering to get permission from one of Parliament's official censors. He followed this transgression the next year with another unlicensed pamphlet, the *Areopagitica*, considered one of the most eloquent essays in English to advocate freedom from prior censorship. Another of his essays justified regicide, and his political activities as Latin Secretary for Oliver Cromwell gave him a ringside seat to a decade of debates about freedom and tyranny. It was a miracle that he escaped execution after the monarchy was restored in 1660. He spent three dark years in seclusion as "the detestable blind republican and regicide who had, by too great clemency, been left unhanged."[9] Banished from political life, he now had time to write, and the result was *Paradise Lost*.

It should be no surprise that Milton's epic turned out to be deeply political. Parliamentarian arguments for freedom are echoed not just in the conversations between Adam and Eve, but in the rhetoric of the fallen angels' councils, where Satan presides as Lord Protector of the damned. Especially political is Milton's version of the crucial moment in heaven when Lucifer convinces a third of the angels to join him in rebellion. They have gathered ostensibly to welcome the newly begotten son of God, anointed to be head of all the angels. Milton's God has proclaimed that before his only son "shall bow/ All knees in heav'n" (V, 607–8). Lucifer's pretext for gathering together the angels is "only to consult how we may best/ With what may be devised of honors new/ Receive him" (V, 779–81). Together they will plan a huge party to celebrate the Son's status as God's other self. Masterfully, Lucifer modulates his planned welcome into an invitation to rebellion against a tyrant God:

> This only to consult how we may best
> With what may be devised of honors new
> Receive him coming to receive from us
> Knee-tribute yet unpaid, prostration vile,
> Too much to one, but double how endured,
> To one and to his image now proclaimed?
> But what if better counsels might erect
> Our minds and teach us to cast off this yoke? (V, 779–86)

Lucifer repeats God's proclamation that all knees in heaven "shall bow" to the Son of God. He reinterprets that gesture, though, not as devotion, but as "knee-tribute yet unpaid, prostration vile." What was presented by Milton's

God as an extension to his son of the worship due God himself, is presented by Lucifer as the "vile" tribute endured by captives under the yoke of a conqueror. The rebellion Lucifer is about to lead will be liberation from this humiliation. Lucifer asks rhetorically, "Who can in reason then or right assume/ Monarchy over such as live by right/ His equals, if in power and splendor less,/ In freedom equal?" (V, 793–96). Luicifer's listeners, his soon-to-be-fallen fellow angels, coauthor this rhetorical question by being receptive to it. In the process, they allow Satan to focus and unify their conception of freedom, filtering out moral complexities in favor of regarding it merely as a capacity for physical domination.

The assumption here is that the only thing that separates God from the angels is his superior might, though even that power is qualified with a hypothetical "if." The language of freedom and equality dominates Lucifer's appeal, as if he were Milton justifying the rights of Parliament before Charles I. The prospect of freedom from a monarch's domination convinces a third of the angels to rebel. Thus, Milton takes his experience of revolution and incorporates it into his epic. This is a risky business, since it puts the very best arguments for rebellion—arguments that have led in England to regicide—into the mouth of Satan. That heaven is not England, and God not a monarch, is something that readers like C. S. Lewis and Douglas Bush believe Milton hopes his readers will realize, but the fact that Satan is an eloquent advocate for negative liberty (freedom from interference) makes him dangerously appealing.[10] A century and a half after Milton wrote his epic, Satan's determination not to be dominated by anyone, not even God, won over Romantic poets like Byron and Blake, who saw him as Milton's unintended hero. Today, Satan's declarations of independence continue to appeal to many readers, while others expose their specious logic or probe the ambiguity of the situation from which they arise.

What seems most clear is that Satan's negative liberty is negative liberty in its most radical and dangerous form. From his perspective, anyone who seeks to be completely free from the domination of someone else will eventually need to dominate everyone else. As he works to persuade others to join his rebellion, Milton's Satan always returns to this vision of freedom based on power, and he invites others to join in a bogus equality that always leaves him in charge. Ironically, when he claims that the angels and God are "in freedom equal," he is right, but the freedom and equality he has in mind, which involve being equally free politically to seize what they think they deserve, are not Milton's God's freedom and equality, which involve being equally free morally to choose between good and evil. *Paradise Lost* presents a constant battle between these mutually exclusive perspectives on freedom, with Satan always reducing moral questions to a matter of power, as if the only aspect of God that matters is the thunderbolt and the only way to be free is to be in charge. Because of Satan's dialogic virtuosity he is remarkably successful at propagating his vision.

## SPEAKING ALL LANGUAGES

Milton's Satan seems comfortable speaking with everyone he encounters. An excellent listener, he can grasp in a moment another creature's needs, fertilize them with visions of freedom as power, and nurture them even as he asks for and gets what he wants. As he navigates his way among angels, monsters, and humans, his ability to understand the perspectives of others and to smoothly shift between the epistemological layers of their various ways of knowing the world, is dazzling. The expectations he either happens upon or helps to shape codetermine his strategies of deception and persuasion. Many people know from Genesis about the serpent's success in persuading Eve to eat the forbidden fruit, but unless you read *Paradise Lost* you miss the full splendor of Milton's presentation of the dark side of dialogic freedom—the ability to exploit for the worst possible purposes the capacity to see from the perspective of just about anyone.

For medieval and Renaissance thinkers, the most frightening thing about evil, whether human or diabolical, was its power to pervert the highest intelligence to serve the darkest ends. Education was important precisely because those with the greatest innate abilities had the most potential to wreak havoc once they went off the tracks. What Shakespeare's Gratiano lacks—the ability to see from another's perspective—is something we find in effective religious leaders, therapists, or poets, but also in con artists and frauds. By being an astute listener who encourages others to trust him, Satan coauthors their words and deeds, even as their responses to him coauthor his words and deeds. By presenting an anthropomorphic Prince of Darkness, *Paradise Lost* explores both his dialogic virtuosity and his horror. His virtuosity leads some readers to conclude that he is the poem's hero. His horror leads others to conclude that like Dante, Milton challenges us to see through the most attractive forms evil can take, so that when our time comes to face it—in ourselves and in others—we will be ready.

We first meet Milton's Satan in the burning lake, where he has been cast down from heaven after his rebellion against God. Not long before, he was Lucifer, the light bearer, chief among the Archangels. Now he lies stupefied in chains, after falling a distance impossible for us to imagine:

> Him the Almighty Power
> Hurled headlong flaming from th'ethereal sky
> With hideous ruin and combustion down
> To bottomless perdition, there to dwell
> In adamantine chains and penal fire,
> Who durst defy th'Omnipotent to arms. (I, 44–49)

These lines beg to be read out loud, almost spit out, taking full advantage of percussive consonants, open vowels, and tumbling rhythms that speed Satan to his doom. His damnation will be eternal and bottomless, and his chains will be so hard that they can never melt, no matter how hot the fires of his punishment burn. His headfirst momentum reflects his own role in the matter, having voluntarily hurled himself headlong into the rebellion that cost him heaven. This momentum also reflects his power, his violence, and the counterforce the Omnipotent had to exert to expel him.

Satan will be allowed to leave the burning lake, but he does not know this when he first speaks to his closest comrade, Beelzebub:

> If thou beest he; but O how fall'n! how changed
> From him, who in the happy realms of light
> Clothed with transcendent brightness didst outshine
> Myriads thought bright: if he whom mutual league,
> United thoughts and counsels, equal hope
> And hazard in the glorious enterprise,
> Joined with me once, now misery hath joined
> In equal ruin: into what pit thou seest
> From what highth fall'n, so much the stronger proved
> He with his thunder: and till then who knew
> The force of those dire arms? Yet not for those,
> Nor what the potent victor in his rage
> Can else inflict, do I repent or change.
> . . . What though the field be lost?
> All is not lost; the unconquerable will,
> And study of revenge, immortal hate,
> And courage never to submit or yield. (I, 84–108)

These are Satan's first words in *Paradise Lost*. They reflect how quickly he gets down to the business of rebounding from defeat to continue his war against God. He is in shock, barely able to recognize Beelzebub, but instantly he begins to demonstrate his characteristic ability to lead/manipulate others.[11] Before Beelzebub says a word, Satan figures out what his lieutenant needs to hear. Thus Satan starts with the language of equality, appealing to Beelzebub's presumed desire for "mutual league" and "equal hope," which soften the blow of "equal ruin." He also presents himself and Beelzebub as epic heroes who are temporarily suffering a setback in a "glorious enterprise." While he flatters his companion as an equal warrior, he also casts doubt on the omnipotence of God. He reasons that without a demonstration of his ability to hurl them out of heaven and chain them in the burning lake, no one could have known how powerful God was. The thunderbolt was just hypothetical until it was used. Though God proved himself stronger in the moment he used it, the implication is that perhaps in some future moment God will not prevail. In fact, physical power is one thing, Satan argues, but mental prowess is quite another. The field may be lost, but the will is unconquerable. God cannot control the rebels' choice to rebel. Thus, the fallen angels can still show what heroes they are, by embracing the challenge of revenge.

The most impressive thing about this logic is Satan's ability to anticipate his silent listener's perspective and supply what he needs to hear. He knows that as soon as Beelzebub opens his eyes he will register how physically changed Satan is in this place of "darkness visible," where all his "transcendent brightness" has disappeared. Satan preempts Beelzebub's shock by deflecting it toward Beelzebub himself, and he distracts him with a flattering sense of equality not just with Satan, but with God, whom only thunder has made stronger. God's perfection, too, is cast in doubt by this logic, since it attributes the punishment of the fallen angels not to justice but to rage. The God Satan frames for Beelzebub cannot control his anger and therefore needs to prove his power. As Satan describes this God, he satisfies his listener's need for a unified narrative to explain that the battle is not lost, that God is vulnerable, that the minds of the fallen angels are beyond God's control, and that heroic action is still possible. In the process, Satan demonstrates not only his ability to imagine and shape Beelzebub's perspective, but also his mastery of logic as his main persuasive tool. Many readers have found Satan's logic so compelling that they conclude with Blake that Milton was "of the Devil's party without knowing it."

Yet just as Dante works to sharpen his readers' abilities to see through the self-serving logic of Francesca, Milton makes it possible for readers to see through Satan. We can heroize Satan by accepting his logic, or we can demonize him by questioning his manipulative language of equality. We can observe that equality with the omnipotent and omniscient Christian God is an impossibility, and that even in Hell Satan does not live up to his word: he is not really open to persuasion, preferring rather to rule like a tyrant. What Satan does not explain to Beelzebub is that the fallen angels are free, not because of their innate strength, but because God has insisted on creating all sentient beings morally free. This insistence is one of the central tenets of *Paradise Lost,* explained by Milton's God himself:

> Not free, what proof could they have giv'n sincere
> Of true allegiance, constant faith or love,
> Where only what they needs must do, appeared,
> Not what they would? What praise could they receive?
> What pleasure I from such obedience paid,
> When will and reason (reason also is choice)
> Useless and vain, of freedom both despoiled,
> Made passive both, had served necessity,
> Not me. (III, 103–11)

Milton's God could have created both humans and angels robotically good, incapable of evil. But such creatures would have seemed "useless and vain," passive rather than active. Milton presents here an idea of "serving"—a word not usually associated with independence—which is paradoxically linked not to blind obedience, but to freedom. The prospect of watching creatures think for themselves and take responsibility for their choices was such a source of pleasure to Milton's God that he decided to take the risk that moral freedom always entails: that they might not choose well. To Milton, there is an important distinction between making something possible and causing it. From the perspective of questioning Satan's claims to heroism, God's insistence on moral freedom makes Satan's rebellion possible, but Satan is responsible for choosing to rebel.

Thus it is that God's insistence on freedom leaves the fallen angels not only free to rebel, but free to continue their rebellion, which is why they will be able to leave the burning lake, and Satan will be able to escape the confines of Hell and enter the Garden of Eden. Beelzebub suspects that the fallen angels might not be altogether free from God's designs in Hell, and he asks Satan, "What if our conqueror . . . Have left us this our spirit and strength entire/ Strongly to suffer and support our pains,/ That we may so suffice his vengeful ire,/ Or do him mightier service as his thralls?" (I, 143–49). What if it is all part of God's plan to let the fallen angels plot in Hell to get God back? What if their continued rebellion just intensifies their suffering? What if even in this extended rebellion they will somehow be serving God? These are good questions, and Milton's Satan does in fact wind up serving God's purposes in the larger plan to redeem man through Christ. But in the conversation at hand, Satan, the perfect listener, is ready to quell the doubts of Beelzebub:

> If then his providence
> Out of evil seek to bring forth good,
> Our labor must be to pervert that end,
> And out of good still to find means of evil. (I, 162–65)

Satan explains that as God's adversaries they will labor not just to destroy what God creates, but to undermine the goodness that God takes pleasure in. Of course, God will try to bring good from their evil, but they can beat him at that game by turning good to evil. In their war against their "conqueror"—a word that implies the temporary imposition of control by an illegitimate, external force—Satan and his crew are to be the epic heroes who undermine God's plan. They will have the strength of Achilles, the wiliness of Odysseus, and the determination of Hector. By anticipating, understanding, and alleviating Beelzebub's fears, Satan inspires him with the mental strength to defy God and the physical strength to create a new subterranean world free from God's interference. To lead/manipulate Beelzebub, Satan needs to embrace a perspective that is unified in a vision of God as despot and of the fallen angels as his heroic and defiant victims. It is particularly easy for Satan to navigate this particular way of knowing, in that it is at the center of his own self-conception. In this conversation, Beelzebub coauthors Satan's choices by needing to witness them, while Satan coauthors those of Beelzebub by being receptive to and inspiring them.

## RECOGNIZING DADDY

Once Milton's Satan assembles the fallen angels, who have been liberated from the burning lake, he convinces them that he is the perfect leader to carry out the dangerous mission of finding Earth and perverting the creatures God has placed there. He alone will take on the risky business of seducing Adam and Eve. To do this, he must travel to the Garden in Eden, which involves making his way past the gates of Hell erected by God as a barrier to the damned, traversing the vast Chaos that separates Hell from the Universe, finding Earth and entering Paradise. The first challenge is to break out of Hell. As Satan approaches its gates, which are "impenetrable, impaled with circling fire,/ Yet unconsumed," he sees two sentries:

> Before the gates there sat
> On either side a formidable shape;
> The one seemed woman to the waist, and fair,
> But ended foul in many a scaly fold
> Voluminous and vast, a serpent armed
> With mortal sting. . . .
> The other shape,
> If shape it might be called that shape had none
> Distinguishable in member, joint or limb,
> Or substance might be called that shadow seemed,
> For each seemed either; black it stood as night,
> Fierce as ten Furies, terrible as Hell,
> And shook a dreadful dart; what seemed his head
> The likeness of a kingly crown had on. (II, 648–73)

Satan confronts two nightmare shapes. One seems to be a beautiful woman, but she is serpent-like below the waist and armed with a deadly sting. The other has no recognizable shape but is menacing the way a pitch-black night can be menacing—filled with invisible, imagined threats. The second shape, which seems to wear a king's crown, is as "fierce as ten Furies" and shakes a deadly dart.

These monsters turn out to be Satan's children, Sin and Death, whom their father does not recognize as his progeny. In fact he almost winds up in an apocalyptic battle with Death, who dares to challenge Satan's claim to pass through Hell's gates, commanding, "Back to thy punishment!" Satan stands his ground, "unterrified." Simultaneously, each makes the decision to fight, but for both of them, that decision is based more on reflex than knowledge. They have heard and responded to the hostility in each other's vaunts, but each is ignorant of the identity of the other. In terms of dialogic freedom, they are both operating within their own circumscribed ways of knowing, unable to see things from each other's perspective. They are about to lock in combat when Sin, who is the only one to recognize the family connection, intervenes:

> "O father, what intends thy hand," she cried,
> "Against thy only son? What fury O son,
> Possesses thee to bend that mortal dart
> Against thy father's head?" (II, 727–30)

Demonstrating his lack of both omniscience and paternal affection, Satan responds, "I know thee not, nor ever saw till now/ Sight more detestable than him and thee" (II, 744–45). That Satan does not recognize Sin is richly allegorical. The very attractive possibility that beneath the surface is a wrong turn—an affair, a slightly more favorable version of the truth, revenge on an enemy—is often recognized as wrong only after the fact. Milton here implies that if it were easy to recognize from the beginning what sin is, more of us would avoid it.

As if to refresh her father's memory, Sin proceeds to give him an account of her birth, at the moment he conceived his conspiracy against God:

> All on a sudden miserable pain
> Surprised thee, dim thine eyes, and dizzy swum
> In darkness, while thy head flames thick and fast
> Threw forth, till on the left side op'ning wide,
> Likest to thee in shape and count'nance bright,
> Then shining heav'nly fair, a goddess armed
> Out of thy head I sprung. (II, 752–58)

Just as Athena, goddess of wisdom, sprang fully mature from Zeus's head, so Sin springs from Satan's. When he makes the decision to rebel against God, Sin, the perversion of wisdom, is born. She is very beautiful—"heav'nly fair"—and a close reflection of her father's splendor. Yet there is also something dangerous about her, "a goddess armed." She is surprised now that her father does not recognize her, because once the rebel angels got used to her, her "attractive graces won/ The most averse, thee chiefly" (II, 762–63). In fact, seeing her as a perfect image of himself, Satan became enamored with his daughter and together they conceived a child.

Now Sin fills her father in on the part of the story he has missed. While the war in heaven arose, she grew large with the burden of her unborn child. After the rebel angels were cast down to Hell, the pregnant Sin was assigned by God to guard its entrance, "with charge to keep/ These gates for ever shut" (II, 775–76). There she sat alone, until she went into a horrendous labor and gave birth to Death:

> At last this odious offspring whom thou seest
> Thine own begotten, breaking violent way
> Tore through my entrails, that with fear and pain
> Distorted, all my nether shape thus grew
> Transformed: but he my inbred enemy
> Forth issued, brandishing his fatal dart
> Made to destroy: I fled, and cried out "Death." (II, 781–87)

Just as Sin has sprung from Satan's brain, Death springs from Sin's womb, the fruit of incest, ready to kill. This image is particularly creepy for any woman who has experienced labor and perhaps even more unnerving for someone contemplating a trip to the delivery room. On an allegorical level, though, it dramatizes Christian doctrine, since Death is the product of Sin. Death is also paradoxically the enemy of Sin, in that the sinner who dies ceases to be able to sin. From Sin's narrative Satan learns that the formless, enraged creature with the deadly dart, with whom he is about to fight, is simultaneously his son and his grandson.

Sin continues with a description of her postpartum experience, which has repeated itself every hour, up until the moment of her father's arrival:

> I fled, but he pursued (though more, it seems,
> Inflamed with lust than rage) and swifter far,
> Me overtook his mother all dismayed,
> And in embraces forcible and foul
> Engend'ring with me, of that rape begot
> These yelling monsters that with ceaseless cry
> Surround me, as thou saw'st, hourly conceived
> And hourly born, with sorrow infinite
> To me, for when they list, into the womb
> That bred them they return, and howl and gnaw
> My bowels, their repast. (II, 790–800)

Allegorically speaking, sin's consequences to the sinner are as endless and horrifying as anything Dante came up with in his *Inferno*. Sin brings death into the world, but the consequences of sin and death together gnaw away at the sinner, over and over, without end. Sin hurts others but is also self-punishing, in a process that repeats itself moment by moment, not only in the repetition of the decision to sin, but in consequences beyond the sinner's control. The lust and rage that characterize these relationships between mother and child emphasize that the punishments of sin are psychological as well as physical, the products of insatiable appetites that grow even as they are indulged.

Sin tells this story to keep Satan from entering into combat with his only son, the third figure in a trinity that parodies the Father, Son, and Holy Spirit of Christianity. She intervenes not just to save her rapist son, but also, by implication, to save the infernal trinity that is Satan's full identity. Without the death that sin breeds, sin would be without consequence, and Satan would be undermined. Thus we see that Sin's intervention and storytelling to Dad is codetermined by his threat to enter into battle with his son. His threat to fight Death coauthors his daughter's narrative by making it absolutely necessary for her to convince him to desist. Her story, in turn, gives Satan information he can mine to convince these two sentries—who have been ordered by God, in no uncertain terms, not to let anyone pass—to open the gates of Hell.

As soon as Sin ends her narrative with an appeal not to fight his only son, Satan once again demonstrates that he is a quick study. With a show of newly discovered paternal affection, he responds, "Dear daughter, since thou claim'st me for thy sire,/ And my fair son . . . I come no enemy, but to set free/ From out this dark and dismal house of pain,/ Both him and thee" (II, 817–24). The fallen angel who was ready a moment ago to do battle has instantly grasped the perspectives of Sin and Death and figured out how to win them over. In order to succeed he must be seen not as a fugitive but as a loving father and liberator who can offer them better lives. Thus, he refers to them as "dear daughter" and "fair son," and he tells them about a "race of upstart creatures" he is on his way to find. He promises that if they open the gates he will return and bring them to "the place where thou and Death/ Shall dwell at ease, and up and down unseen/ Wing silently the buxom air, embalmed/ With odors; there ye shall be fed and filled/ Immeasurably, all things shall be your prey" (II, 840–44). These promises are well received, as "Death/ Grinned horrible a ghastly smile, to hear/ His famine should be filled" (II, 845–46). Sin, too, is pleased, and decides that she owes God a lot less than she owes her own father. She decides to open the gates.

In this conversation with his children Satan once again illustrates his resourcefulness at coming up with the perfect logic to appeal to his listeners. Death's appetite is insatiable, so the prospect of a whole universe of soon-to-be-dead things is irresistible. Sin, too, is attracted to the prospect of a larger empire. Because he reads their ambitions so clearly, Satan is able to use them to get what he wants. Though surprised by paternity, he embraces it, converts Hell's sentries from hostile enemies to receptive subjects, and inspires them with their great expectations. The new information they provide, as well as the desires they express, coauthor Satan's promises of greener pastures on Earth, while his ability to assess and respond to their desires coauthors Sin's decision to open the gates. As figures that are at the same time monologically allegorical and dialogically anthropomorphic, Sin and Death simultaneously represent chaotic forces to be unleashed on earth and children to be placated. Satan smoothly navigates his way through their perspectives, learning from them how best to proceed on his journey toward Paradise.

# NEGOTIATING WITH CHAOS

Having escaped Hell's gates, Satan now confronts the immense region separating him from the Universe: Chaos, "the womb of Nature and perhaps her grave" (II, 911), where the elements of air, earth, fire, and water clash randomly. According to Milton, God created Earth not out of nothing, but by ordering the disordered elements of Chaos. After the Apocalypse, the universe will perhaps return to this primordial stew. Having entered the disorienting atmosphere of Chaos, Satan has no idea where Earth and man are. He stops to ask directions from the "anarch" (as opposed to monarch), who, like Sin, Death, and the fallen angels, is both an allegorical and a dramatic figure. Just as Satan appealed to Beelzebub by offering equality, glory, and freedom, and to his children by offering new victims to devour, he appeals to the anarch with the hope of regaining the real estate God confiscated when he created the universe. All the anarch has to do is tell Satan where to find the newly created universe:

> Direct my course;
> Directed, no mean recompense it brings
> To your behoof, if that region lost,
> All usurpation thence expelled, reduce
> To her original darkness and your sway
> (Which is my present journey) and once more
> Erect the standard there of ancient Night;
> Yours be th' advantage all, mine the revenge. (II, 980–87)

Satan realizes that the way to appeal to this listener is to offer him the possibility of regaining lost territory. He also demeans God's act of creation by referring to it as usurpation, which emphasizes the injustice of God's project and the justice of the anarch's claim. Satan argues that if he succeeds, he stands to gain nothing but the satisfaction of revenge, while the anarch will regain a lost portion of his empire. This argument prevails, showing that once again Satan has grasped in an instant his listener's perspective, responding to it with resourceful passion. Whether we see this virtuosity as evidence of great leadership or evil manipulation depends on whether we see Satan in general as heroic or corrupt.

The anarch of Chaos coauthors and calls forth Satan's appeal by being receptive to it. Meanwhile, Satan coauthors the anarch's cooperative instructions by convincing him that the project to corrupt man will help restore the anarch's empire. Already irritated that Hell was carved out of his territory, the anarch is only too glad to let someone try to rectify his most recent loss—when God created the universe and man—because "Havoc and spoil and ruin are my gain" (II, 1009). He gives Satan directions to the universe, which hangs by a golden chain "To that side of heav'n from whence your legions fell" (II, 1006). As an anthropomorphic and dramatic character, the anarch is leader of an empire being chipped away as God creates one thing after another, while allegorically he represents the centrifugal force for disorder that opposes all centripetal efforts to create order. From an anthropomorphic perspective, Satan understands well the anarch's political indignation at the loss of his empire, while he also shares the anarch's allegorical orientation toward undermining God's order. Thus he can lead/manipulate him to take part in the mission to corrupt man. As was the case with his encounter with his children, Satan's anthropomorphic identity as the sympathetic rebel against God's tyranny makes his encounter with the anarch of Chaos richly dialogic.

## TRICKING THE SHARPEST SIGHTED SPIRIT

Satan does not hang around long enough to thank the anarch for giving him excellent directions for reaching the universe. Rather, he "Springs upward like a pyramid of fire/ Into the wild expanse" (II, 1013–1014). He works his way toward the lower link of the golden chain connecting the universe to heaven. From there he throws himself down through the universe, past "other worlds,/ Or other worlds they seemed, or happy isles . . . but who dwelt happy there/ He stayed not to inquire" (III, 566–70). Milton pauses to imagine life beyond Earth, then propels Satan toward the Sun, where he must once more stop to ask for directions. Here, too, there is a sentry, the Archangel Uriel, who was a witness to creation, when "order from disorder sprung." Uriel's job is to watch for Satan—who is expected to try to get into Paradise—and also to oversee angelic tourism between heaven and earth, as angels like Raphael (the Sociable Spirit) come down to check out the new creatures. The blinding brightness of the sun is an emblem for Uriel's perfect vision. Realizing that the "Sharpest-Sighted Spirit" is not about to let him pass, Satan, who, like all the angels, can change his form, disguises himself as "a stripling Cherub":

> Not of the prime, yet such as in his face
> Youth smiled celestial, and to every limb
> Suitable grace diffused, so well he feigned. (III, 637–39)

Pretending to be one of the legions of angels, who, according to Milton, go back and forth between heaven and earth before the Fall, the Cherub asks Uriel where he can find this "new happy race of men," who have been created to "repair that loss" when the rebel angels were driven from heaven. Uriel directs Satan to Paradise.

Whereas Satan used logic to appeal to Beelzebub, Sin, and the anarch of Chaos, here he realizes that there is no argument that could persuade the unfallen angel to let him pass. Uriel, who has already rejected whatever logic Satan used to convince a third of heaven's angels to rebel, would see through any appeal Satan might now make, either to his vanity, or to his desire for freedom as power. By his anticipated resistance to Satan's logic, Uriel coauthors Satan's decision to refrain from making the kind of appeal that has worked so well with others, and to resort instead to the Cherub disguise, which easily deceives the Sharpest-Sighted Spirit:

> So spake the false dissembler unperceived;
> For neither man nor angel can discern
> Hypocrisy, the only evil that walks
> Invisible, except to God alone,
> By his permissive will, through heav'n and earth:
> And oft though wisdom wake, suspicion sleeps
> At wisdom's gate, and to simplicity
> Resigns her charge, while goodness thinks no ill
> Where no ill seems. (III, 681–89)

How is it that this angel with keen vision cannot see through such a simple deception? What happened to the vigilance Dante warned readers about, in the face of sin? Milton seems to be saying that whoever can view with suspicion the very emblem of innocence—a Cherub—would view every creature with suspicion. Under such circumstances, you would successfully arm yourself against evil, but also against good. If you always suspected that beneath the appearance of innocence lay the prospect of guilt, there would be no possibility for friendship or love. The trust upon which they are based would always be undermined by suspicion. If you could never trust that what seems good is good, you could never love anyone, and your isolation would be Hell.

Uriel does recognize Satan, but only later, after he has revealed to him how to locate Adam and Eve, and Satan lands outside Eden. The Archangel has watched the Cherub descend to Earth, but suddenly he notices that instead of cherubic joy his face is filled with the painful contortions of despair: "Horror and doubt distract/ His troubled thoughts, and from the bottom stir/ The hell within him, for within him hell/ He brings" (IV, 18–21). Confronted with God's newest creation, Satan rethinks his lost happiness and "heav'n's free love dealt equally to all" (IV, 68). He curses God's love, then himself: "Me miserable! Which way shall I fly/ Infinite wrath, and infinite despair?/ Which way I fly is hell; myself am hell" (IV, 72–75). Satan realizes that although he has escaped the physical environment of Hell, his true damnation is mental and portable. Unless he abandons his rebellion against God, he will carry Hell with him wherever he goes. That being the case, he wonders, "is there no place/ Left for repentance?" (IV, 79–80). This is an important question for a Christian, because as long as the sinner chooses to repent, there is no sin too terrible for God to forgive. But Satan decides that even if he could repent and be readmitted to heaven, he would just become dissatisfied all over again, and he would once again choose to rebel. By his own decision he

abandons the possibility of repentance. "All hope excluded thus," Satan concludes, "all good to me is lost;/ Evil be thou my good" (IV, 109–10).[12] As
these thoughts run through his head his face contorts with anger and misery,
and Uriel suddenly recognizes him, "For heav'nly minds from such distem-
pers foul/ Are ever clear" (IV, 118–19).

Milton seems to be saying that the very trust that good people extend
toward others who seem good carries dangers, because it is an open invitation to deception. Thus it is that we can use deception to hide our evil
intentions, but we cannot hide the despair that those who choose to hurt
others carry with them as their own personal hell. We will eventually be
recognized for what we are. Milton also seems to be saying that revenge is its
own punishment, its own hell. Having landed on earth, Satan brings with him
his remarkable ability to see things from others' perspectives, which includes
the ability to see the beauty and love in this new world. But the more beautiful this world seems, the more isolated he feels in his despair. It is in this
state of mind, lamenting what he has lost, certain that he would do it all
again, aware that the love between Adam and Eve is both beautiful and
inaccessible, that Satan manages to locate Eve. Despite the elasticity of Satan's ability to perceive from multiple vantage points, he recognizes his own
decision to cut himself off from repentance and to reduce his own perspective to one epistemological layer: despair. This lens paradoxically allows him
still to grasp the perspectives of those who are not despairing, while at the
same time he recognizes the impossibility of ever again sharing their hope.
One of the most interesting things about Satan's encounter with Uriel and its
aftermath, when Uriel recognizes him because of his despair, is that this
episode blends so completely the allegorical Satan who deceives the Sharpest-Sighted Spirit, and the anthropomorphic Satan, who experiences the soul-
searching and despair of one who knows he is choosing wrongly but insists
on following that path.

## PERSUADING EVE

Until Satan encounters Eve, his conversations are always with other supernatural beings: angels, fallen angels, or allegorical entities like Sin, Death,
and Chaos. As a human being, Eve presents a new challenge, because her
human perspective has many facets. As Adam's perfect partner, worshipper
of God, gardener, queen of Paradise, and curious student of life, Eve goes
about the business of tending flowers, plants, and the first human community. In dealing with her, Satan will use his ability to imagine these various
aspects of her life and the perspectives they entail. He will also use the
techniques of logic, manipulation, and deception that have worked so well
with his previous listeners. He starts out with the technique that worked on

Uriel: deception. In the form of a serpent, he begins his appeal without even speaking: "oft he bowed/ His turret crest, and sleek enameled neck,/ fawning, and licked the ground whereon she trod" (IX, 524–26). Here the once majestic Lucifer debases himself by bowing, fawning, and licking the ground beneath Eve's feet. Then he dazzles Eve with the miracle of speech:

> Wonder not, Sovran mistress, if perhaps
> Thou canst, who art sole wonder, much less arm
> Thy looks, the heav'n of mildness, with disdain,
> Displeased that I approach thee thus, and gaze
> Insatiate, I thus single, nor have feared
> Thy awful brow, more awful thus retired.
> Fairest resemblance of thy Maker fair,
> Thee all things living gaze on, all things thine
> By gift, and thy celestial beauty adore
> With ravishment beheld. (IX, 532–40)

The amazed Eve asks, "What may this mean? Language of man pronounced/ By tongue of brute, and human sense expressed?" (IX, 553–54). She is no more ready to see through Satan's physical disguise than Uriel was. Yet she works to understand the significance of this miracle.

Beyond "wondrous" speech, Satan also employs the flattery that worked so well with Beelzebub. He refers to Eve as "Sovran," "sole wonder" and "Fairest resemblance of thy Maker fair," whose "celestial beauty" makes all creatures adore her. Eve is stunned that the snake can talk at all, let alone string together these extravagant compliments. She asks him how it is that he can speak, and he explains that he ate a magical fruit that endowed him with both speech and reason. Under its influence he pondered "speculations high and deep" and "all things fair and good":

> But all that fair and good in thy divine
> Semblance, and in thy beauty's heav'nly ray
> United I beheld; no fair to thine
> Equivalent or second, which compelled
> Me thus, though importune perhaps, to come
> And gaze, and worship thee of right declared
> Sovran of creatures, universal dame. (IX, 606–12)

Eve is dubious about the effects of such a fruit if the only thing the serpent can think to do after eating it is to worship her. With a sense of humor that catches us by surprise, she says, "Serpent, thy overpraising leaves in doubt/ The virtue of that fruit" (IX, 615–16). Yet, she is curious and wants to see this magical tree.

Satan leads Eve to the Tree of Knowledge, at which point she exclaims:

> Serpent, we might have spared our coming hither,
> Fruitless to me, though fruit be here to excess,
> The credit of whose virtue rest with thee

Wondrous indeed, if cause to such effects.
But of this tree we may not taste nor touch;
God so commanded, and left that command
Sole daughter of his voice; the rest, we live
Law to ourselves, our reason is our law. (IX, 648–54).

Here, Eve accepts Satan's ocular proof of the tree's power to perform mira-
cles, but she also explains that she answers to other voices besides the one
presently speaking to her. She answers to God, who has commanded her on
pain of death not to eat the fruit from this tree, and to reason, the law that
governs Adam and her in Paradise. These two authorities she acknowledges
as superaddressees who coauthor her decisions. Her reply turns down Satan's
offer, but it also shows him the way to renew his effort to seduce her to his
way of thinking. All he needs to do is argue that eating the fruit is more
reasonable than not eating it, and that God's command is not to be taken
seriously. He must pit one superaddressee against the other, promoting one to
preeminence while undermining the prohibition declared by the other. A few
lines later Milton refers to Eve as "yet sinless." Her reverence for reason is
thus sanctioned by the poet and by Christian doctrine. Nonetheless, Eve's
statement is like a green light for Satan to do what he does best, construct
logical arguments that persuade others to do what he wants. Eve coauthors
the rest of Satan's appeal by giving him to understand that through logic he
can prevail, since "reason is our law." The choices he makes to use one
argument rather than another reflect his sense of her receptivity to particular
logic and particular evidence.

Thus, Satan presents Eve with a blizzard of logical arguments, all in the
form of questions:

Do not believe
Those rigid threats of death; ye shall not die:
How should ye? By the fruit? It gives you life
To knowledge. By the Threat'ner? Look on me,
Me who have touched and tasted, yet both live,
And life more perfect have attained than fate
Meant me, by vent'ring higher than my lot.
Shall that be shut to man, which to the beast
Is open? Or will God incense his ire
For such a petty trespass, and not praise
Rather your dauntless virtue, whom the pain
Of death denounced, whatever thing death be,
Deterred not from achieving what might lead
To happier life, knowledge of good and evil;
Of good, how just? Of evil, if what is evil
Be real, why not known, since easier shunned? (IX, 684–99)

How could the fruit possibly cause death, when the serpent, who has eaten it,
is obviously alive? Would a thing be permitted to beasts and not to man?

Aren't courage and ambition virtues? Won't God be impressed by your willingness to take initiative? How could it be prohibited to know about good? Conversely, if evil should be avoided, shouldn't we know more about it, too, so we can shun it more easily? These are all great questions, and they carry the force of logic. We might say that Satan models for Eve advanced critical thinking skills, urging her to ask questions and look for logical explanations.

These questions are also presented in such a way as to undermine Eve's obedience to God. The threats of death are described as "rigid." God himself has been demoted to "Threat'ner," a source of power rather than spirituality, no longer perfect, but capable of "ire." The lowly status from which the serpent has been elevated through speech was determined in the first place not by God but by "fate." Here Satan places the Christian God within a pagan religious framework of multiple gods, most of whom could not interfere with the ancient force of fate. Perhaps Satan's most brilliant touch is his parenthetical remark, "whatever thing death be," which guts God's threat by casting doubt on the existence of the threatened punishment, death. Since death has never been a reality in Eve's world—mortality will exist only after the Fall—how can she be expected to take seriously a concept she cannot possibly understand, which may not even exist? Satan makes the same point with regard to sin by the parenthetical remark, "if what is evil be real." Evil, like death, is not yet present in Adam and Eve's world. How can we say something is real if it doesn't yet exist?

These are clever arguments, which Milton has anticipated by sending down Raphael, the Affable Archangel, to have lunch with Adam and Eve before Satan has a chance to enter Paradise. Raphael tells Adam and Eve all about Satan's rebellion in heaven, including the logic he used to convince a third of the angels to rebel. He also tells them how the faithful Abdiel saw through Satan's logic and denounced him, illustrating that it is possible to resist Satan's eloquence. Raphael encourages questions, satisfying his hosts' curiosity about how angels eat, how the universe was created, and how "time may come when men/ With angels may participate. . . . Your bodies may at last turn all to spirit,/ Improved by tract of time, and winged ascend/ Ethereal, as we, or may at choice/ Here or in heav'nly paradises dwell" (V, 493–500). Raphael holds out the possibility that humans can become like angels and "by steps . . . ascend to God." Included in this information is the warning that Satan is trying to get into Paradise in order to corrupt the first humans. Milton is very careful, then, to present Adam and Eve as knowledgeable about Satan's evil and prepared by Raphael's visit to resist it. Like the angel Abdiel, they have been created "Sufficient to have stood, though free to fall" (III, 99).

Thus Eve has been forewarned, and the field of forces within which she operates is rich with perspectives on good and evil. From Raphael she knows about Satan's manipulative logic, and she knows that Satan is expected to arrive in Paradise at any moment. But she knows about evil the way most of us know about murder. We have heard about it. We know that it is bad. We also know that we do not need to find out how bad it is by killing someone ourselves. A crucial part of Satan's argument, therefore, is to persuade Eve that she needs to know about evil in a new way. He continues his seduction by saying to her, "ye shall be as gods./ Knowing both good and evil as they know it./ . . . So ye shall die perhaps, by putting off/ Human, to put on gods, death to be wished" (IX, 708–13). Raphael had already dangled before Adam and Eve the possibility that she and Adam could "ascend to God," but he had qualified the offer with the caution: "improved by tract of time." The implication is that the process will not be quick. In the forbidden fruit, Satan is offering Eve a shortcut. Referring to "gods" rather than "God," Satan casts Eve's ambition in pagan terms, once again demoting the Christian God to the status of one god among many. In the process, he offers Eve what he offered Beelzebub: equality. He also neutralizes the threat of death, turning it into a metaphor and an advantage. The higher consciousness to come, proportionately greater for man than for the serpent, will make Eve happy to leave behind humanness for divinity. Instead of taking years to achieve enlightenment, she can achieve it all in a moment.

Satan's final strike is against God's omnipotence. He asks Eve, "What can your knowledge hurt him, or this tree/ Impart against his will if all be his?" (IX, 727–28). This is a brilliant question. If God is omnipotent and omniscient, Satan suggests, man cannot hurt him or do anything that God does not permit. Technically, Satan's logic is sound. If an omnipotent God wanted to prevent Eve from eating the fruit, he could do it. He could paralyze her arm; he could make her suddenly realize that the serpent is Satan; or he could have Adam show up at the last second and intervene. But we know that Milton's God insists on leaving all sentient beings free to choose well or poorly. Thus we have been prepared by Milton to see through Satan's logic. It would be as if a murderer were to submit as his defense, "if God did not want me to slay my victim, he would have stopped me." Readers of *Paradise Lost* are in a different position from Eve's, though. We know all along that the serpent is Satan, and we also inhabit a postlapsarian world where in the twenty-first century we are accustomed to Internet scams, lying politicians, and fraudulent investors. By contrast, Eve is in Uriel's position, unable to see through Satan's disguise. She has also invited his very logical arguments by saying, "reason is our law."

As Eve ponders the serpent's words, noon approaches and hunger colludes with reason and deception to coauthor Eve's decision to taste the fruit. First she runs through the serpent's arguments: the fruit gave "elocution to the mute"; "good unknown, sure is not had"; the serpent "hath eaten and lives"; and it seems unlikely God would reserve "intellectual food only for beasts." She then adds evidence from her own experience: how can this be a bad thing if the fruit's effect on the serpent is not to make him envy man but rather to inspire him to share "with joy/ the good befallen him . . . far from deceit or guile" (IX, 748–72). Just before Eve eats, she concludes:

> What fear I then, rather what know to fear
> Under this ignorance of good and evil,
> Of God or death, of law or penalty?
> Here grows the cure of all, this fruit divine.
> Fair to the eye, inviting to the taste,
> Of virtue to make wise; what hinders then
> To reach, and feed at once both body and mind? (IX, 772–79)

Pleading the innocence of ignorance, Eve for the first time imitates the manipulative, self-serving logic of Satan. She is not ignorant of good and evil, thanks to Raphael's visit. Rather, she is ignorant of knowing good by means of evil, a problem she is about to remedy. From the starting point of "reason is our law," she has arrived at her decision to choose a quick fix, a "cure of all."

Many would argue that the logic that Satan uses to seduce Eve would seduce anyone—that she is no more blameworthy than Uriel, the Sharpest-Sighted Spirit, who was tricked by Satan's Cherub disguise and not blamed by God afterwards. Others would say that given Raphael's forewarning Eve should have done a little more critical thinking about the serpent's ability to speak, and in any case she should have chosen obedience to God over logic, evidence, and hunger. The point here is not to resolve that debate but to emphasize that Milton's text gives readers an opportunity to think through the complexities of Eve's situation, including the attractions of evil. If it were easy to be good, the world would not be filled with suffering. He also wanted to show that reason, our most valuable tool for interpreting evidence, constructing arguments, and arriving at conclusions, is capable of becoming our most dangerous tool, when it is employed in the service of evil.

## THE DOWNSIDE OF DIALOGIC FREEDOM

Satan's ability to anticipate the arguments that will be most persuasive with his listeners—to calibrate their receptivity to him by presenting himself as totally receptive to them—constitutes a kind of dialogic virtuosity. With Beelzebub, he can imagine the best argument in favor of equality; with Sin and Death, the advantages of a new domain for satisfying their appetites; with the anarch of Chaos, a convincing justification for restoring his lost empire; with Uriel, a credible reason why a young angel would want to see firsthand God's newest creatures; and with Eve, a multitude of reasons why tasting the fruit should not be forbidden. As he navigates his interlocutors' ways of knowing, his ability to listen inspires their trust and fuels his own imagination. Thus, they coauthor his efforts to persuade them, even as he coauthors their responses. That he is so good at what he does is one of the most exhilarating yet frightening things about *Paradise Lost.*

This dialogic virtuosity is also a source of Satan's suffering. When he first sees Eve working alone the effect on him is almost overpowering:

> Her every air
> Of gesture or least action overawed
> His malice, and with rapine sweet bereaved
> His fierceness of the fierce intent it brought:
> That space the Evil One abstracted stood
> From his own evil, and for the time remained
> Stupidly good, of enmity disarmed,
> Of guile, of hate, of envy, of revenge;
> But the hot hell that always in him burns,
> Though in mid-heav'n, soon ended his delight,
> And tortures him now more, the more he sees
> Of pleasure not for him ordained: then soon
> Fierce hate he recollects. (IX, 456–71)

For a moment, Satan is so receptive to Eve's beauty, innocence and goodness, that it freezes him in his tracks. He is "stupidly good"—not "stupid" in the sense of "unintelligent," but in the sense of "stupefied," impotent, suddenly wordless. Seeing Eve, Satan is briefly disarmed of hate, deception, envy, or revenge, for a moment incapable of evil. Such is the power of Eve's presence that it calls forth Satan's "rapine sweet," a kind of rapture. Without even being aware of him, Eve coauthors in Satan a benign paralysis. Her presence unleashes forces that disarm his malice, calling to him with an invitation to share in her goodness. In the process, she comes close to coauthoring in him a desire to abandon his infernal project, since his ability to register her perspective is potent enough to threaten his whole enterprise. This threat is fleeting, though, because the "hot hell that always in him burns" breaks the spell. His hate is stronger than her "every air." He resists the temptation to abandon his project and recommits to the "fierce hate he recollects." Yet, the greater his momentary delight in Eve's purity, the more intense Satan's pain of remembering how impossible it is for him to share in a "pleasure not for him ordained." This recommitment, something that he chooses in the face of the alternative clearly embodied by Eve, "tortures him now more." Satan's response to Eve's "graceful innocence" illustrates that his capacity to see things for a moment from a different, more innocent, perspective only makes him more miserable, as he rededicates himself to his decision to destroy goodness. Thus, one source of his misery is that he remembers the ability to see from and appreciate more innocent ways of knowing, even as he uses his dialogic virtuosity to achieve the darkest possible ends.

Bakhtin's concept of "pure empathizing" casts light on Satan's crisis.[13] Bakhtin distinguishes "pure empathizing—that is, the act of coinciding with another"—from "active empathizing," where "I do not lose myself complete-ly."[14] According to him, "pure empathizing," which calls for me to complete-ly identify with another, so that I lose myself in the identification, is danger-ous. We can think of Satan's "abstraction" as a moment when he comes closest to "pure empathizing" with Eve. When he is momentarily stunned by her innocence and beauty, he almost loses himself, "abstracted . . . from his own evil." Of course, Satan's empathy is not the same as the human empathy Bakhtin imagines—a sympathetic identification with a sufferer who needs help. Satan is not human, and Eve is not suffering, at least not yet. Still, Satan's momentary pleasure in Eve's innocence is as powerful as the empa-thetic bond Bakhtin imagines, in which "I project myself" into someone else.[15] Bakhtin cautions that my ability to help another depends upon not empathizing too completely, but rather preserving my separate identity so that I can take responsibility for the actions I choose in the way of offering aid or consolation. He explains, "If this return into myself did not actually take place, the pathological phenomenon of experiencing another's suffering as one's own would result—an infection with another's suffering and nothing more" (AH, 26). For him, the phenomenon is pathological and self-destruc-tive, because one who empathizes purely with another gets lost in that iden-tification and can only repeat the other's suffering, forfeiting the ability to help.

Satan's situation is perversely different from the one Bakhtin imagines. In his moment of paralysis, Satan's empathy is directed not toward Eve's suf-fering (which does not yet exist) but toward her beauty and innocence. Yet, the loss of self threatened by being rendered "stupidly good" is as potent a danger to Satan as if he were caught up in Eve's suffering. Bakhtin explains, "a pure projection of myself into the other, a move involving the loss of my own unique place outside the other, is, on the whole, hardly possible; in any event, it is quite fruitless and senseless" (AH, 26). Satan himself seems to recognize both the unusualness and the danger of his "rapine sweet," which threatens not just to derail his enterprise, but to undermine his very identity. He masters his empathetic impulse toward Eve in time to resist this "sweet/ Compulsion" (IX, 473–74). He rejects what Bakhtin would call the "patho-logical" in favor of a return to the hate that is from his rebellious perspective normal and healthy. Putting it differently, we might say that the anthropo-morphic Satan, who is capable of being tempted by "pure empathy," gets absorbed back into the allegorical Satan, who masters that impulse. In any case, Milton's Satan gathers his wits and returns to his project to corrupt mankind. In the process, he uses the *appearance* of empathy as an instrument to undermine Eve's vow of obedience. Yet he cannot altogether shake his close encounter with Eve's innocence. It lingers in the "hot hell that always in him burns/ . . . And tortures him now more the more he sees/ Of pleasure not for him ordained" (IX, 467–70). With Satan's return to himself comes a renewed commitment to coauthoring Eve's decision to defy God, but also a deepening misery.

Milton's Satan illustrates that dialogic freedom is a potent force, but it is not always a force for good. It opens the door to understanding others better and coauthoring action with them, but this action can be destructive. The ability to see from the perspective of another can lead to empathy and inspiration, but it can also tempt us to take advantage of the vulnerable or the innocent. Those who heroize Milton's Satan focus on his ability to use his great persuasive powers to unmask a tyrant God and liberate subjects from his yoke. From their perspective, Satan, the true hero of *Paradise Lost*, illustrates the power freedom unleashes in the hands of a leader who can inspire others to break God's tyrannous grip. Those who demonize Milton's Satan focus instead on his manipulative genius, which needs to be unmasked by wary readers. From this perspective, Satan epitomizes the threat freedom poses in the hands of one who would undermine the potential for goodness in others. However we wind up judging Milton's Satan, the contradictory interpretations that he inspires reveal that dialogic virtuosity can be dangerous, not just in his hands, but in yours and mine. If dialogic freedom is a two-sided act, involving deliberation from multiple perspectives, Milton's radical commitment to moral freedom calls upon readers to embrace a difficult project. He calls upon us to see through deception, yet to trust that those who appear good really *are* good. How are we supposed to manage that particular balancing act? He calls upon us to navigate the perspectives of others, but to resist the temptation to manipulate them. In those moments when our intimacy is greatest and the trust invested in us is most complete, will we be able to resist the temptation to shade the truth just a bit and with the lightest hand steer someone toward the decision that is best not for him or her, but for us? Generations of readers have taken up Milton's challenge to exercise strenuously our intellects and hearts to navigate ways of knowing that seem alien, risking both their attractions and their dangers, as we coauthor decisions in a fallen world.

## NOTES

1. William Zunder, ed., *Paradise Lost: Contemporary Critical Essays* (New York: St. Martin's Press, 1999), 1.

2. A. J. A. Waldock, *Paradise Lost and Its Critics* (Cambridge, UK: Cambridge University Press, 1966), 1.

3. In 1737 Alexander Pope set off a firestorm of reinterpretations that burns still today, when he said that in *Paradise Lost* "God the Father turns School-divine." "Epistle I of Horace," *The Works of Alexander Pope Esq.* (London, 1751), 4:127, quoted in *The Critical Response to John Milton's Paradise Lost*, ed. Timothy Miller (London: Greenwood Press, 1997), 100. In

twentieth-century Milton criticism, there was a long-standing debate between Douglas Bush and C. S. Lewis, on the one hand, who saw *Paradise Lost* as upholding the traditional Christian view that disobedience to God is the source of all evil, and William Empson and A. J. A. Waldock, on the other, who saw Milton's epic as presenting a distasteful God and a heroic Satan. Stanley Fish was the first to suggest that these two opposing traditions could be reconciled if we were to understand the way Milton deceives "the reader" through an experience in which he "is brought to a better understanding of his sinful nature and is encouraged to participate in his own reformation." *Surprised by Sin* (1967; rev. ed., Cambridge, MA: Harvard University Press, 1998), lx. Fish explained that through this process "the reader is continuously surprised by sin" (44). According to Fish, as readers we reason with Satan, or Adam, or Eve, then are corrected by Milton's narrator until we realize the importance of "accepting on faith what we are unable to understand" (245). In a later work he added, "Centrifugal forces are in constant motion and vie for our attention," but "the poems and much of the prose are engaged in an act of containment, in the forcible undoing and dispelling of energies . . . that are protean in their resourcefulness even though they are finally illusory and without substance." *How Milton Works* (Cambridge, MA: Harvard University Press, 2001), 11. John P. Runrich takes issue with Fish's ingenious solution. He suggests instead that "Milton was the poet of indeterminacy." *Milton Unbound* (New York: Cambridge University Press, 1996), 24. Runrich argues that "when we look closely enough into *Paradise Lost* . . . we find instability and excess; we find incoherence and undecidability" (118). Peter Herman agrees, proposing that "Miton is, in fact, a poet of deep incertitude." *Destabilizing Milton: Paradise Lost and the Poetics of Incertitude* (New York: Macmillan, 2005), 21. For an overview of interpretive approaches to Milton's *Paradise Lost*, see *A Companion to Milton*, ed. Thomas N. Corns (Oxford: Blackwell, 2001), 329–410.

4. 4 Nicholas von Maltzahn, "Milton's Readers," in *The Cambridge Companion to Milton*, 2nd ed., ed. Dennis Danielson (Cambridge, UK: Cambridge University Press, 1999), 245.

5. William Blake, "The Marriage of Heaven and Hell," in *The Complete Poetry of William Blake*, ed. David Endman (New York: Doubleday, 1988), 5.

6. William Empson, *Milton's God* (1961; reprint, London: Cambridge University Press, 1981), 25.

7. John Milton, *Paradise Lost* (1674). Thomas H. Luxon, ed. The Milton Reading Room. Accessed March 2012,http://www.dartmouth.edu/~milton. Citations of *Paradise Lost* are to this edition.

8. David Masson, "A Brief Life of Milton," in *Paradise Lost*, ed. Scott Elledge (New York: Norton, 1975), 322.

9. Masson, "A Brief Life of Milton," 343.

10. In his introduction to the 1998 edition of *Surprised by Sin*, Stanley Fish catalogues Milton's efforts to correct readers' impressions of Satan, so that they will come to see through rhetoric that at first deceives them. Fish points out that the lens through which Satan saw the elevation of the Son was shaped by envy and pride: "Pride and obedience name the positions perceiving agents already occupy, and it is within those positions that the shape of events emerges" (xxvii). Fish continues, "If [Satan] begins by conceiving of God as a paternal tyrant whose reign is an accident of time and power, that conception will structure his understanding of everything that happens subsequently" (xxxiii). In *Milton Unbound* John Runrich argues instead that Milton finds ways "to incorporate the uncertain and the evolving" (24). Readers like William Blake, William Empson, and A. J. A. Waldock would see in this speech not Satan's duplicity but his unmasking of Milton's God.

11. Satan's rhetoric can be described either positively or negatively, depending on whether you see him as hero or villain. My shorthand for this ambiguity is the occasional split verb "lead/manipulate."

12. Here Satan neatly illustrates the double meaning of Dante's "Lasciate ogne speranza, voi ch'intrate," usually translated "Abandon all hope, you who enter here!" (*Inferno*, Canto 3, line 9). He abandoned all hope of redemption when he rebelled against God, and he is abandoning it now, as he witnesses the love of Adam and Eve in Paradise and realizes he can never be part of it.

13. See chapter 1 for a discussion of "pure empathizing."

14. Mikhail Bakhtin, *Toward a Philosophy of the Act*, ed. Vadim Liapunov and Michael Holquist; trans. Vadim Liapunov (Austin: University of Texas Press, 1993), 15.

15. Mikhail Bakhtin, "Author and Hero in Aesthetic Activity," in *Art and Answerability: Early Philosophical Essays by M. M. Bakhtin*, ed. Michael Holquist and Vadim Liapunov; trans. Vadim Liapunov (Austin: University of Texas Press, 1990), 26. Citations to "Author and Hero in Aesthetic Activity" are to this text, with the abbreviation AH.

## Chapter Six

# Shaping the Master's Vision in "Benito Cereno"

Dialogic freedom: a two-sided act, chosen within *a field of unifying and frag-menting forces along a continuum of minimal to maximal layers of knowing that are never final.*

"Benito Cereno" may be Herman Melville's most provocative creation. Although its first appearance in *Putnam's* magazine (1855) and its publication among the *Piazza Tales* (1856), drew very little attention, in the twentieth and twenty-first centuries, this violent tale of a slave rebellion at sea has become one of Melville's most studied and debated works.[1] You could say that it has read each new generation, even as readers have puzzled over its deliberately misleading words. In the aftermath of World War II, "Benito Cereno" seemed to be a study of good and evil—the good American Captain Delano, who recaptures the monstrous slave leader, Babo.[2] The cultural revolution of the 1960s drew out new perspectives, in which race and class became central.[3] By the 1980s a blizzard of scholarship had reconsidered the tale's historical context in terms of the slave trade, imperial destiny, and the documents on which the story was based. It began to seem that in "Benito Cereno" Melville showed contempt for his contemporary readers,[4] creating a work that would require future generations to probe the depths of its irony.

The reception of this story illustrates Mikhail Bakhtin's remark, "There can be neither a first nor a last meaning; it always exists among other meanings as a link in the chain of meaning. . . . In historical life, this chain continues infinitely, and therefore each individual link in it is renewed again and again, as though it were being reborn."[5] My reading of "Benito Cereno" is intended as one more "link in the chain of meaning" created by Melville's words and his readers. I explore the field of forces for unity and chaos that involve an American sea captain's racist assumptions, a Spanish captain and crew's terrorized behavior, and the shifting circumstances of a slave rebellion. In Melville's tale the slave Babo enacts his dialogic freedom by exploiting the master's racist perspective in order to conceal the rebellion he has led to take over a Spanish merchant ship. Amasa Delano, the American sea captain who comes aboard, is oblivious to this rebellion, blinded by his own racism, which disarms his suspicions moment by moment, before they can rise to the level of thought. Babo manipulates Delano by playing the role of the attentive servant, even as he terrorizes the Spanish captain and crew. Meanwhile, Melville's complex narratorial perspective invites readers to share Delano's racism, then pulls the rug out, unmasking the compromised dialogic freedom of racists who fail to see what is happening before their eyes.

The plot of the story seems straightforward—slave rebellion quelled at sea—which led Melville's contemporaries to see it as one more "sea-romance" or "mystery."[6] An American merchant ship lies docked in the bay of a deserted island off the southern coast of Chile. Its captain, Amasa Delano, sees a Spanish merchant ship approaching the harbor dangerously close to a reef, and he concludes that the pilot needs help bringing it in. The San Dominick is not showing its flag, which is odd, and it is unkempt, apparently the victim of bad weather at sea. Captain Delano, a typical American of the late eighteenth century—optimistic, generous, and ready to act—decides to board the vessel and navigate it to safety. Melville's narrator presents the unfolding events from Delano's perspective, so it is not until very late in the story that readers learn that the ship has been taken over by its slaves. At the moment when Delano boards the San Dominick, ignorant of this turn of events, the slave leader Babo has already controlled for months every move of the ship's captain, Benito Cereno. In fact, all on board the San Dominick enact a drama improvised by Babo, who pretends to be the captain's faithful body servant, while the Spanish captain pretends that scurvy and unexpected calms have wiped out most of his crew. This elaborate charade is possible only because Babo has discovered a way to completely intimidate the Spanish captain and crew, even as that intimidation masquerades to Delano as the obedience of a devoted slave. The irony afforded by a second reading of the tale derives from the stark contradiction between the master and slave roles that Babo simultaneously enacts.

"Benito Cereno" has been called a racist tale, in that it presents an overtly racist narrator who seems to express Melville's own views.[7] This narrator parades uncritically the self-satisfaction of the racist perspective that pervaded the author's white society. The reader assumed by this narrator shares the assumptions implicit in this perspective. Late twentieth-century readers began to dissent from the theory of the racist Melville, focusing more on the author's irony in "uncovering the secrets" of Amasa Delano's sentimental and blinding racism.[8] Melville's evasive writing continues to provoke debates about who is the hero of the tale and why. I will argue that "Benito Cereno" eventually presents a reality that demolishes sentimental racist assumptions about slaves who love to serve, but only after Melville has allowed his narrator to present the myth of the contented slave in its most attractive light. The tale's conclusion risks replacing this myth with its mirror image: the nightmare that once the shackles are removed, the savage will cut your throat. By presenting the dialogic relationships between Amasa Delano, Benito Cereno, and Babo, Melville exposes the limitations of racist thinking, even as he presents the exploitation of that thinking by the slave who would be free.

Melville displayed a remarkable audacity in presenting an ironic portrait of both idyllic and nightmarish racist visions, just five years before the Civil War broke out. He was an abolitionist and the son-in-law of Massachussetts Chief Justice Lemuel Shaw, who in 1850 had enforced the Fugitive Slave Act, in spite of his own antislavery leanings. Melville first published "Benito Cereno" in 1855, during a slave insurrection panic that was sweeping the South, three years after *Uncle Tom's Cabin* had appeared. His source was a memoir, the 1817 *Narrative* of the historical figure Captain Amasa Delano, who had put down a mutiny in 1805 aboard the Spanish slave ship *Tryal*.[9] The slaves, led by a leader named Babo, had seized control of the vessel and murdered most of the crew. The historical Captain Delano came to the aid of the ship, distributing water and other provisions, ignorant of the rebellion, while the captive Spanish pretended that nothing was amiss. As Delano was leaving the *Tryal*, its Spanish captain jumped into the American's boat and called to his own sailors to flee. Once Delano realized that the slaves had seized the Spanish ship, he used his guns and crew to retake it and to return them to captivity, in the process saving the life of Captain Bonito Cereno. Melville included in his story these key elements of Delano's 1817 *Narrative*, at times quoting verbatim parts of the legal depositions it included. Yet he also made significant changes which eventually turned this self-satisfied diary into an ironic masterpiece.

When Melville fictionalized Delano's *Narrative*, he made two apparently insignificant changes: he altered the Spanish ship's name from the *Tryal* to the *San Dominick*; and he shifted the date of the rebellion back in time, from 1805 to 1799. In doing so he laid the groundwork for an intense focus on race. Santo Domingo was the first place in America discovered by Christopher Columbus and also the island where in 1493 the Spanish introduced slavery into the Western Hemisphere. In 1799, midway through the French Revolution, there was a rebellion on the island, in which slaves slaughtered whites in what was referred to as "a theatre of blood." Using the captured ship's name to reference both slavery and the fiercest slave rebellion in anyone's memory would have raised the blood pressure of Melville's white

Southern readers, many of whom lived in fear of an eruption from the slaves in their midst. Those who regard Melville's story as racist can cite his decisions to set the tale in 1799 and to name the Spanish ship the *San Dominick* as evidence that "Benito Cereno" exploited and exacerbated Southern whites' fears of slaves. Viewed from this perspective, these changes emphasize that without the restraining influences of the institution of slavery, blacks revert to savagery. There is another way to look at these changes, though. They draw attention to the institution of slavery itself and to the violence it breeds, in both slaveholders and slaves. From this perspective the violence of Babo and the other slaves seems no worse than the violence of white slaveholders and traders. In fact, from this perspective, Babo seems heroic for finding resourceful ways to fight back in a war beyond his control.[10]

Three larger changes in Melville's source materials help clarify Melville's focus not on the bestiality of the slaves but on the debilitating prejudice of the slaveholders. These changes involve the relationship between the two sea captains, the composition of Amasa Delano's American crew, and the role of the slave leader, Babo. Much of Delano's original 1817 *Narrative* had been devoted to the Spanish captain's lack of gratitude and integrity, after being saved from the slave revolt on the *Tryal.* Instead of voluntarily repaying his debt for food, water and aid, Bonito Cereno needed to be petitioned before the colonial authorities and forced to cough up the appropriate sum to Delano. Furthermore, Delano's 1817 *Narrative* explains that after the slave rebellion was quelled, while the surviving slaves lay disarmed, wounded, and shackled, Delano had caught the Spanish captain in "the act of stabbing one of the slaves." In the face of such "barbarity," Delano explains, "I immediately caught hold of him, took away his dirk [daggar], and threatened him with the consequences of my displeasure" (103). In Melville's story, by contrast, a genteel Benito Cereno never wavers in his gratitude toward the generous Amasa Delano, he never lays a hand or dagger on a slave, and the two captains enjoy a warm, though brief, friendship. We have to wonder why Melville chose to excise Benito Cereno's darker side from the tale.

The author makes a similar change for the better in his presentation of the American captain's crew, who are rarely described, but rather taken for granted as able, competent seamen, who hunt seals, gather provisions, or retake a slave ship, as needed. We see a different view in Amasa Delano's 1817 *Narrative,* in which the American captain complains that during his voyage he lost some of his best crew members, and after leaving New Holland he discovered among the new recruits seventeen men, "most of whom had been convicts at Botany Bay," who had "secreted themselves on board," without his knowledge. He laments, "After making this bad exchange, my crew were refractory; the convicts were ever unfaithful, and took all the advantage that opportunity gave them" (97). Delano constantly fretted about the reliability of these former inmates of the British penal colony established in New South Wales in 1788, and as soon as he docked at St. Maria, three of the convicts took the opportunity to flee. Later, in depositions supporting Bonito Cereno's efforts to shirk his debt, they would swear that the American captain was a pirate (104). As with Melville's portrait of the Spanish captain, we have to wonder why the author chose to expurgate the dark side of Delano's crew.

While Melville eliminated key characteristics of the whites, he significantly expanded the role of the slave leader, Babo. Both the 1817 *Narrative* and "Benito Cereno" identify him as leader of the rebellion, but Amasa Delano's *Narrative* does not mention him directly by name. Only the deposition from Bonito Cereno, appended to the *Narrative*, makes brief references to Babo as "the ring leader" (108). Melville's tale expands those references to a role of chilling psychological intimidation that dominates the story's central scene, where Babo, parading himself as the attentive body servant, gives Benito Cereno a shave. In that scene he appears to Delano and the narrator as Benito Cereno's faithful servant, while in reality he is his inquisitor, terrorizing the Spanish captain with every move of the razor at his throat. Readers who consider "Benito Cereno" the creation of a racist author can point to all these changes as evidence that in this tale Melville draws attention to the innocence of the whites and the treachery of the blacks, thus presenting a racist vision of whites as good and blacks as evil. When we examine the irony of the shaving scene, however, it becomes clear that Melville's alterations in his source materials are part of the risky, indirect path he chose for his exploration and critique of the racist perspective.

## RACIST BENEVOLENCE

At the center of Melville's portrait of racism in this tale is the generous American captain, Amasa Delano. Near the beginning of the story, the narrator describes Delano's surprise as he observes the damaged Spanish vessel approaching the harbor:

> Captain Delano's surprise might have deepened into some uneasiness had he not been a person of a singularly undistrustful good nature, not liable except on extraordinary and repeated incentives, and hardly then, to indulge in personal alarms any way involving the imputation of malign evil in man. Whether, in view of what humanity is capable, such a trait implies, along with a benevolent heart, more than ordinary quickness and accuracy of intellectual perception, may be left to the wise to determine. [11]

Captain Delano's good nature—his benevolence, his generosity, his tendency not to be suspicious of the motives of others—is his most salient feature. This faith in others deviates broadly from the skepticism of the historical Delano, who had to be vigilant to manage his largely convict crew, never "daring to let my whale boat be in the water for fifteen minutes unless I was in her myself, from a fear that some of my people would run away with her" (98). Melville's Amasa Delano is innocent of such skepticism. After Melville deliberately erases the historical Delano's distrustfulness, Melville's narrator, with some ambiguity, implies that the fictional Delano's "undistrustful good nature" may be evidence that he is less than brilliant. Not likely to distrust the motives of others, he may also be unlikely to uncover those motives, once he embarks down the path of speculation. The very convolutedness of the word "undistrustful," instead of "trusting," puts us on guard about the amount of intelligence we as readers will need to devote to understanding this story. From the beginning, we are told to observe the goodness of Captain Delano, yet made uneasy about what that goodness might imply. We are given a narratorial perspective that invites us to look behind Delano's back, yet presented a narrative in which that same narrator sees uncritically only what Delano sees.

Even before Captain Delano meets Benito Cereno, he observes the slaves on board the *San Dominick*. Melville's narrator, who has already undermined our confidence in Delano's "quickness and accuracy of intellectual perception," now prefaces his subsequent narrative with a description of the "enchantment" that this strange spectacle of a ship in distress creates "in contrast with the blank ocean which zones it" (148). The implication is that the none-too-intelligent Delano may be entering, or expecting, a sort of magical experience, which the narrator is about to present from Delano's enchanted perspective. In spite of warning us about Delano's limitations, the narrator will now see what Captain Delano sees, no more nor less. Delano sees, and the narrator describes, "six hatchet-polishers" who are "intent upon their task." Using a kind of indirect free style that channels Delano's perspective uncritically, the narrator describes "the peculiar love in Negroes of uniting industry with pastime," as " two and two they sideways clashed their hatchets together, like cymbals, with a barbarous din" (149). This description employs racist clichés about song, dance, and loving to serve. The word "barbarous" is the icing on the cake. The implication is that enslaving Africans quells their barbarism, teaches them industry, and opens the door to happiness through service. The flip side to the myth of the contented slave is the barbarism that justifies enslaving someone in the first place. Believing in the basic goodness of slavery, the white racist looks for evidence of contentment in "the peculiar love" of uniting "industry with pastime." Melville's narrator uncritically presents this racist epistemology that is at the heart of Delano's good-natured generosity.

We hear more of the same after Benito Cereno is introduced, "bearing plain traces of recent sleepless cares and disquietudes." He stands passively leaning against the mainmast with a "dreary, spiritless look," while at his side stands Babo, "a black of small stature, in whose rude face, as occasionally, like a shepherd's dog, he mutely turned up into the Spaniard's, sorrow and affection were equally blended" (149). The racism persists in the phrase "rude face" and in the comparison of Babo to an obedient dog. The animal-like slave will be civilized and softened by his servitude. A reader coming at the story a second time catches the irony in the phrase, "sorrow and affection equally blended." They are equally blended all right, but not because Babo feels sorrow and affection for his master. Rather, there is no sorrow. There is no affection. They are equally blended only in the sense that they are equally absent and equally feigned for the American captain's benefit. What Delano sees as fidelity is really Babo's tight surveillance, making sure the Spanish captain enacts his prescribed role in the drama that has been created, directed, and produced by his captor. While Babo plays his own role of happy slave, he is ready in an instant to kill Benito Cereno, should he deviate from the script.

Ironically, the effectiveness of this dramatic fiction—that Babo is the faithful slave rather than the intimidator—depends entirely on the cooperation of Amasa Delano's racist expectations. Amasa Delano coauthors Babo's pageant by being receptive to it. Despite a growing sense of uneasiness at the unruly, chaotic behavior he witnesses on the Spanish vessel, Delano is generally able to calm his centrifugal fears by reminding himself of the docility and harmlessness that characterize happy slaves. Invited to join Benito Cereno on the poop deck, he must reach it by passing between the hatchet-polishers. He steps gingerly, "and in the instant of leaving them behind, like one running the gantlet, he felt an apprehensive twitch in the calves of his legs" (158). He reassures himself by glancing back and seeing "the whole file, like so many organ-grinders, still stupidly intent on their work, unmindful of everything beside." Reinterpreting hatchet-polishers as organ-grinders makes Delano "smile at his late fidgety panic" (148–49). He quells his fears with the harmlessness of the organ-grinder image, the Africans reduced to entertainers, incapable of noticing the world around them, circumscribed by limited roles created and controlled by others, and eager to please. The centripetal force of this unifying vision outweighs the centrifugal force of the visceral fears threatening to undermine his calm. That Delano has just come within an inch of death is just barely registered in the animal reaction of his calves, which twitch. His racist perspective is an anesthetic that bolsters his confidence. It also protects him physically as well as mentally, because if he were to see the truth, the rebel slaves would need to kill him. As it stands, Delano's racist perspective is the means by which Babo sustains his drama of helpfulness and helplessness, gathering the provisions provided by the generous Captain Delano, while he lays groundwork for an assault on Delano's ship, planned for later that night. By seizing the American ship, the slaves hope to advance their goal of reaching freedom in Senegal. Thus Delano's racist perspective is a matter of life and death for everyone aboard the *San Dominick*.

Melville's examination of this perspective becomes most ironic in his elaborations on the master-slave relationship. Channeling Delano's perspective, the narrator marvels at how Babo performs his offices "with that affectionate zeal which transmutes into something filial and fraternal acts in themselves but menial, and which has gained for the Negro the repute of making the most pleasing body servant in the world; one, too, whom a master need be on no stiffly superior terms with, but may treat with familiar trust—less a servant than a devoted companion" (151). Here, Melville confronts head-on the unifying myth of the contented slave, which insulated slaveholders from the centrifugal panic they might otherwise feel should they ponder the likelihood that the enslaved might want to be free. The slave who enjoys slavery is like a child (filial) and a "devoted companion," who can be treated with "familial trust." Instead of trying to regain his liberty, the contented slave will be fulfilled by quasi-familial love. This coherent narrative represents the "repute" of the African among many of Melville's readers. From this perspective, the rebel slave is framed not as a captive who seeks freedom, but as a violator of trust and familial bonds. The zeal that "transmutes" the menial into the fraternal emphasizes the power of a mentality that transforms imprisonment into contentment. Just as medieval alchemists sought to transmute lead into gold, invariably failing, nineteenth-century slaveholders sought to transmute restive African captives into contented American slaves, succeeding only until some act of violence, from slaveholder or slave, broke the spell.

## THE DOWN SIDE OF BENEVOLENT RACISM

The imagined zeal of the contented slave is a racist projection that turns out to be dangerous not just for the slave but for the slaveholder. Under Babo's watchful gaze, Benito Cereno explains to Delano that his friend Alexandro Aranda, the owner of the slave cargo transported on the *San Dominick*, "was quite right in assuring me that no fetters would be needed with his blacks" (156). Instead of chaining his slaves in the ship's hold, as was common practice in the crossings, Aranda left them to range freely, which made it possible for them to execute their rebellion. Oblivious to this turn of events, Delano observes Babo's attentions to his captain, the "black upholding the white," and ponders "the beauty of that relationship which could present such a spectacle of fidelity on the one hand and confidence on the other" (156). At that moment Delano has no idea that Babo and his comrades have not only killed Aranda but replaced the ship's figurehead on the prow, Christopher Columbus, with Aranda's skeleton. The rebels have shown each surviving Spanish crewmember—one by one—both the skeleton and the inscription below it, "FOLLOW YOUR LEADER," after which they have had no trouble controlling the whites on board. The myth of the contented slave has created the conditions both for rebellion and for the deception of Delano. Unmasking this myth has been at the root of the terror used to control the Spanish on board the *San Dominick*. Every time captain or crew see or contemplate Aranda's skeleton, they confront anew the acute disparity between their assumptions about the harmlessness of the slaves and the real threat they pose.

In *The Second Treatise of Government* (1680), John Locke laid out the case for the inalienable rights to life and freedom, as well as the connection between them. He argued that "freedom from absolute, arbitrary power is so necessary to, and closely joined with, a man's preservation that he cannot part with it but by what forfeits his preservation and life together." According to Locke, a person will fight to the death to avoid being held in slavery. Furthermore, "a man . . . cannot by compact or his own consent enslave himself to any one."[12] Here Locke emphasizes that not only is it a violation of Nature to enslave another, but a person cannot agree voluntarily to be enslaved, because freedom is inalienable—it can't be given away. Whoever seeks to enslave another confronts the potential slave's natural desire to remain free and enters into a state of war with that person, which lasts as long as the slavery lasts. Force will be required both to enslave someone and to sustain that person's captivity. By Locke's logic, the slave is by definition in a state of war initiated and perpetuated by the slaveholder. The slave who resorts to violence against the master is therefore responding to this state of war, not initiating it. According to Locke, every slave can be expected to try to escape captivity. Hence, only a fool would seek to transport slaves on a ship without securing them in chains. Benito Cereno and his surviving crew members are in the process of learning just how big a fool Alexandro Aranda was when he claimed "no fetters would be needed." The myth of the happy slave conceals from view, yet perpetuates, the state of war that Locke characterizes as the relationship between master and slave.

In the shaving scene of "Benito Cereno," Melville dramatizes the full alchemical power of the racist perspective that justified enslaving blacks and transporting them without chains. As Babo prepares his captain by draping his shoulders with the Spanish flag and loosening his cravat, Delano pauses to contemplate to himself the beauty of the scene, which Melville's narrator uncritically conveys:

There is something in the Negro which, in a peculiar way, fits him for avoca-
tions about one's person. Most Negroes are natural valets and hairdressers,
taking to the comb and brush congenially as to the castanets, and flourishing
them apparently with almost equal satisfaction. There is, too, a smooth tact
about them in this employment, with a marvelous, noiseless, gliding briskness,
not ungraceful in its way, singularly pleasing to behold, and still more so to be
the manipulated subject of. And above all is the great gift of good humor. Not
the mere grin or laugh is here meant. Those were unsuitable. But a certain easy
cheerfulness, harmonious in every glance and gesture, as though God had set
the whole Negro to some pleasant tune. (186)

There is no Lockean state of nature here, requiring freedom from "absolute,
arbitrary power." On the contrary, for "the Negro" in this passage, the state
of nature is slavery. Slaves are "natural valets and hairdressers." God's own
hand is behind the harmonious tune that animates the "smooth tact" of the
slave. Babo is described here not as an exception, but as the best of breed,
who most fully realizes the potential of his nature. He illustrates, in their
most refined form, characteristics common to his species: cheerfulness, con-
geniality, and a sort of efficient unobtrusiveness that prevents the recipient
from feeling embarrassed by such attentive ministrations. The pleasure of the
experience is downright physical, a joy to behold, and an even greater joy "to
be the manipulated subject of." The narrator transmits perfectly the self-
satisfaction of a mind at peace with itself, beaming benevolence upon a lower
species.

   The unapologetic racism of this passage, described from Amasa Delano's
point of view and representative of prevailing sentiments in Melville's
American South, contrasts sharply with the reality being experienced here by
Benito Cereno and Babo. With a razor at his throat—the only part of his face
besides his upper lip that actually needs shaving, since he wears a beard—the
Spanish captain describes the gales and calms which have supposedly extended the voyage of the *San Dominick* and exhausted the ship's provisions.
Amasa Delano finds the tale hard to believe, "For here, by your account, you
have been these two months and more getting from Cape Horn to St. Maria, a
distance which I myself, with a good wind, have sailed in two days" (189).
Just at that moment, the razor at Benito Cereno's throat draws blood, and
Babo says, "But answer Don Amasa, please, master, while I wipe this ugly
stuff off the razor, and strop it again" (190). While Babo pauses to sharpen
his weapon, Benito Cereno thinks of more plausible explanations for the
ship's distress and delay. The Spanish captain continues haltingly, but more
convincingly, providing details of "obstinate currents," as well as praise of
"the blacks, for their general good conduct." Meanwhile, Babo remains attentive: "The servant, at convenient times, using his razor, and so, between
the intervals of shaving, the story and panegyric went on with more than
usual huskiness" (190). The strength of Delano's racism blinds him to the

protracted torture he is witnessing, so that all he sees are a devoted servant's ministrations to his frail master. A first-time reader is invited to fall in with Delano's perspective, but a re-reader of this scene witnesses both the Spanish captain's horror and the slave captain's improvisational virtuosity, as he terrorizes Benito Cereno, draws out the tale that needs to be heard, plans the next stage of the rebellion, and watches for any hint that the American captain has perceived the truth. [13]

## UGLY PASSIONS

The shave finished, Delano returns to the main deck, where he runs into Babo and sees "the Negro, his hand to his cheek. Advancing, Captain Delano perceived that the cheek was bleeding." Babo explains that his master has cut him "because, only by accident, Babo had given master one little scratch" (191). Shocked at such treatment, Amasa Delano muses to himself, "Ah this slavery breeds ugly passions in man" (191). This statement reverberates for the rest of the tale. The "ugly passions" to which Delano refers—Benito Cereno's anger and spite against "this poor friend of his"—are a figment of Delano's imagination, guided by Babo. To perpetuate the drama he is acting out for Delano's benefit, the rebel leader has cut his own cheek. Yet Amasa Delano's spontaneous phrase about "ugly passions" resonates with readers precisely because there are other ugly passions to consider, bred by slavery. Beyond the slave's desire for revenge, there is the master's contempt for the humanity of the slave, manifest in the slave trader's willingness to treat human beings as cargo to be bought, stored, transported, and sold. Ironically, even the white racist's complacency, which the racist sees as benevolence, is also an "ugly passion" in its denial of the slave's humanity. Delano embodies this complacency in the very good-naturedness of his own relations with African Americans: "Like most men of a good, blithe heart, Captain Delano took to Negroes, not philanthropically, but genially, just as other men to Newfoundland dogs" (187). This geniality, which dehumanizes people as dogs, is all the more ugly for its good-natured self-satisfaction and its imperviousness to its own ugliness.

The remainder of the story explores the implications of the genial racist paternalism that both the narrator and Amasa Delano embrace uncritically. When Benito Cereno jumps into Captain Delano's boat to make his escape from the *San Dominick*, the American captain's first reaction is to think that the Spanish captain is attacking him. Only when Babo, who has followed his master in the leap, aims a knife at Benito Cereno's heart, does Delano realize that the slaves have seized control of the Spanish vessel:

> Captain Delano, now with scales dropped from his eyes, saw the Negroes, not
> in misrule, not in tumult, not as if frantically concerned for Don Benito, but,

with mask torn away, flourishing hatchets and knives in ferocious piratical revolt. Like delirious black dervishes, the six Ashantees danced on the poop. (204)

At this moment Captain Delano experiences a paradigm shift. He no longer suffers from the complacency that has blinded him to the slave rebellion, but this complacency has been replaced by another "ugly passion," a racist vision of delirious, ferocious barbarians. The flip side of the fantasy of the happy slave was always the savage African that needed to be enslaved, and this barbarian has now been unleashed. With the mask torn away from the body servant and his fellow slaves, Delano sees for the first time African savages flourishing hatchets. Yet there is irony in the phrase, "scales dropped from his eyes," because this fantasy of the barbaric savage will be no more successful than the fantasy of the contented slave, when it comes to explaining the intelligence and subtlety of Babo's stratagem.

Aiming to recapture the *San Dominick*, Delano turns his cannons on the Spanish vessel and sends his crew to chase it down, armed with guns and sealing spears against the slaves' hatchets and knives. To inspire his men to recapture the slaves alive, Delano explains that the proceeds from the sale of the ship's human cargo, worth more than a thousand doubloons and now considered lost, will be shared with the crew. With this financial incentive, they attack the *San Dominick*. In the battle that ensues, the two sides seem evenly matched:

> For a time, the attack wavered, the negroes wedging themselves to beat it back, the half-repelled sailors, as yet unable to gain a footing. . . . They were almost overborne, when, rallying themselves into a squad as one man, with a huzzah they sprang inboard. . . . Soon, in a reunited band, and joined by the Spanish seamen, the whites came to the surface, irresistibly driving the Negroes toward the stern. (207)

In the end the white attackers gain the upper hand: "Exhausted, the blacks now fought in despair. Their red tongues lolled, wolflike, from their black mouths" (208). This description, which begins neutrally enough, with "negroes wedging themselves" to beat back an attack, ends by echoing the theme of savagery, presenting the slaves as animals reduced to tongues and mouths. One is tempted to conclude that Melville shares his narrator's view of these conquered slaves as beasts who have reverted to their pre-enslavement savagery. Certainly those who read "Benito Cereno" as a racist tale, reach this conclusion.

Several details of the story work against this interpretation, however. First, there is the question of atrocities, which seem to be equally divided between blacks and whites. Among the blacks, the females are in favor of torturing, not merely killing, the Spanish, and must be restrained from doing so by the other slaves (220). Among the whites, "beside the Negroes killed in action some were killed after the capture and reanchoring at night, when shackled to the ringbolts on deck. . . . These deaths were committed by the sailors, ere they could be prevented" (222). Ugly behavior is thus contemplated or committed by both blacks and whites, then restrained by other members within each community. On the level of leadership, there are also atrocities on both sides. Aboard the *San Dominick*, Babo and his colleagues arrange to reduce Alexandro Aranda's body to a skeleton, which they display as the figurehead on the ship's prow. Back in Lima, after a trial in which Babo refuses to speak, he is executed: "Dragged to the gibbet [gallows] at the tail of a mule, the black met his voiceless end." After he is tortured and hanged, "for many days, the head, that hive of subtlety, fixed on a pole in the plaza, met, unabashed, the gazes of the whites" (226). Readers are left to speculate which is more barbaric: the skeleton on the prow, or the head on a spike. Which death is more brutal? In terms of atrocities and punishments, Melville seems to present rough parity between blacks and whites. If the conquered slaves act as beasts, so do the whites.

The story ends with a description of Babo's severed heard, but not before Amasa Delano tries one last time to cheer up Benito Cereno. He says to the devastated Spaniard, "The past is passed; why moralize upon it? Forget it. See, yon bright sun has forgotten it all, and the blue sea, and the blue sky; these have turned over new leaves." The American's celebrated resilience on display, he shakes off an unpleasant experience and prepares to go on with his life. The "bright sun, " "blue sky," and "new leaves" are just the optimistic clichés we would expect from a person of "undistrustful good nature." Amasa Delano cannot imagine why Benito Cereno does not just put the whole thing behind him, as the American so obviously can. The Spanish captain is impervious to this optimism, however, reminding Delano that the sun, sea, and sky can forget it all, only "because they have no memory . . . because they are not human" (225). To be human is to be conscious and to remember. When the American asks, "What has cast such a shadow upon you?" Benito Cereno enigmatically replies, "The Negro." This is the end of their conversation. There is no more explanation—not from Delano, not from the narrator, not from Melville. A reader winds up stranded on that phrase.

Is it that Babo represents an evil so terrifying to Benito Cereno that the consciousness of its very existence kills him? Those who read the story as a tale of good and evil reach this conclusion. "The Negro," synonymous with evil, destroys the Christ-like Benito Cereno. [14] According to this view, Amasa Delano cannot possibly understand what Benito Cereno has been through, since he has not experienced the horror of the knife at his throat or of his best friend reduced to a skeleton on the prow. Or is it that Benito Cereno has been forced to rip the mask away from both sides of the slaveholder's myth—the contented slave and the barbarous savage—only to find both sides inadequate to contain the "hive of subtlety" that is Babo's mind? Neither the happy slave nor the menacing savage seems capable of finding a way, without weapons, without navigation skills, without funds, and without the supporting structures of laws, governments, and fleets at sea, to take control of a ship, disarm its crew, and intimidate them into carrying out the tasks necessary for escape and survival at sea. Neither the slave nor the savage seems capable of fabricating in two hours the only charade that can dupe the American captain, buy time, assemble provisions, and lay groundwork for seizing the American ship. If Babo does not fit into the ways of knowing that have sustained Benito Cereno until now, unifying mental categories that have enabled him to think well of himself and his friends, as they carried out the business of transporting human cargo from one country to another, what other elements of the scaffold upon which he has erected his certainties about the meaning and purpose of life might now collapse?

Melville does not answer these questions. He merely leaves us to contemplate in an open-ended way the incompatibility between Amasa Delano's good-natured, generous optimism, Benito Cereno's horrified, depressed despair, and Babo's "unabashed" manipulative genius. Delano and Cereno are technically the winners—they get back the ship, much of its cargo, and some of its crew—and Babo, returned to slavery, tried, and executed, is definitely the loser. Yet he denies to them the one thing they most crave: an explanation that fits into their worldview. They have no way to navigate the epistemological layers of his defiance, even though he has penetrated their racism and manipulated both their condescension and their fear. The narrator describes Babo in defeat: "Seeing all was over, he uttered no sound, and could not be forced to. His aspect seemed to say: since I cannot do deeds, I will not speak words" (225). It is up to each reader to figure out the significance of Babo's final silence and "that hive of subtlety, fixed on a pole in the plaza" which meets "unabashed, the gazes of the whites."

## DIALOGIC FREEDOM IN "BENITO CERENO"

In terms of dialogic freedom, the two most interesting characters in "Benito Cereno" are Amasa Delano and Babo, the former because his racism limits his ability to see what is happening before his eyes, the latter because he manipulates that racism to advance his quest for freedom. Having been victimized by a racist world that regards him as less than human, Babo exploits the nuances of that perspective to conceal his plot from Delano, even as he intensifies the intimidation that allows the rebel slaves to dominate the Spanish captain and crew. Thus, he uses his ability to navigate the ways of knowing of the American captain, the Spanish captain, and the crew of the *San Dominick*, to coauthor his own strategy for escape. Their expectations, fears, and anticipated reactions all coauthor his improvisations. Each decision—to concoct the story of hardship at sea, to reduce Aranda's body to a skeleton for the ship's prow, to invite the American captain to chat with the Spanish captain while he gets shaved—is coauthored by the relevant listeners, both anticipated and present. Without the ability to imagine how Delano sees the world, or what scenario will simultaneously intimidate Cereno and charm Delano, Babo would not be able to concoct the tale of suffering that buys him time and that he hopes will lay the groundwork for capturing the American's ship. He navigates with agility ways of knowing that include his own escaped slave's perspective and the various forms of racism to be found in his former owner's benevolence, the Spanish captain's terror, and the American captain's good-natured generosity. Able to imagine what it is like to know the world from each of these perspectives, he coauthors the decisions and actions of others, even as they coauthor his. Thus, he exploits events moment by moment aboard the *San Dominick*, in order to enact his dialogic freedom.

Babo's grasp of Delano's racism is especially helpful. Even as Babo's words answer in advance Delano's expectations, they are also coauthored by Benito Cereno, the captive who must seem captain and who must, in any event, be kept in line. In his simultaneous deception of Delano and intimidation of Cereno, Babo successfully anticipates, responds to, and reinforces Delano's vision of the contented slave; he also anticipates, responds to, and guarantees Cereno's fear of the savage lurking beneath the surface. His coauthorship of both Delano's complacency and Cereno's fear, his understanding of his fellow slaves' desires for freedom, and his awareness of the overwhelmingly hostile context of law, money, and power that perpetuates their slavery, all reflect a multivalent dialogic flexibility that grows even as it is exercised in his improvised drama of the perfect slave. In a world whose laws, traditions, and attitudes all conspire to thwart him, Babo uses his grasp of the various forms of the racist perspective represented by Aranda, Delano, and Cereno to create a parenthesis within which he can enjoy the only freedom he will ever experience.

Amasa Delano deliberates and acts from multiple perspectives as well, which reflect the various roles he fills and relationships he enjoys. Among other things, he is a white American, a sea captain, a bachelor, a businessman, a traveler, a speaker of Spanish, a man of action, an optimist, a lover of nature and honesty, and a friend. These and other aspects of his identity (dog lover, citizen of Duxberry, Massachusetts, etc.), orient his efforts to unify the chaos of daily reality and to deliberate upon a course of action. Each perspective helps him construct unified meaning from the centrifugal chaos of daily reality. Each role he inhabits has the centripetal effect of unifying experience in terms of a particular perspective, and his multiple perspectives work congruently in the meaning-making process as long as they do not suggest contradictory ways of making sense of events and taking action, and as long as he is not overwhelmed by efforts to think from all possible perspectives at once or to notice every detail, which would lead to chaos. His complacency may be threatened from time to time, but the coherence of his dominating vision of the contented, spaniel-like slave always rescues him from the chaos of uncertainty. Even after he confronts the fact that the slaves have seized control of the *San Dominick*, he is able to incorporate that inconvenient truth into a coherent, unified vision of the slave's bestiality beneath the veneer of civilization. Amasa Delano is remarkably successful at reconciling the various roles he fills as he coauthors decisions with others within the context of the slave trade.

As a captain, Delano knows to look for the flag that will identify another ship at sea. As a businessman, he knows to seek reimbursement for provisions distributed aboard a ship in distress. As a man of action, he does not hesitate to offer aid to a disabled vessel, or to quell a mutiny. In each case, the action he takes is two-sided, involving other people—his crew, his investors, the people he encounters—as well as the laws, rules, and values that constitute the superaddressees to which he feels answerable. He follows the customs of hospitality that call for hosting a fellow captain, he follows the maritime law that governs the distribution of recovered cargo. He embraces the values of generosity, optimism, and benevolence, which also help him decide what to do. His dialogic freedom is a function of his ability to see things from the multiple perspectives created by these roles and reinforced by these values, as he answers to investors, crew, and others who coauthor the decisions he makes. To the extent that these multiple perspectives operate congruently they contribute to a unified sense of reality that might be summarized as Amasa Delano's good-natured optimism and generosity.

As he witnesses the puzzling events aboard the *San Dominick*, Delano draws on these various forces for meaning making. At one point, for example, he contemplates the apparent incivility of the Spanish captain, who seems sometimes eager to talk, other times curiously contemptuous: "The singular alternations of courtesy and ill-breeding in the Spanish captain were unaccountable, except on one of two suppositions—innocent lunacy, or wicked imposture" (164). Delano is eager to find a way to explain the behavior he is witnessing, and to fit it into the various narratives he has become accustomed to in his efforts to make sense of his life within a context of other people. But the centripetal categories he has for meaning making, which have so far worked to orient his decisions, now threaten to become inadequate. The eventness of the reality Amasa Delano is caught up in on the *San Dominick* is not to be explained in terms of either the lunacy or the vice of the Spanish captain. To put it another way, Amasa Delano may consider the two alternative explanations he poses adequate, but a second-time reader of the tale will not. Though the various perspectives from which Delano experiences his situation contribute to the way he goes about registering reality and making decisions, Melville is particularly interested in the ways in which Amasa Delano's benevolent racism undermines his ability to register the reality before him on board the *San Dominick*.[15]

Delano's racism limits his dialogic freedom by narrowing his capacity to see what is happening before his eyes. Since he fails to recognize Benito Cereno for the captive that he is, and Babo for the captor that he is, the two-sidedness of his interactions with both of them becomes distorted. He constantly misunderstands both the words and the body language of the Spanish captain. Racking his brain for explanations, he interprets Benito Cereno's frailness, taciturnity, and apparent lack of interest in his own cargo and crew, variously as sullenness, rudeness, the enervated weakness of the Old World, or a piratical conspiracy with his crew to take over Delano's ship. In the face of a persistently inexplicable reality, the more energetic his search for explanations, the further afield Delano wanders, illustrating the power of a single, unifying constellation of racist misconceptions to derail the processes of logic and evidence. At one point "the mad idea now darted into Captain Delano's mind that Don Benito's plea of indisposition, in withdrawing below, was but a pretense: that he was engaged there maturing his plot." When this disturbing possibility enters Captain Delano's mind, his paranoia is fanned by his certainty that "the whites, too, by nature were the shrewder race." He briefly entertains the possibility that the Spanish captain is in league with the slaves: "Could Don Benito be any way in complicity with the blacks? But they were too stupid. Besides, who ever heard of a white so far a renegade as to apostasize from his very species almost, by leaguing in against it with Negroes?" (177). Here, Delano exhibits no shortage of curiosity in confronting and trying to solve a mystery. The problem is that his racist assumptions—that the blacks are too stupid to participate in a plot, let alone hatch one; that they belong "almost" to another species—undermine Delano's ability to process the evidence before him. Thus, the effects of his racist perspective multiply with the energy devoted to sustaining it. Amasa Delano's racism limits his dialogic freedom by preventing him from comprehending the complexities of the events transpiring before and around him. He misunderstands almost every word, gesture, or action contemplated, taken, or not taken. Benito Cereno and Babo coauthor Delano's decisions, in that he acts in response to what he thinks they need and want, but his racism limits his perspective to taking in only those details that are consistent with the epistemology of his expectations. Thus, his racism limits the arena within which his dialogic freedom can be enacted.

Chapter 1 discusses what Bakhtin calls "participative thinking," "active empathizing," "sympathetic understanding," and the "willingness to listen." That discussion includes speculation about obstacles that might undermine a person's ability to experience these perspectives, that is, to navigate and return from the epistemological layers of another person's way of knowing.

These obstacles (hostility, indifference, sexism, racism, etc.) undermine the dialogic freedom of someone who might otherwise empathize with a sufferer. In "Author and Hero in Aesthetic Activity," Bakhtin describes the suffering person as one who "does not see the agonizing tension of his own muscles, does not see the entire, plastically consummated posture of the body, or the expression of suffering on his own face. He does not see the clear blue sky against the background of which his suffering outward image is delineated for me."[16] (25). Only the observer can see these things and fulfill the centripetal task of completing, consummating, or filling in the image of the sufferer. According to Bakhtin one friend helps another by completing his image of himself. In chapter 1, I argued that this process can derail: "The more an observer's ability to see behind another's back, or to see the expression on his or her face, contributes not to a fuller image of that person, but to a reduced or distorted image, the more that observer reduces his or her own opportunities for navigating and returning from the ways of knowing entailed in that person's experience. " Over and over, Melville explores how Delano's racism radically limits his capacity to grasp what Babo is up to.

Melville also explores how Delano's racism undermines his ability to empathize with Benito Cereno. Seeing the Spanish captain's weakness, dejection, and constant need to be propped up by his faithful servant, Captain Delano is filled with a desire to reach out in friendship and empathy. Seeing through Delano's eyes, Melville's narrator describes the suffering captain:

> A prey to settled dejection, as if long mocked with hope he would not now indulge it even when it had ceased to be a mock, the prospect of that day, or evening at furthest, lying at anchor, with plenty of water for his people, and a brother captain to counsel and befriend, seemed in no perceptible degree to encourage him. His mind appeared unstrung. . . . No wonder that, as in this state he tottered about, his private servant apprehensively followed him. (148)

Here, the narrator channels Delano's efforts to see what Benito Cereno cannot see—the agonizing expression on his face, the weakness in his faltering step. Delano fills in or "consummates" for Benito Cereno a portrait of the "brother captain" he would "befriend," drawing conclusions about why the Spaniard's mind appears "unstrung." The totalizing power of Delano's racist horizon—from which Babo can be seen only as the faithful servant and Benito Cereno can be seen only as the debilitated master—undermines the American captain's ability to penetrate to the core of Benito Cereno's suffering. Delano's fantasy of comrade ships, lying at anchor, restored to peace and plenty, while the brotherly captains share a glass of wine, comforts him but has nothing to do with Benito Cereno's situation. The well-meaning American places Babo and Benito Cereno within a narrative that is capable of identifying either the contented slave or the barbarian beneath the surface, either the weak captain or the potential scoundrel, but not the human beings standing before him on deck. Racism establishes powerful categories for who can be considered intelligent or even human, but this totalizing effect comes at great cost. Delano's racism derails his analytical powers by eliminating possibilities and reducing his options for understanding the world, empathizing with Benito Cereno, and acting on the basis of that understanding.

Even as Captain Delano's racism limits his dialogic freedom, it serves also to protect him. A major irony of Melville's tale is that Delano's failure to grasp the reality of his situation saves his life. He carries such a potent expectation of the happy slave's benevolence that he is blind to the torture he is witnessing. Yet had he penetrated Babo's scheme, the honest man of action in him would not have been able to dissemble. As the only outsider aboard the *San Dominick*, waiting for his whaling boat to return with provisions, outnumbered by the hatchet-polishers, he would have been the next victim in the "theatre of blood." When later he learns of the danger he was in, rather than being unnerved by it in retrospect, Delano is cheered by his constitutional optimism and good humor, which allow him to enjoy his role as savior, compartmentalize the negative aspects of the experience as exceptional, and get on with his life. There is no indication in Melville's text that Delano's brush with mortality and a slave rebellion modifies in any way his views about the world. He may have been wrong about who was in command on the *San Dominick*, but his myth of the happy slave, the flip side of which is the ferocious savage, remains intact when the rebel slaves are unmasked to him as savages in piratical revolt. In order for Delano to see things differently—in order for him to grasp the genius of Babo's charade—he would have to relive the whole experience from an ironic perspective, like a second-time reader of Melville's tale. This possibility is out of the question for "a man of such native simplicity as to be incapable of satire or irony" (163). Delano's racism saves his life, but it does not save him from the narrowness of a worldview that obfuscates reality and undermines the possibilities for "empathy," "participative thinking," and dialogic freedom.

Like Amasa Delano, Babo deliberates and acts from multiple perspectives. He is an African, formerly a black man's slave, a white man's escaped slave, a small person, the leader of the slave rebellion, an actor, a director, an improviser, and the mastermind of both Benito Cereno's intimidation and Amasa Delano's deception. We know that he values freedom enough to kill for it, that he wants to get to Senegal, and that he understands the white racist myth of the happy slave and the barbarous savage well enough to impersonate the perfect servant and to install on the ship's prow a human skeleton. We know that he is a multitasker, organizing the other slaves and torturing Benito Cereno, even as he flatters and deceives Amasa Delano, always thinking ahead. These roles, experiences, and values contribute to the decisions he makes and the actions he takes among other people who are their coauthors. For example, because his second in command, Atufal, was an African king,

Babo seems to enjoy creating a special role for him in the Delano deception drama. The majestic Atufal appears in chains to stand mutely before Benito Cereno, ostensibly to beg the Spanish captain's pardon (which he stubbornly refuses to do, remaining mute), but actually to be ready in an instant to strike. Seeing Atufal stand at attention with an iron collar around his neck, "from which depended a chain thrice wound round his body" (161), Delano observes that "he has a royal spirit in him, this fellow" (162). Babo responds, "those slits in Atufal's ears once held wedges of gold" (163). True, Atufal has agreed to this charade, which allows him to be close by if needed, but Babo must take special satisfaction in the pageant of the chained former king standing mutely, ready for Babo's next command. When Babo comments on the slits in Atufal's ears, the remark is not just for Delano's benefit. Atufal, too, coauthors it by being the target of Babo's reminder that in the meritocracy of rebellion, the former king serves the former black man's slave.

Unlike Delano's thoughts, which the narrator tracks and largely mirrors, Babo's thoughts are inaccessible to the narrator, except through the deceived eyes of Delano, and hence mostly inaccessible to readers. Just as Chaucer presents the Canterbury pilgrims by giving only the surface details of their lives—how they dress, what they say and do, the stories they tell, not what they speculate about—Melville presents only Babo's surface: his dress, gestures, words, and deeds. Thus, it is difficult for readers to penetrate inside his mind. We see only what he presents to Delano, and we know that this is a charade, not because he confesses in some Shakespearean soliloquy, but because of his actions. Even restricted to these surface details, a reader can gather from his words and deeds that Babo has mastered Delano's racist perspective, and that he sees not only what Amasa Delano misses, but much more, because he also sees Delano failing to see. His virtuosity in playing Delano's racism like a flute is coauthored by Delano, who calls forth Babo's deceptions by being ripe for them. When Delano offers to buy him, Babo's response is, "Master wouldn't part with Babo for a thousand doubloons" (172). Delano's question coauthors Babo's answer, in that Babo uses it to stoke the fires of Delano's fantasy of the contented slave. At the same time, Babo is brazen enough to know that Delano will miss his irony—Benito Cereno is not in a position to part with Babo under any circumstances—and he takes this opportunity to rub in the truth to the Spanish captain who is his prisoner. Thus, his statement is also coauthored by Benito Cereno, whom it tortures.

This complex dynamic allows Babo for a time to enact his dialogic freedom, understanding and manipulating the limitations of Amasa Delano's thinking, watching for some indication that the American captain is wising up, dominating the words and actions of Benito Cereno and crew, directing the assignments of various slave leaders, improvising new plans amid shifting circumstances, and planning the raid on Amasa Delano's ship. Within a field of forces for unity and chaos that involve Delano's racist assumptions, the captain and crew's terrorized behavior, and the shifting circumstances of a slave rebellion that at any moment might be exposed, Babo decides his actions within a context of other people. If, following John Locke's lead, we think of slavery as a continuation of the state of war, and the slaves' rebellion as unmasking that war, we see Babo as the leader who for a time replaces one form of slavery with another, until he is defeated. His elaborate stratagem breaks down only when he leaps after Benito Cereno into Delano's whaling boat, aiming to stab the Spanish captain. At that point Babo is swiftly taken prisoner, and the only further choice we see him make involves his decision not to speak. His refusal to explain himself—to confess, to repent, or to beg for mercy—is itself dialogic, in that it is coauthored by his captors, as a response to their efforts to torture him into speech. His last independent act is his refusal to play the role of suppliant perfected by the Trojan king Priam in the *Iliad*. Though Babo dies a slave, he demonstrates that under the most unlikely conditions, without any of the instruments that we normally associate with a life of freedom—citizenship, education, wealth, possessions, professional training, legal rights—a person can at least for a time coauthor what others see and do, and can respond resourcefully to the coauthorship of others within a field of forces for unity and chaos.

## READING FOR AND WITH DIALOGIC FREEDOM

Its trick ending and irony make each reader a major participant in "Benito Cereno." On a first reading, restricted by the narrator mainly to Delano's racist perspective, readers are invited by that narrator to share Delano's assumptions.[17] The more good-natured Amasa Delano seems, the more innocuous and representative of his time and place his assumptions seem. Readers in 1855 might have fallen in with these ideas, while readers 150 years later are more likely to condemn them or to dismiss them as anachronistic, whether or not readers identify these ideas with Melville. Whether five years before the civil war, or a century and a half after, each reader is invited by Melville's narrator to share the racist perspective presented right up until the story's trick ending, which destabilizes that perspective and inspires readers to start over from page 1. A second-time reader, whether in 1855 or 2013, has the opportunity to witness the moment-by-moment discrepancy between the myth of the happily domesticated savage and the reality of the complex rebellion in process aboard the *San Dominick*. A second-time reader is tempted to ponder the inadequacy of either image—the devoted slave or the barbaric savage—to explain the subtlety of Babo's project. In terms of dialogic freedom, as a reader comes to grasp Amasa Delano's or the narrator's limitations, there is a growing understanding of multiple perspectives that

Melville presents as if behind the narrator's back. Delano is seen not just as good-natured but as obtuse; Benito Cereno is seen not just as fragile but as terrorized. A second-time reader can read the exact same words as before and remember his or her first response, even as that response is being revised. Chief among the perspectives gained by a second-time reader is an appreciation for Babo's ability to act as an author finalizing Amasa Delano's conception of himself, Benito Cereno, and the slaves on board. A second-time reader experiences moment by moment both the memory of the first reading and the complexities of the second, as that reader witnesses Babo's grasp of how Delano goes about seeing what is not there (docile slaves), and how he goes about not seeing what *is* there (a slave rebellion).

A second-time reader who also reads Amasa Delano's 1817 *Narrative* is in a good position to consider the implications of Melville's changes to his source materials. Linking the timing of the rebellion aboard the Spanish ship, as well as its name, to the French Revolution, the establishment of slavery in the Western Hemisphere, and the bloody slave rebellions on the island of Santo Domingo encouraged Melville's contemporaries to focus on both the violence of slavery and the international movements to embrace freedom. Expurgating the dark sides of the Spanish captain and crew, at the same time emphasizing Delano's gullibility, allowed Melville to focus on the "ugly passions" that include the self-satisfied benevolence of the white racist image of the natural black slave, civilized by his happy servitude. If Melville had focused instead on the mistreatment of blacks by cruel overseers, he would have helped perpetuate the fantasy that the elimination of such cruelty could cure the evils of slavery—that if we take away the beatings, rapes, and lynchings, slavery could be a civilized and civilizing institution. By making his slaveholders decent, benevolent, people, Melville explodes this fantasy of benevolent slavery, which degrades slaves by underestimating their need and capacity for freedom, even as it anesthetizes slaveholders to the dangers in their midst. Conversely, by expanding the role of Babo, so that moment by moment he juggles the many challenges of his precarious rule, Melville also emphasizes the inadequacy of the happy slave/barbaric savage dichotomy to explain Babo's intelligence and audacity. Second-time readers with a knowledge of the narrative on which Melville's story was based, as well as the historical events Melville chose to emphasize, enjoy the nuanced perspectives this information contributes.

Readers today face the challenge of calibrating the irreconcilable perspectives of Amasa Delano, Benito Cereno, and Babo, then confronting the disjunction between their own first and second readings. Amasa Delano's good-natured racism, a point of view that survives into the twenty-first century, is held out to each reader like a bright red lollipop, then smashed on the ground. At the end of the tale, Delano holds on to his confident vision, bracketing off the rebel slaves as piratical savages among an otherwise happy lot. A reader steeped in Melville's moment-by-moment irony can have no such illusions. In the twenty-first century, most second-time readers entertain Amasa Delano's perspective only to reject it.[18] Benito Cereno's despair seems more realistic, acknowledging the human capacity to be haunted by disturbing memories. Yet, what reader wants to be crushed by the Spanish captain's depression, or his refusal even to look at Babo when confronted with him in the courtroom?[19] A second-time reader is likely to grasp Benito Cereno's pained perspective, too, only to reject it. Babo's insight, creativity, and defiance seem more attractive. Yet what reader wants to sympathize with a torturer?[20] A second-time reader may grasp the virtuosity of Babo's multiple perspectives without really seeing into his soul (withheld from us by the narrator) or embracing whatever is at the heart of his "unabashed" stare.

By inviting rereaders to rethink the events on board the *San Dominick*, Melville enhances our capacity to see things from mutually exclusive perspectives. In the process he invites us to make our first-time-reader selves answerable to our second-time-reader selves, so that even as we rethink Amasa Delano's racism or Babo's dialogic virtuosity, we also reevaluate our own first-time-reader selves. If, for example, we reread the shaving scene, where Babo uses the Spanish flag as a bib, we might think, "How did I miss that?" With detail after detail, we wind up interrogating our first-time-reader selves, not always in a friendly way. You might say that we coauthor with our earlier reading selves our own rereading experience, or we become our own superaddressees, to which our earlier reading selves would have responded as to a god, if they had only had the chance. The dialogic relationship between a second- and first-time-reader self—as a rereader remembers the first reading and responds not just to the text, but to that earlier experience—must be very personal, taking each of us face to face with our own expectations, prejudices, preferences, and attitudes toward being manipulated or surprised. If we imagine dialogic freedom and the multiple perspectives that it entails, on a continuum between one and ten, a rereader of "Benito Cereno" lies closer to ten than he or she did the first time around. A second-time reader of "Benito Cereno" is also more capable than any character in the tale, and more capable than its biased narrator, of engaging in the two-sided act of choice, which involves deliberation from multiple perspectives within a field of forces for unity and chaos.

Melville's tale invited his contemporaries first to indulge in the complacent racism that dominated his white culture—enhancing that invitation by expunging from Amasa Delano's 1817 *Narrative* most of the negative characteristics of the whites, even as it fanned white readers' fears of violence—then to rethink the mental limitations of that same racism.[21] In the twenty-first century "Benito Cereno" still invites readers to reach beyond the mental limitations of that "ugly passion"—all the uglier for its self-satisfaction—that continues to distort our perceptions of others. The brilliance of Melville's appeal is that rather than focusing on the violated rights of victims, he focuses on the compromised freedom of racists. When they fail to see what is happening before their eyes, they narrow the range of choices that they can coauthor with others. In "Benito Cereno," Herman Melville calls on us all to avoid the fate of the good-natured Delano, who survives only by being a slave to his limited horizon. Melville also seems to imply that if we are to avoid Delano's fate we will need to be willing to commit ourselves to the project of endlessly revising our first impressions. This project will call for an enormous effort, possibly dangerous, never final, to reread the decisions we coauthor in a world shared with others.

## NOTES

1. Mike Davis observes that "the scholarship on 'Benito Cereno' is some of the best work yet on Melville." "Rhetorical Razors: 'Lurking Significance' in the 'Vexatious Coincidence' of 'Benito Cereno,'" in *Reading the Text That Isn't There: Paranoia in the Ninteenth-Century American Novel* (New York: Routledge, 2005), 71. Some of the most interesting recent readings of this tale are Carolyn Karcher, *Shadow over the Promised Land: Slavery, Race, and Violence in Melville's America* (Baton Rouge: Louisiana State University Press, 1980), and Carolyn Karcher, "The Riddle of the Sphinx: Melville's 'Benito Cereno' and the Amistad Case," in *Critical Essays on Herman Melville's "Benito Cereno,"* ed. Robert Burkholder (New York: Hall, 1992), 196–227. Also in Burkholder's collection are Eric Sundquist's "'Benito Cereno' and New World Slavery," 146–67, and H. Bruce Franklin's "Past, Present, and Future Seemed One," 230–46. Particularly useful on the subject of Melville's difficult narrator is Sundquist's "Suspense and Tautology in 'Benito Cereno,'" in *Modern Critical Interpretations of Billy Budd, Benito Cereno, Bartleby, and Other Tales,* ed. Harold Bloom (New York: Chelsea House, 1987), 81–106. William Spanos calls "Benito Cereno" Melville's "anticanonical masterpiece," in *Herman Melville and the American Calling: The Fiction after Moby-Dick, 1851–1857* (Albany: State University of New York Press, 2008), 116.

2. Rosalie Feltenstein, "Melville's 'Benito Cereno,'" *American Literature* 19 (1947): 245–55, and Ivor Winters, "'Benito Cereno': A Late Masterpiece," in *In Defense of Reason* (New York: Routledge, 1947), both argue that evil, not slavery, is Melville's subject in this tale. For Sidney Kaplan, on the other hand, the story reflects the racism of Melville's era. Kaplan argues that "it seems highly improbable that Melville in writing *Benito Cereno* was not thinking within the framework of the cultural concerns of his time." "*Benito Cereno*: An Apology for Slavery," in *Melville's Benito Cereno: A Text for Guided Research*, ed. John P. Runden (Lexington, MA: Heath, 1965), 170.

3. See H. Bruce Franklin, "'Apparent Symbol of Despotic Command': Melville's *Benito Cereno,*" in *Critical Essays on Herman Melville's "Benito Cereno,"* ed. Robert Burkholder (New York: Hall, 1992), 50–56, and Kermit Vanderbildt, "'Benito Cereno': Melville's Fable of Black Complicity," in *Critical Essays on Herman Melville's "Benito Cereno,"* ed. Robert Burkholder (New York: Hall, 1992), 65–75.

4. H. Bruce Franklin, in "Past, Present, and Future Seemed One," speaks of Melville's "estranged relationship with his audience" (238); Charley Swan, in "'Benito Cereno: Melville's De(con)struction of the Southern Reader," quotes from Melville's letters in 1856, where the author laments, "What a madness and anguish it is that an author can never—under no conceivable circumstances—be at all frank with his readers" (176).

5. Mikhail Bakhtin, *Speech Genres and Other Late Essays*, ed. Caryl Emerson and Michael Holquist, trans. Vern McGee (Austin: University of Texas Press, 1986), 146.

6. See unsigned reviews from the *New York Tribune*, June 23, 1856, and the *Knickerbocker*, September, 1856, in *Melville: The Critical Heritage*, ed. Watson G. Branch (London: Routledge, 1974), 330, 357–59.

7. Sidney Kaplan and Newton Arvin lead this group.

8. Elizabeth Hardwick, *Herman Melville* (New York: Viking, 2000), 106. See also Sandra Zagarell, "Reenvisioning America: Melville's 'Benito Cereno,'" in *Critical Essays on Herman Melville's "Benito Cereno,"* ed. Robert Burkholder (New York: Hall, 1992), 129, and Karcher, "The Riddle of the Sphinx," 198.

9. Amasa Delano, *A Narrative of Voyages and Travels, in the Northern and Southern Hemispheres: Comprising Three Voyages Round the World, Together with a Voyage of Survey and Discovery in the Pacific Ocean and Oriental Islands* (Boston: E. G. House, 1817), in *Melville's Benito Cereno: An Interpretation with Annotated Text and Concordance*, ed. William D. Richardson (Durham, NC: Carolina Academic Press, 1987), 95–122. Citations to Delano's 1817 *Narrative* are to this text.

10. The violence of the slave rebellion can be seen as heroic, rather than savage. Sundquist, in "'Benito Cereno' and New World Slavery," describes Babo as "a heroic figure" (156); Arnold Rumpersad calls Babo "the most heroic character in Melville's fiction." "Melville and Race," in *Herman Melville: A Collection of Critical Essays*, ed. Myra Jehlen (Englewood Cliffs, NJ: Prentice Hall, 1994), 165.

11. Herman Melville, "Benito Cereno," in *"Billy Budd" and Other Tales* (New York: Signet, 1998), 164–65. Citations to "Benito Cereno" are to this edition.

12. John Locke, *The Second Treatise of Government*, ed. Thomas P. Peardon (Indianapolis: Bobbs-Merrill, 1952), 17.

13. In "The Riddle of the Sphinx," Carolyn Karcher observes that in this scene Melville promotes Babo to "the rank of co-author" in his improvisations (220). In "New World Slavery," Eric Sundquist quotes Melville's narrator in this scene, "Nor . . . could he [Delano] resist the vagary, that in the black he saw a headsman, and in the white a man at the block." Sundquist notes that the conceit of decapitation, uniting "Jacobin terror, the Inquisition and slave vengeance—has here more actuality than the literal barbering that is taking place" (182).

14. According to Guy Cardwell, in "Melville's Gray Story: Symbols and Meaning in 'Benito Cereno,'" "The Negro" compacts "all the imagery associated with blackness into a summation of horror at evil rampant," while the white Benito Cereno is presented as "the good, the Christlike man" (70).

15. Carolyn Karcher explains, "I do not believe that 'Benito Cereno' is primarily a dramatization of a slave revolt . . . but rather an exploration of the white racist mind and how it reacts in the face of slave insurrection." *Shadow over the Promised Land*, 128.

16. Mikhail Bakhtin, "Author and Hero in Aesthetic Activity," in *Art and Answerability: Early Philosophical Essays by M. M. Bakhtin*, ed. Michael Holquist and Vadim Liapunov, trans. Vadim Liapunov (Austin: University of Texas Press, 1990), 25.

17. In "Past, Present, and Future," H. Bruce Franklin argues that Melville's "strategy depends on a narrator who cannot comprehend what he sees" (241). Eric Sudquist argues in "Suspence and Tautology" that the "narrator merges with then withdraws from Delano's point of view" (93) with a voice filled with "cagey manipulation" (83). For him there is a "perplexing distance between the narrator and Delano, a distance that continually collapses and expands" (86). This element of free indirect discourse poses one of the story's biggest challenges. We never know quite where Melville stands in relationship to his slippery narrator.

18. What Guy Cardwell in 1959 saw as Delano's "innocent perceptiveness" (73), Joyce Adler saw in 1981 as "the outlook of the average white eighteenth-century American" ("The Monastic Slaver: Images and Meaning in 'Benito Cereno,'" in *Critical Essays on Herman Melville's "Benito Cereno,"* ed. Robert Burkholder [New York: Hall, 1992], 85), and Carolyn Karcher saw in 1980 as Delano's "obtuse . . . intelligence" (*Shadow over the Promised Land*, 121). What we now debate is the degree to which Melville ironizes Delano's outlook through the actions in the tale and through the words of a narrator whose distance from Delano Eric Sundquist calls "perplexing" ("Suspense and Tautology," 86). Karcher explains, "The central critical problem the story poses is that of distinguishing between Melville's interpretation of the events that transpire on the *San Dominic* and the interpretation he ascribes to his chief protagonists, the Yankee captain Amasa Delano and the Spaniard Benito Cereno" (*Shadow over the Promised Land*, 128).

19. Although in 1947 Roselie Feltenstein saw Don Benito as belonging "to that class of good harmless men and women" ("Melville's 'Benito Cereno,'" 252), by 1980 Karcher would dismiss Benito Cereno's self-image as the cruelly betrayed martyr and describe him instead as a "stereotype of the southern gentleman," or "southern Hamlet," who "proves incapable of facing the murderous rage that seethes beneath the Negro's apparent submission to enslavement that threatens to erupt again and again in furious revolt as long as he remains a slave" (*Shadow over the Promised Land*, 136–37).

20. See note 10 above. Karcher describes Babo as "a favorable portrayal of a black rebel, . . . by far the most intelligent character in 'Benito Cereno'" (*Shadow over the Promised Land*, 140).

21. William Spanos sees in "Benito Cereno" Melville's "great refusal to be answerable to . . . the American Calling" (*Herman Melville and the American Calling*, 7). According to him, Melville wrote "stories of the obsessive efforts of the custodians of the dominant . . . American culture . . . to repress . . . (anti)Americans who simply *do not answer to* or *refuse to be answerable to* the *call* of the *American narrative*" (10), which Spanos describes as the "liberal capitalist problematic" (111).

# Chapter Seven

# The Grand Inquisitor's Silent Christ

> Dialogic freedom: a two-sided act, chosen within a field of *unifying* and fragmenting forces along a continuum of minimal to maximal *layers of knowing that are never final.*

In *The Brothers Karamazov*, Fyodor Dostoevsky explores the complexities of coauthorship between characters with mutually exclusive perspectives on freedom: one view that doubts man's capacity to handle moral freedom, the other that insists on it as essential to life. In parallel battles of the will, the Grand Inquisitor attempts to force Christ to speak, while Ivan Karamazov attempts to derail his brother Alyosha[1] from becoming a priest. In both cases, the speaker's words are coauthored by his silent listener, while the listener's actions are coauthored by the speaker to whom he responds. When Christ kisses the Grand Inquisitor and Alyosha kisses Ivan, those acts are codetermined by their opponents' arguments against freedom. Conversely, the kiss "glows" in the recipient's heart, challenging his intellectual ideal with a spiritual one. In the end, Ivan and his creation the Grand Inquisitor both must live with the tension between two conflicting perspectives, neither of which they can finally jettison or embrace. The superaddressee—a force like God, or "the law," or "the spirit of forgiveness"—usually functions as an incontestable, unifying absolute, or the perfect standard to which a speaker is answerable. In these conflicting perspectives, however, Dostoevsky suggests that there can be competing superaddressees—in this case, Christ's choice to forgive, as opposed to the Grand Inquisitor's belief that the choice between good and evil is a burden too great for man to bear. The superaddressee is such a potent force in human life that this competition proves deeply disturbing for the human characters involved. For readers who witness these characters' attempts to hold on to their most important values, in the face of challenges too potent to ignore, the effect is also unsettling.

129

# MILTON, MELVILLE, AND DOSTOEVSKY

The two hundred years that elapsed between the publication of Milton's *Paradise Lost* in 1667 and Dostoevsky's *The Brothers Karamazov* in 1880 encompassed major historical and cultural shifts. Yet in some ways these years constitute a short leap, in that both Milton and Dostoevsky were obsessed by the connections between Christianity, politics, and freedom. Dostoevsky's political activities came earlier in life than Milton's, but they were no less dangerous. The details are well known to biographers.[2] In 1849, he was only twenty-eight years old when he and a group of utopian socialist friends who were producing an underground newspaper that would be considered tame by modern standards were arrested, jailed, and condemned to die by Czar Nicholas I. The czar would not have been impressed by Milton's defense of free speech in the *Areopagitica*. After eight months in prison, Dostoevsky and the other "conspirators" were taken to the public square, hooded, and prepared for execution. At the last minute, in a carefully orchestrated but sadistic drama, a courier from the czar brought a reprieve that commuted the sentence to four years of hard labor in Siberia.[3] The posttraumatic effects on Dostoevsky of this simulated execution are a matter of speculation, but the experience drove at least one of his comrades insane. When it came time thirty years later to write *The Brothers Karamazov*, the author mined this ground to create one of the brothers: Ivan Karamazov, a young utopian socialist. By this time Dostoevsky had rejected the radicalism of his youth and embraced his own version of Christianity, but just as Milton turned to his parliamentary experience for some of Satan's best arguments, Dostoevsky turned to his political past for some of Ivan's most powerful ideals.

In the process, Dostoevsky, like Herman Melville, who was born two years earlier and outlived him by a decade, came to focus on the "human moral distortion" of "the prevailing social order and its institutions."[4] Such "moral distortion," all too evident in the racist mentality that justified the institution of slavery on the *San Dominick*, would take a different form in the Grand Inquisitor's utopian vision. Generations of Dostoevsky's readers have debated the nature and significance of that vision, with some identifying the author with the nihilism of Ivan,[5] others confident of Dostoevsky's Christianity,[6] still others convinced that the author struggled throughout his life with doubts about the most profound spiritual questions.[7] Part of the problem is that the Grand Inquisitor's assault on freedom, an interpolation in *The Brothers Karamazov*, is several times removed from the author. It is presented as the direct expression not of Dostoevsky to you or me, nor of a narrator to a presumed reader, nor even of Ivan Karamazov to his brother. The Grand Inquisitor's tirade is presented as his own direct speech to Christ, as told by Ivan to Alyosha. Because of the layers in this narrative process, there is tremendous potential to conflate the views of the various "creators," a danger Dostoevsky himself was aware of and went to considerable lengths to defuse. In a letter to his publisher, N. A. Liubimov, he said " [in "The Grand Inquisitor"] it is not I who am speaking . . . but a character in my novel, Ivan Karamazov."[8] Although Dostoevsky has created Ivan, Ivan is the creator of the ninety-year-old cardinal of the sixteenth-century Spanish Inquisition, who arrests and interrogates Christ. Despite Dostoevsky's disclaimer, readers often disagree about whether the Grand Inquisitor speaks for Ivan, and whether either of them speaks for Dostoevsky.

No matter what position you take on these questions, there is no way to avoid the unsettling presence in "The Grand Inquisitor" of Dostoevsky's silent Christ. Whether or not this Christ is thought to refute the Grand Inquisitor's arguments against freedom, with either his silence or his kiss, those responses are central features of the legend. In "Benito Cereno," Melville merely glances at the power of silence. After the rebellion on the *San Dominick* is quelled and Babo is re-enslaved, he refuses to speak. We are told very little about his intransigence—only that "he uttered no sound," and somewhat menacingly, he "could not be forced to" (225). We can only speculate about his motives in going mute. Defiance? Despair? Diabolical resolve? Courage? One brief sentence is all the attention this gesture gets in Melville's narrative. Yet the fact that Babo remains silent even under torture creates a powerful image of a conscious, sustained, difficult decision not to speak, codetermined by the torture meant to break that resolve. Remaining silent means something different when it is sustained even under stressful conditions designed to end it. Melville's problematic narrator does not speculate about Babo's motives, but the phrase "could not be forced to" rattles in a reader's brain long after the book is closed.

The silence of Dostoevsky's Christ in the face of the Grand Inquisitor's relentless questioning occupies a much larger parcel of narrative real estate. Whether this silence seems to reveal love, acquiescence, or the apophatic unknowability of God, no reader of "The Grand Inquisitor" can afford to ignore it. In "The Grand Inquisitor" there is also silence beyond Christ's: the silence broken by both Ivan Karamazov and the Inquisitor when they decide at last to speak out; and Alyosha's silence, as he listens to his brother's "poem," a silence that Ivan succeeds in shattering. Where Melville only glances at the dialogic aspects of silence as a response to aggressive efforts to provoke speech, Dostoevsky dwells on these dialogic possibilities as he reexamines—some might say subverts—Milton's project "to justify the ways of God to man."

## CHILD ABUSE

Ivan prefaces the legend of the Grand Inquisitor with several anecdotes of child abuse, which he considers real-life evidence of why the moral freedom that Milton's God insists on in *Paradise Lost* is too great a burden for man to bear. This argument is, of course, blasphemy, but the fictitious Grand Inquisitor has devoted his life to undoing the damage done by God in creating man morally free. Ivan explores this premise with such relentlessness and passion that generations of readers have had trouble logically refuting the Grand Inquisitor's point: that human beings cannot handle moral freedom.[9] In "Rebellion," the chapter that precedes "The Grand Inquisitor," Ivan presents Alyosha with examples of child abuse, each of which, according to Dostoevsky, comes directly from current newspapers. Desperate to evade censorship, he had written to his publisher, "All the anecdotes about children took place, existed, were published in the press, and I can cite the places, I invented nothing."[10] The Grand Inquisitor is a fabrication, Dostoevsky explains, but the justification for the Grand Inquisitor's ideas lies in the real world.

Ivan's final example of child abuse involves an eight-year-old serf boy who "threw a stone in play" and hurt the paw of a dog that belonged to his master, the owner of a large estate, "a general of aristocratic connections." He is "one of those men . . . who, retiring from the service into a life of leisure, are convinced that they've earned the power of life and death over their subjects" (223). The general has the boy seized and shut up overnight, then brought before him the next morning, "a capital day for hunting":

> The general orders the child to be undressed; the child is stripped naked. He shivers, numb with terror, not daring to cry. . . . "Make him run," commands the general. "Run! Run!" shout the dog-boys. The boy runs. . . . "At him!" yells the general, and he sets the whole pack of hounds on the child. The hounds catch him, and tear him to pieces before his mother's eyes. (224)

Ivan watches intently his younger brother's reaction to this narrative, asking him afterwards what the general deserved for this crime against a child: "Well—what did he deserve? To be shot? To be shot for the satisfaction of our moral feelings? Speak, Alyoshka!" (224). When Alyosha murmurs, "To be shot," Ivan shouts, "Bravo!" He has succeeded in getting the priest in training to reject forgiveness in favor of vengeance.

Ivan's triumphant point is that all the fervent talk in Christianity about heaven, hell, God, and forgiveness is not worth the suffering of one innocent child. He proclaims, "I renounce the higher harmony altogether" (225).[11] He adds, "What do I care for a hell for oppressors?" According to him, there is no circle in Dante's *Inferno* where the general could adequately atone for this child's death, because there is no punishment that can bring the child back to life or undo his suffering. What's more, argues Ivan, Christian forgiveness is a joke: "I don't want the mother to embrace the oppressor who threw her son to the dogs! She dare not forgive him! Let her forgive him for herself, if she will. . . . But the sufferings of her tortured child she has no right to forgive" (226). Ivan makes two points here about moral freedom. The first is that as long as human beings are free to choose between good and evil, someone, somewhere, will choose to inflict pain on an innocent child. They can blame it on drugs, or rage, or mental illness, but if God did not leave humans morally free to choose to act one way or another, there would be no child abuse. According to Ivan, the moral freedom God insists on is too great a burden for man to bear. Ivan's second point about freedom is that the forgiveness Christ calls on us to extend to our enemies—which involves the choice to love in the face of the temptation to hate—is also too much to ask. We can forgive our own sufferings, but we have no right to forgive injuries to innocent children. Better to prevent them in the first place. According to this logic, both punishment and forgiveness are inadequate responses to those who harm the innocent. The only solution is to lift the burden of moral freedom that allows one to choose poorly. This conclusion is implicit in Ivan's stories of child abuse, which lay a foundation for the Grand Inquisitor's dramatic confrontation with Christ.

## FORCING CHRIST TO SPEAK

Ivan sets his legend of the Grand Inquisitor in the midst of the sixteenth-century Spanish Inquisition, where one day earlier the Inquisitor has burned nearly one hundred heretics at the stake. Into this scene walks Christ, who stops before the steps of the Seville cathedral, among mourners who carry the open coffin of a seven-year-old girl. Somehow the crowd instantly recognizes the Son of God: "'He will raise your child,' the crowd shouts to the weeping mother. The priest, coming to meet the coffin, looks perplexed, and frowns, but the mother of the child throws herself at His feet with a wail, 'If it is Thou, raise my child!'" Christ says, "Maiden, arise!" and the little girl "sits up in the coffin and looks round, smiling with wide-open wondering eyes, holding a bunch of white roses they had put in her hand" (230). At this moment the Grand Inquisitor passes by. He sees everything, and the upshot is that he arrests Christ and hauls him off to prison. That night he comes to him in his cell, promises to burn him at the stake the next day, and proceeds to harangue him about man's inability to handle moral freedom. Attacking God for insisting that man be free to choose between good and evil, the Grand Inquisitor asks Christ question after question, trying to force him to justify God's plan. It is a frustrating conversation for the Inquisitor, because Christ never says one word. Yet he listens intently.

The prisoner's silence is the silence of someone who could speak at any moment. The Grand Inquisitor grows more and more resourceful in his attempts to provoke Christ to speak, while Christ, without saying anything, coauthors the Grand Inquisitor's words by inspiring him to attempt one argument after another. It is only in retrospect that we as readers know that Christ will not speak. In the presentness of the encounter, and from the Grand Inquisitor's dramatic perspective, the possibility is always open that Christ will speak, if only the Inquisitor can find the right trigger. On one level the Inquisitor accepts his prisoner's silence, saying, "Thou mayest not add to what has been said of old, and mayest not take from men the freedom which Thou didst exalt when Thou wast on earth. Whatsoever Thou revealest anew will encroach on men's freedom of faith; for it will be manifest as a miracle" (232). The Grand Inquisitor knows that if Christ were to speak, this would be a miracle that would alter scripture and undermine the freedom of faith. Confronted with a miracle, one has no choice but to believe in the divinity of the being that performs the miracle. Hence a miracle is coercive. If Christ were to speak, that miracle would force the Grand Inquisitor to abandon the path he has chosen, thus undermining his freedom. This outcome would be worth it to the Grand Inquisitor, because although he would no longer be free to pursue his mission, he would have succeeded in forcing Christ to acknowledge that the burden of moral freedom, in this case the Grand Inquisitor's, should be lifted.

The Grand Inquisitor taunts Christ, "For fifteen centuries we have been wrestling with Thy freedom, but now it is ended and over for good. . . . Now, today, people are more persuaded than ever that they have perfect freedom, yet they have brought their freedom to us and laid it humbly at our feet" (234). According to the Inquisitor, people think of themselves as free—more free than ever before—even though he has destroyed the moral freedom God was at great pains to create. At the center of the Grand Inquisitor's argument is the idea that moral freedom is "insupportable" for man—that although people want to think of themselves as free, they do not really want to handle the responsibility of making moral choices: "Man prefers peace, and even death, to freedom of choice in the knowledge of good and evil" (235). Moral freedom is to be avoided at all costs precisely because it is "exceptional, vague and enigmatic . . . utterly beyond the strength of men." It is a source of incalculable suffering. According to this logic, if God had really loved man, he would not have insisted on imposing this burden. Claiming to love man more than God does, the Grand Inquisitor has a solution to the problem: a way of life managed by the Grand Inquisitor and his followers, who take on this burden for everyone else. He boasts to Christ, "We are ready to endure the freedom which they have found so dreadful" (234).[12]

In the Inquisitor's plan, "the ages will pass, and humanity will proclaim by the lips of their sages that there is no crime, and therefore no sin; there is only hunger." When every crime is explained as the result of hunger, poverty, or some other environmental factor, all sense of moral responsibility will be lifted from mankind, and with it the burden of moral freedom. People will raise a banner that says, "Feed men, and then ask of them virtue!" (233). This cryptic command postulates that only with a full stomach can a person indulge in the luxury of morality. Whoever can fill stomachs, provide jobs, and manipulate the promise of material wealth or the threat of hunger, will be able to inspire people to behave in a way we might call virtuous. If someone could end world hunger, for example, that would be seen as a miracle, and everyone would bow down before the miracle worker. Under these circumstances, the cooperative masses would no longer function as adults making choices, but rather as children huddling close, "as chicks to the hen," for "a childlike happiness is the sweetest of all" (239). The Grand Inquisitor's vision of happiness is of a perpetual childhood. There will be contentment for all but the Inquisitor and his enlightened army of enforcers, who reserve to themselves the burden of moral choice. This utopian vision, couched here in religious terms, Dostoevsky meant as code for "the future reign of socialism . . . the total enslavement of the freedom of conscience."[13] He explained to his publisher, "My socialist (Ivan Karamazov) is a sincere man, who admits openly that he agrees with the 'Grand Inquisitor's' view of humanity and that Christ's faith (seemingly) raised man much higher than he in fact is. The question is brought to a head: 'Do you despise humanity or respect it, you, its future saviors?'"[14]

At every stage of his monologue the Grand Inquisitor peppers Christ with questions, trying to provoke him, hoping his listener will interrupt and set him straight. Yet Christ remains steadfastly silent. At one point the Grand Inquisitor asks him, "Is the nature of men such, that they can reject miracle, and at the great moments of their life, the moments of their deepest, most agonizing spiritual difficulties, cling only to the free verdict of the heart?" (236). For the old man, this is a rhetorical question, whose clear answer is "No!" But Dostoevsky wants readers to ponder it. In fact, all of his novels depict characters caught in intense situations in which they must choose to do one thing or another, within a context of friends, lovers, family, and community. These are "great moments" of "agonizing spiritual difficulties," in which they suffer or inflict terrible wrongs, then must decide whether to forgive, to confess, to take revenge, or to flee. These are the moral decisions that are referred to here as "the free verdict of the heart." The Grand Inquisitor asks, as do all of Dostoevsky's novels, "Can man handle the burden of such a choice?"

In this encounter with Christ, the Grand Inquisitor himself is experiencing "agonizing spiritual difficulties," as he confronts the decision whether or not to execute his prisoner as promised. Through his relentless interrogation, he is also attempting to create "agonizing spiritual difficulties" for Christ, as he goads him to perform the miracle of intervention. In the end, the Grand Inquisitor fails to force Christ to speak, but he does get a response:

> He suddenly approached the old man in silence and softly kissed him on his bloodless aged lips. That was all his answer. The old man shuddered. His lips moved. He went to the door, opened it, and said to Him: "Go, and come no more. . . . come not at all, never, ever!" And he let him out into the dark squares of the town. (243)

The meaning of this kiss has been much debated. D. H. Lawrence called it the "kiss of acquiescence," Christ's recognition of his own inadequacy in the face of the Grand Inquisitor's logic.[15] Jacques Catteau asked instead, could the kiss signify "forgiveness? Absolution, because the Inquisitor's sin is motivated by an excess of love? . . . But it is certainly a refusal to judge, to condemn."[16] Whatever the kiss means, that meaning is codetermined by the Inquisitor, who has worked so strenuously to provoke a response from Christ, and by Christ, who now responds.

Clearly the kiss means something to the Inquisitor, because he shudders, and then instead of following through with the threat to execute Christ, he lets him go. According to the "kiss of aquiescence" theory, the Grand Inquisitor releases Christ because he concludes that Christ is no longer a threat. According to the "kiss of forgiveness" theory, the Inquisitor releases Christ because he has been touched by Christ's love, even after the old man has admitted, "We are not working with Thee, but with *him*—that is our mystery . . . We took from him what Thou didst reject with scorn, that last gift he offered Thee, showing Thee all the kingdoms of the earth" (238). The "kiss of forgiveness" theory suggests that Christ loves the Grand Inquisitor, even though the old man thinks that when Satan offered the three temptations in the wilderness, the last of which was the promise of unlimited political power, Christ should have taken him up on the offer. The Grand Inquisitor believes that he has rectified Christ's mistake by embracing political power. He proclaims the vision Dostoevsky calls socialist: "We shall triumph and shall be Caesars, and then we shall plan the universal happiness of man." Perhaps because of, perhaps in spite of, the Inquisitor's plan to create universal happiness by destroying freedom, Christ kisses him. In any event he leaves the Grand Inquisitor free to pursue his ideals.

Ivan explains the effect of the kiss on the Inquisitor: "The kiss glows in his heart, but the old man adheres to his idea" (243). The kiss seems to be a sign of love, since it "glows" in the old man's heart. The implication is that it will continue to burn there, reminding him of the strength of Christ's choice to love him and to leave him free. Yet it also seems to be a sign of acquiescence, precisely because it leaves the Grand Inquisitor free to adhere to his idea. Christ's kiss intensifies the Grand Inquisitor's state of "agonizing spiritual difficulty" by simultaneously illustrating the aspect of moral freedom that is the capacity for love, and recognizing the power of the Grand Inquisitor's commitment to his own ideas. The effect of the kiss is like the equal and opposite forces on a jet whose engine has been revved to high levels just before takeoff, while at the same time the brakes are locked in place. Intellectually the Grand Inquisitor remains committed to his logic, while spiritually and physically he experiences the forgiveness that is the noblest manifestation of the moral freedom he seeks to destroy.

Whatever its significance, Christ's kiss is the culmination of his enigmatic silence. According to Malcolm Jones, the silence of Christ in "The Grand Inquisitor" stems from an apophatic religious tradition that focuses on "the ultimate unknowability of Godhead" (53). This tradition is fundamentally unstable, in that the unknowable can be interpreted in contradictory ways, on a continuum that runs from atheism to the most orthodox Christianity. Jones views Christ's silence in this legend as infinitely rich, but also ambiguous, because it can be seen as "fullness or an absence" (71). He distinguishes between two types of silence: *molchanie* (absence or cessation of conversation), the silence of someone who might have spoken but has declined to; and *tishina* (tranquility or absence of sound), the silence of someone who is fully at peace and has no need to speak. Jones associates the first type of silence with Ivan, who has held back performing his "poem" until he pours it out to Alyosha, his first listener; and with the Grand Inquisitor whose "long obsessive guarding of a secret " is "broken in a torrent of words" to Christ (144). Jones associates the second type of silence with Christ and with Alyosha, both of whom exude "inner peace and tranquility" (144).

This distinction between silence as tranquil fullness and silence as agitated, withheld speech is especially interesting from a dialogical perspective. The silence of the spiritual leader so filled with peace that he or she feels no need to speak is very different from the silence of the sufferer who struggles to hold back an outburst. The first silence seems godlike in its transcendence, a monologic mystery. The second seems all too human to anyone who has ever tried not to respond to a provocation or tried not to blurt out a confession or a complaint. Yet both the silent, tranquil spiritual teacher and the silent, agitated guarder of secrets coauthor decisions with others. In the case of the Grand Inquisitor, it could be that Christ's quiet tranquility and his resurrection of a child agitate the old man so much that he must break his own silence. At the moment when he decides not just to defy God or to rebel against him as superaddressee but actually to arrest and interrogate Christ, the Inquisitor takes upon himself the challenge of destabilizing Christ's tranquil silence, transmuting *tishina* into *molchanie*. Of course he fails. Ivan's Christ responds to the Grand Inquisitor's attack only with more *tishina*, which the Inquisitor registers not as transcendence but as provocation. [17]

Christ's tranquility cannot be disturbed by the Grand Inquisitor, but not because it is static, or because Christ is deaf to the Grand Inquisitor's appeals. The kiss Christ gives him is evidence that the prisoner has been listening, and in response to the priest's tirade he has decided to act. In Bakhtinian terms, his kiss can be seen not only as dialogic—coauthored by the Grand Inquisitor's eagerness for a response—but also as empathetic. In the early philosophical texts discussed in chapter 1, Bakhtin describes empathy as the ability to "penetrate" the sufferer "and almost merge or become one with him from within."[18] In these texts Bakhtin discusses not literature or religion, but human beings like you and me. He is careful to add the word "almost," emphasizing that we must take care not to completely "merge" or "become one with" a sufferer. He warns against any attempt at "pure empathizing" or "experiencing another's suffering as one's own," which he calls "pathological." Losing oneself in another's suffering is for Bakhtin a kind of insanity. According to him, what empathy calls for is a return to ourselves so that we can actually help the sufferer instead of just duplicating his or her distress. If you or I disappear into the suffering of a friend, we damage ourselves and we fail to help.

As God, Christ does not need to worry about the pathological dangers of "pure empathizing" that Bakhtin warns about, because he is by definition immune to them. In his apophatic, unknowable silence, he can presumably experience the Grand Inquisitor's ways of knowing, without running any risk of being infected by them or losing himself in them (the Grand Inquisitor's goal). Where a human being might be won over by the Grand Inquisitor's arguments or driven to despair by his isolating pride, Christ as God is not vulnerable to those possibilities. He can afford to penetrate to the depths of the old man's vision and return whole, responding to the Grand Inquisitor from his own apophatic depths. Christ's kiss is ambiguous, but it may achieve best what Bakhtin describes as the goal of empathy: responding to a "cry of pain" with "an act of assistance."[19] If we consider the Grand Inquisitor's tirade not just as an assault on freedom but as a "cry of pain" in the midst of his "agonizing spiritual difficulties," we can regard Christ's kiss not only as a sign of forgiveness or acquiescence but also as "an act of assistance." As the Grand Inquisitor "adheres to his idea," in whatever is left of this ninety-year-old's future, his actions will be codetermined by the kiss that is the "act of assistance" he has coauthored.

With this moment of highly charged ambivalence, Ivan ends his fable. His younger brother responds by imitating Christ: "Alyosha got up, went to him and softly kissed him on the lips.[20] "'That's plagiarism,' cried Ivan, highly delighted. 'You stole that from my poem. Thank you though'" (244). Just as Christ insists on loving the Grand Inquisitor despite his defiance, Alyosha insists on loving his brother despite his blasphemy. Alyosha's love is human, rather than divine, and his empathy too is human. He illustrates

Bakhtin's dictum: "I empathize actively into an individuality and, consequently, I do not lose myself completely, nor my unique place outside it, even for a moment."[21] Alyosha does not embrace Ivan's ideas; he does not lose himself in the epistemological layers of his brother's perspective. In response, Ivan says to Alyosha, "It's enough for me that you are somewhere here, and I shan't lose my desire for life yet. . . . When at thirty, I want to 'dash the cup to the ground,' wherever I may be I'll come to have one more talk with you, even though it were from America" (244). Ivan expects to pay a high price for his ideas, which cut him off from his family, his spiritual roots, even his homeland, and have led to the isolation of despair. Yet he promises to return for one more conversation with Alyosha, one more attempt to make himself comprehensible to his brother, one more effort to be accepted or rejected, condemned or forgiven, hated or loved. Ivan's promise to return is itself a sign that although his ideas undermine the possibility of love, his actions, coauthored by the memory of Alyosha's kiss, will keep that possibility alive.

## READING "THE GRAND INQUISITOR" FOR AND WITH DIALOGIC FREEDOM

The encounter between the Grand Inquisitor and Christ is dialogic not just for them but for the brothers Alyosha and Ivan, because at the same time that the Grand Inquisitor is attempting to provoke Christ, Ivan is attempting to provoke Alyosha. In both cases, the listener codetermines what the speaker says and does, merely by listening with rapt attention. The drama of the situation is intense, in that at any moment Ivan might convince Alyosha not to enter the monastery, and at any moment the Grand Inquisitor might convince Christ to speak. Thus both situations feel open-ended for the participants, as speakers and listeners codetermine words spoken and actions taken. Until the actions are taken, this outcome is uncertain. In the face of this uncertainty, two competing theories of human behavior are in tension with each other. One theory, shared by Ivan and the Grand Inquisitor, holds that moral freedom is an impossible burden for mankind. The other, shared by Alyosha and Christ, holds that moral freedom is not only possible but essential.[22] Both theories attempt to impose a unified vision on an open-ended reality where anything might happen. Both theories, by presenting a unifying, coherent explanation for human behavior, make it easier for their adherents to take action.

These unifying theories are also mutually exclusive. One is intellectual, the other spiritual. As long as a person embraces one or the other, that theory can serve a centripetal, unifying function in authorizing action. It can serve as a superaddressee, to whom the speaker is answerable above all else. But if a person attempts to embrace both theories at once, the situation becomes paralyzing. When Ivan seeks to impose his intellectual perspective upon Alyosha, and the Grand Inquisitor seeks to impose that same perspective upon Christ, they both fail, which is the significance of the kiss from a Christian perspective. It stands for the choice to love and in doing so, to affirm the necessity for moral freedom. Yet, failing to impose their intellectual vision on a listener does not require either Ivan or the Grand Inquisitor to abandon that vision. Both adhere to their ideas, their unifying theories about the necessity to eliminate moral freedom. At the same time, however, for each of them, "the kiss glows in his heart." The consequence of their attempts to impose their theories has been to elicit a response that challenges these theories, not intellectually and logically, but physically and spiritually. Thus, the kiss is a response coauthored by their attempts at persuasion, a response that challenges the intellectual framework of Ivan and the Grand Inquisitor with a competing spiritual framework that entails its own unifying explanation of the chaotic reality of human life. That the kiss will continue to glow in their hearts indicates that even as they recommit themselves to their assault on freedom, Ivan and the Grand Inquisitor will carry within them the spiritual counterargument that threatens that commitment. They will be in an impossible situation, answering to two mutually exclusive superaddressees, living with the tension of the jet plane under full throttle and fully braked. This tension will be open-ended, unfinalized, its consequences unforeseeable.[23]

Few people would be able to endure such pressure without imploding, which is why Ivan and the Grand Inquisitor are characters in a novel rather than our next-door neighbors, and why it is more fun to read about them than to be them. These characters represent the extreme possibility of registering contradictory orientations on life. If the experience does not destroy you, it will strengthen you, expanding your ability to navigate alien ways of knowing. If freedom is in part a function of our ability to know the world from a variety of perspectives, the intense confrontations between the Grand Inquisitor and Christ, and between Ivan and Alyosha, stretch to the limits these characters' abilities to be free. In the process, their confrontations enhance readers' abilities to experience conflicting perspectives without that experience becoming a matter of life and death. Hence, a reader's dialogic freedom develops through the intellectually strenuous process of penetrating the arguments of the Grand Inquisitor, the spiritually challenging process of interpreting Christ's kiss, and the integrative effort that goes into processing these mutually exclusive orientations.

"The Grand Inquisitor" invites readers to consider seriously the arguments of a self-proclaimed enemy of freedom and Christianity, rather than just to reject them without thinking them through. Just as Dante presents the attractions of sin in the *Inferno*, and Milton gives the devil his due in *Para-*

*dise Lost,* Dostoevsky articulates the Grand Inquisitor's arguments against freedom in their most potent form. The author's letters reveal that he feared he had succeeded all too well in this enterprise. The book was being published in serialized form in the *Russian Herald,* chapter by chapter, with early chapters published before later chapters were even written. Under these circumstances, Dostoevsky intended to follow Book Five, which included "The Grand Inquisitor," with Book Six, which would focus on "something completely opposite to the world view expressed earlier,"[24] the perspective of the Russian monk, Father Zosima. Dostoevsky wrote to his publisher, "I consider this *sixth* book as the culminating point of the novel."[25] Two weeks later he wrote to a friend that the section about Father Zosima was intended to be "the answer to the whole *negative side.* And for that reason I tremble for it in this sense: will it be answer enough?"[26] This question had worried Dostoevsky for three months, ever since he had explained to his publisher, "My hero's blasphemy will be triumphantly refuted in the next (June) issue, on which I am now working with fear, trembling, and veneration, since I consider my task (the destruction of anarchism) a civic deed."[27] When Dostoevsky refers to his task as a "civic deed," we see the seriousness of this enterprise for him, three months before he was to worry that the answer he provided to the Grand Inquisitor's arguments might not be answer enough.

Generations of readers of *The Brothers Karamazov* have debated whether the novel as a whole and the figure of Father Zosima in particular adequately refute the logic of the Grand Inquisitor. My point is not to resolve this question, but to observe that with the Grand Inquisitor Dostoevsky enters the ranks of Dante and Milton, to show enough faith in his readers to present them with the most compelling possible arguments for a perspective that he considers dangerous. Dostoevsky had written to his publisher that the "future reign of socialism" would replace "the law of Freedom and Enlightenment" with "the law of chains and enslavement by bread."[28] But instead of making his case in a political tract, he created a fable that would force not just the characters in the novel, but the readers of the novel, to work through every nuance of the argument against moral freedom—and to witness the passion of its perspective—as preparation for finding it inadequate. In doing so Dostoevsky took a great risk—the same risk taken by Dante and Milton—that readers would embrace rather than reject an attractive but flawed way of thinking. That risk was the price to pay for amplifying his readers' abilities to see things from this dangerous perspective, in the hope that their own perspectives would become richer, deeper, more resilient.

Dostoevsky models this risk in the reaction of Alyosha to Ivan's presentation. Ivan's nihilistic intellectual framework centers on the idea that since moral freedom is impossible for most people to handle, they cannot be held responsible for their actions, and "all is lawful." His creation, the Grand Inquisitor, shows how well Ivan has been able to unify his thinking according to this perspective and to justify tyranny in the face of human weakness. In presenting Alyosha with stories of child abuse before he tells him the legend of the Grand Inquisitor, Ivan's unified intellectual framework comes up against his brother's equally unified Christian orientation, which insists that all people are capable of handling moral freedom. Confronted with Ivan's relentless logic and the question "What did the general deserve? To be shot?" Alyosha acknowledges his own inability to live up to the Christian call to "love thine enemy." He murmurs, "To be shot," thus illustrating that at least for this moment he finds Ivan's logic persuasive. In the case of the general, Alyosha chooses execution over forgiveness. Yet confronted later with Christ's kiss of the Grand Inquisitor, Alyosha "plagiarizes" it, as if to say to his brother, "I can't logically refute your ideas, but I can still choose to love you." Thus the spiritual perspective Alyosha represents can respond to the intellectual perspective that attacks it; it just cannot respond intellectually. Both brothers seek to unify the chaotic material of reality, one intellectually, the other spiritually, and both experience the tensions that arise when they find themselves unable finally to jettison one of these mutually exclusive perspectives in favor of the other.

That the legend of the Grand Inquisitor is meant to provoke Alyosha can be seen from the younger brother's interruptions of Ivan's presentation. After the Grand Inquisitor brags to Christ that the very people who today cheered him for raising the little girl from the dead will tomorrow "rush to heap up the embers of Thy fire" at the stake, Alyosha interrupts: "I don't understand, Ivan. What does it mean? . . . Is it simply a wild fantasy, or a mistake on the part of the old man?" (231). Later, Alyosha asks about Christ, "Does He look at him and not say a word?" and of the Grand Inquisitor, "Is he jesting?" (232). Toward the end of the narrative, Alyosha "seemed several times on the point of interrupting, but restrained himself. Now his words came with a rush. 'But . . . that's absurd!' he cried, flushing. 'Your poem is in praise of Jesus, not in blame of Him—as you meant it to be. And who will believe you about freedom? . . . Your suffering inquisitor is a mere fantasy'" (241–42). In advance, Ivan had foreseen and disarmed this criticism, by calling "The Grand Inquisitor" "a ridiculous thing" and "a poem in prose. . . . I was carried away when I composed it." What is important is that Alyosha will be Ivan's first listener, and though the Grand Inquisitor will fail to force Christ to interrupt him, Ivan will succeed in provoking that response from his little brother. Ivan asks Alyosha, "'Why should an author forego even one listener?'" (227). As he tells the story, his brother's interruptions testify to his high level of engagement as a listener and to the effectiveness of Ivan's presentation, even as these interruptions help shape what Ivan presents. That Alyosha decides in one direction in the case of the general and in another in the case of his own brother, shows that he is as conflicted as Ivan is about which perspective should prevail. If Christ's silence is the silence of *tishina* (calm, transcendent, spiritual fullness), Alyosha's silence is both *tishina* and *molchanie* (suppressed struggle bursting forth). He is Zosima's protégé but also Ivan's brother.

## MORAL FREEDOM, POLITICAL FREEDOM, AND DIALOGIC FREEDOM

In "The Grand Inquisitor" Dostoevsky explores freedom on a number of levels. On the level of the moral freedom—the choice between good and evil—not merely advocated but insisted upon by Milton's God in *Paradise Lost*, Ivan and the Grand Inquisitor both argue that this freedom should never have been imposed upon man by God. By contrast, Alyosha and Christ illustrate a spiritual commitment to this moral freedom as the choice to love and forgive. On the level of political freedom, Ivan's and the Grand Inquisitor's rejection of moral freedom lead them to reject also the "negative liberty" of John Stuart Mill, in that they do not consider man capable of avoiding harming others when he is left to do as he pleases. Ivan and the Grand Inquisitor embrace instead "positive liberty," the freedom to be enlightened, but they embrace it only for themselves and for the elite followers who can understand and implement the Grand Inquisitor's vision.

In addition to these explorations of moral and political freedom, Dostoevsky explores dialogic freedom as a two-sided act that involves deliberation from multiple perspectives, within a field of forces for unity and chaos. Perhaps more clearly than any other novelist, Dostoevsky presents the two-sidedness of freedom as Alyosha and Ivan coauthor each other's words and choices by advocating, listening, interrupting, and acting in response to each other, even though their perspectives could not be more different. Without Alyosha as Ivan's audience and interrupter, the legend of the Grand Inquisitor would not be the same story. Ivan chooses the direction the story will take, but always in response to his listening brother. The two-sidedness of Ivan and Alyosha is mirrored by the two-sidedness of Christ and the Grand Inquisitor, who also coauthor each other's words (or lack thereof) and choices by advocating, listening, and acting. That Christ is silent makes him no less active in coauthoring the Grand Inquisitor's words, which are always a response to him, and the kiss that Christ gives him is his direct response to the Grand Inquisitor's tirade.

In addition to exploring this two-sidedness, Dostoevsky explores how dialogic freedom involves the ability to see from an alien perspective. The two perspectives at war with each other in this novel, one intellectual and one spiritual, both seek to unify and make sense of a world full of chaotic complexity. Dostoevsky presents them as competing, mutually exclusive visions, but also as theories in tension with each other when experienced by one person. When the kiss glows in the heart of either Ivan or the Grand Inquisitor, yet they adhere to their ideas, we see them struggling to contain contradictory perspectives on the world, to answer to incompatible superaddressees. When Alyosha says the general should be shot, yet kisses his blaspheming brother, we see him, too, struggling to contain contradictory perspectives on forgiveness. Only Christ sees from a single, unifying perspective, but even he appears to understand completely what the Grand Inquisitor is saying. Most importantly, readers of this novel are invited to experience, ponder, and debate the merits of these competing perspectives, just as Milton's readers debate the heroism of Satan and Dante's readers debate the attractions of Paolo and Francesca. To the extent that we can resist demonizing the enemy and we can attempt to register an alien perspective, penetrate it, absorb it, risk embracing it, then argue against it, we will be the citizens Dante, Milton, and Dostoevsky were reaching out to and in some sense hoping to create.

At the center of the idea of dialogic freedom is the observation that when we coauthor decisions we coauthor meaning in an open-ended world. Our ability to do this is a function of being able to enter conversations and make choices among others, to empathize with others without being lost in "pure empathy," which is "pathological." Sometimes that process is easy—with friends, family, or colleagues. Other times it is more difficult—with strangers, opponents, or enemies. The more difficult the circumstances, the more there is at stake, the more important it is that we hear and be heard, rather than merely imposing our wills by force, or falling victim to manipulation or domination. To attempt to achieve a lasting resolution to some great problem, my opponent must allow me to be heard, but my ability to speak and act effectively will also depend on my ability to listen, to penetrate the depths of an alien perspective that codetermines my response to it, and to codetermine by the nature of my listening what is said and done by others. In "The Grand Inquisitor" Dostoevsky presents no final resolution to the problem of choosing between good and evil, but he helps us explore the complexities, the risks, and the benefits of struggling to see from alien, hostile, even mutually exclusive perspectives on that problem. In the process his fable presents a reading experience that expands our capacity for dialogic freedom.

## NOTES

1. Recent scholars (Malcolm Jones, Susan Amert, and Caryl Emerson, among others) prefer the spelling Alesha to Alyosha. I follow the spelling in Richard Pevear and Larissa Volokhonsky's translation of *The Brothers Karamazov* (Alyosha), which is also used in the Constance Garnett translation revised by Ralph Matlaw. Citations to *The Brothers Karamazov* are to Fyodor Dostoevsky, *The Brothers Karamazov*, trans. Ralph Matlaw (New York: Norton, 1976), with the abbreviation "BK Norton" for letters of Dostoevsky and literary criticism quoted from this edition.

2. Konstantin Mochulsky, *Dostoevsky: His Life and Work* (Princeton, NJ: Princeton University Press, 1967), 140–54; and Joseph Frank, *Dostoevsky: The Years of Ordeal, 1850–1859* (Princeton, NJ: Princeton University Press, 1990), 6–66.

3. Ralph Matlaw, "Introduction," in Fyodor Dostoevsky, *Notes from Underground. The Grand Inquisitor*, trans. Ralph Matlaw (New York: Dutton, 1960), vii–viii. Frank clarifies, "Dostoevsky, initially condemned to eight years of hard labor, enjoyed a reduction of his period of penal servitude to four years" (*Years of Ordeal*, 50).

4. F. D. Reeve, *The White Monk: An Essay on Dostoevsky and Melville* (Nashville, TN: Vanderbilt University Press, 1989), 14.

5. The Norton critical edition of the novel edited by Matlaw in 1976 includes remarks by D. H. Lawrence in which he famously concludes, "We cannot doubt that the Inquisitor speaks Dostoevsky's own final opinion about Jesus . . . You are inadequate" (BK Norton, 830). W. J. Leatherbarrow agrees that in *The Brothers Karamazov* Christ's kiss "inadequately counters the force of the Inquisitor's arguments." Leatherbarrow argues that "the figure of the Son of God, by virtue of the kiss he plants on the Inquisitor's 'bloodless aged lips,' is intended implicitly to condone the latter's rejection of divine justice in favor of man's." *A Devil's Vaudeville: The Demonaic in Dostoevsky's Major Fiction* (Evanston, IL: Northwestern University Press, 2005), 72, 153. Victor Terras disagrees. He argues that "The Grand Inquisitor" is "an intricate web in which the unwary are caught too easily." According to him, "Sophisticated readers have mistaken for his own ideas what Dostoevsky was in fact trying to refute." *Reading Dostoevsky* (Madison: University of Wisconsin Press, 1998), 121, 6.

6. Malcolm Jones discusses "the resurgent Orthodoxy that regards Dostoevsky as a great Christian prophet." *Dostoevsky and the Dynamics of Religious Experience* (London: Anthem Press, 2005), x. Indeed, the final volume of Joseph Frank's biography has the subtitle *The Mantle of the Prophet. Dostoevsky: The Mantle of the Prophet, 1871–1881* (Princeton, NJ: Princeton University Press, 2002). René Welleck expresses the view of many who regard Dostoevsky's novels to be the work of a devout Christian: "No doubt could be left that he had become the spokesman of conservative religious and political forces." *Dostoevsky: A Collection of Critical Essays*, ed. René Welleck (Englewood Cliffs, NJ: Prentice Hall, 1962), 2. This tradition goes back at least as far as Nicholas Berdyaev, in 1923, who wrote that "The Grand Inquisitor" was "an extremely powerful vindication of Christ." *Dostoevsky*, trans. Donald Attwater (Cleveland, OH: Meridian Books, 1965), 188.

7. One of Dostoevsky's earliest commentators, Vasily Rozanov, describes the legend of the Grand Inquisitor as an expression of "a most ardent thirst for religion with a total incapacity for it." *Dostoevsky and the Legend of the Grand Inquisitor*, 1891, trans. Spencer E. Roberts (reprint Ithaca, NY: Cornell University Press, 1972), 190. According to his translator, Spencer E. Roberts, "Rozanov sees Dostoevsky as a man who is without faith but longs for it deeply" (x). According to Malcolm Jones, "Dostoevsky's novels are so constructed that they do not privilege one point of view over another" (*Dynamics of Religious Experience*, 22), as they explore the rebellions of "the mutinous crew" (104) and the "ultimate unknowability of Godhead" (53). Robert Louis Jackson explains, "Dostoevsky's heroes are endlessly trying to resolve the unresolvable." *Dialogue with Dostoevsky: The Overwhelming Question* (Stanford, CA: Stanford University Press, 1993), 280.

8. Frank, *Mantle of the Prophet*, 431–32.

9. Two of the best summaries of the Grand Inquisitor's arguments against freedom are to be found in Martin Beck Matusik's *Radical Evil and the Scarcity of Hope* (Bloomington: Indiana University Press, 2008), 257–58; and Malcolm Jones's *Dynamics of Religious Experience*, 119–20.

10. Fyodor Dostoevsky, Letter No. 660, "To N. A. Lyubimov. Staraya Russa, May 10, 1879," BK Norton, 757–58.

11. There is considerable debate about Ivan's renunciation of God in this statement. Is he an atheist, not believing in God, as he himself proclaims more than once in this novel? Or does he accept the existence of God, heaven, and hell, but reject the moral system that God has created? Joseph Scanlan, like many readers, considers Ivan an atheist. According to him, Dostoevsky was offering his critique of "the Western cult of the person" which "transformed the individual will from being a morally suspect phenomenon to being a prime value, held up as the ideal of

human development. The curse of the West was that it not only misunderstood good and evil but created a culture that systematically produced evil people." *Dostoevsky the Thinker* (Ithaca, NY: Cornell University Press, 2002), 42, 242. For a dissenting view, see Matustik, who argues, "The Grand Inquisitor's defiance reveals that neither he nor Ivan could be called ordinary atheists, as they freely decide to give back the entry ticket to God's world, recognizing but rejecting the world's Creator, thereby relating to God personally yet without faith." Matustik, *Radical Evil*, 259.

12. In Dostoevsky's *Notebooks for The Brothers Karamazov* is the entry, "Inquisitor: I LOVE HUMANITY MORE THAN YOU DO." *Notebooks for The Brothers Karamazov*, ed. and trans. Edward Wasiolek (Chicago: University of Chicago Press, 1971), 75.

13. Letter No. 664. "To N. A. Lyubimov. Staraya Russa, June 11, 1879," BK Norton, 759.

14. Letter No. 664. "To N. A. Lyubimov. Staraya Russa, June 11, 1879," BK Norton, 759.

15. See note 5 above.

16. Jacques Catteau, "The Paradox of the Legend of the Grand Inquisitor in *The Brothers Karamazov*," in *Dostoevsky: New Perspectives*, ed. Robert Louis Jackson (Englewood Cliffs, NJ: Prentice-Hall, 1984), 252.

17. Those who conflate Ivan's views with the Inquisitor's fail to take into account that in this legend Ivan creates not just the Grand Inquisitor but also Christ. He creates not only the figure of defiance but also the figure of silent response to this defiance that so unsettles the Inquisitor.

18. See chapter 1.

19. Mikhail Bakhtin, "Author and Hero in Aesthetic Activity," in *Art and Answerability: Early Philosophical Essays by M. M. Bakhtin*, ed. Michael Holquist and Vadim Liapunov; trans. Vadim Liapunov (Austin: University of Texas Press, 1990), 26.

20. Robin Feuer Miller argues that Alyosha's kiss, in imitation of Christ's kiss in Ivan's "poem," testifies to "the most fundamental power of literature (the word); it offers up an artistic model that can inspire one in life." *The Brothers Karamazov: Worlds of the Novel* (New York: Twayne, 1992), 70.

21. Mikhail Bakhtin, *Toward a Philosophy of the Act*, ed. Vadim Liapunov and Michael Holquist; trans. Vadim Liapunov (Austin: University of Texas, 1993), 15.

22. Scanlan describes Dostoevsky's image of man as "a free moral creature with two con-flicting 'natures'—a materialistic, selfish nature . . . and a spiritual, altruistic nature cognizant of the moral demand to obey the law of love" (*Thinker*, 232).

23. Robin Feuer Miller points out that it is Ivan, not the narrator, "who describes how the kiss glowed in the old atheist's heart" (*Worlds*, 70). She argues that in "The Grand Inquisitor," Ivan may be "in the midst of a genuine conversion" (*Worlds*, 54).

24. Letter No. 694. "To K. P. Pobedonostsev. Ems, August 24, 1879," BK Norton, 762.

25. Letter No. 685, "To N. A. Lyubimov. Ems, Germany, August 7, 1879," BK Norton, 760.

26. Letter No. 694. "To K. P. Pobedonostsev. Ems, August 24, 1879," BK Norton, 761.

27. Letter No. 660, "To N. A. Lyubimov. Staraya Russa, May 10, 1879," BK Norton, 758.

28. Letter No. 664, "To N. A. Lyubimov, Staraya Russa, June 11, 1879," BK Norton, 759.

# Chapter Eight

# Goading the Reader of "In the Penal Colony"

Dialogic freedom: a two-sided act, chosen within a field of unifying and fragmenting forces along *a continuum* of minimal to maximal layers of knowing that are never final.

If we imagine dialogic freedom on a continuum between zero and ten, with zero representing the choices of a prisoner chained and gagged, and ten representing the options of one who perfectly negotiates multiple perspectives, balancing the need for unified explanation with the chaos of reality, Franz Kafka's "In der Strafkolonie" ("In the Penal Colony") explores the end of the scale closest to zero. At the same time, it challenges readers to embrace an experience of dialogic freedom that eludes every character in the story. This tale of an execution gone amok dramatizes how people function within a perverse reality. In the process, it shows that even as the dialogic freedom of various characters breaks down, a reader witnessing that process is inspired to desire, embrace, and enact that missing freedom. Two years after the publication of this story, Kafka wrote to his friend Oskar Baum, "It's as though the reader were crouching forgotten in the corner of the room where he can participate all the more intensely in what is happening there."[1] "In the Penal Colony" demands that a reader "crouching forgotten in the corner" feel the greatest possible pressure to "participate all the more intensely in what is happening." While different readers can be expected to bring a variety of values, experiences, and perspectives to reading this tale, and to react in different ways to the events it unfolds, they share the experience of being pressured by the presentation of these events to want to intervene in a monstrous process that seems to be accepted all too calmly by its perpetrators, victims, and observers, including Kafka's curiously aloof narrator.

147

"In the Penal Colony" is a strange tale, although it seems less strange, post–Guantanamo Bay[2] and Abu Ghraib.[3] It presents the adventure of a man "sent out to study criminal procedure in all the countries of the world."[4] He visits a penal colony on an island in the South Pacific, where an unnamed officer attempts to perpetuate with reverence a torture and execution program put in place by the old Commandant who has recently died, and challenged by the new Commandant who has replaced him. The traveler[5] has been invited to witness an execution to be carried out over a twelve-hour period, during which an elaborate machine with three parts—the Bed, the Harrow, and the Designer—will use glass needles to penetrate deeper and deeper into the condemned man's body to inscribe upon it in ornate, unreadable script, both his crime and his punishment. In charge of the execution will be the officer, the last and most passionate follower of the old Commandant, who invented the machine and used it for hundreds of executions. In years gone by, appreciative throngs had vied with each other for good seats, saving the best up front for their children. Now the new Commandant is making it difficult to get spare parts for the machine, though not yet banning the procedure. The officer sees this execution as an opportunity to enlist the visitor's support to save from extinction the tradition he venerates. When his listener ultimately refuses, the officer lies down in the apparatus, with gruesome consequences.

This tale is considered by many to be Kafka's most important short story,[6] not just for its arresting narrative, but for its elements of allegory, parable, and fable. Perhaps because of these elements, there is no consensus about how the tale should be read. In fact, there has been a "pandemonium of critical interpretation,"[7] including, but not limited to, readings of it as a meditation on the crucifixion; a prophecy of the advent of Nazism; an indictment of Western culture's Enlightenment skepticism; an anti-colonial or anti-technological exposé; reflections on good and evil, innocence and guilt, or tradition and change; a sexual fantasy; a critique of the death penalty and state-sponsored terror; or an examination of the processes involved in reading or writing.[8] My aim is not to evaluate these diverse approaches but rather to explore the dialogic relationships that Kafka's narrator draws our attention to, and in some cases withholds, as readers witness a series of events that call for intervention before it is too late.

## THE FANATIC

One of the most striking things about this story is the insanity of the officer's perspective, which it opens with in the officer's own words: "It's a remarkable piece of apparatus" (140). With a fanatic's zeal, he shares his devotion to the execution machine and to the creator he describes, whose "organization of the colony was so perfect that his successor . . . would find it impossible to alter anything, at least for many years to come" (141). This devotion is all the more creepy, because it elicits a strange indifference from both the traveler and the narrator, who seem to lack an emotional response appropriate to the horror of the officer's delusions. The promised execution, without indictment or trial, is to be perverse, involving, among other things, "a little gag of felt," which, the officer explains, will be forced into the condemned man's mouth, "for otherwise his neck would be broken by the strap" (143). But the traveler seems curiously unaware that he is about to witness cruel and unusual punishment. He is attending the execution "merely out of politeness," and he walks "up and down behind the prisoner with almost visible indifference," while the colony as a whole does not "betray much interest in the proceeding" (140). Meanwhile, the officer's enthusiasm compensates for this apathy. He scampers "with great zeal" up and down the machine, inspecting it, making last-minute adjustments (140). He boasts to the traveler, whose attention keeps wandering, "Up till now a few things still had to be set by hand, but from this moment it works all by itself" (141).

Kafka's narrator does not do much to help readers get their bearings as witnesses to this bizarre encounter, in which the officer and his visitor often "speak or even think past one another."[9] We learn a few facts: the prisoner has been condemned for falling asleep on guard duty and thus failing to salute his captain's door every hour on the hour. Caught in the act and punished, the man grabbed his captain's whip, about to be used on him, and said, "Throw that whip away or I'll eat you alive" (146). There have been no formal charges, no trial, just the captain's complaint to the officer an hour earlier, and now the man is condemned to have "HONOR THY SUPERIORS!" inscribed upon his body by needles that penetrate deeper and deeper until a moment arrives when, according to the officer, "Enlightenment comes to the most dull-witted" (150). Confronted with the horror and absurdity of this situation the narrator can only observe that the condemned man "was a stupid-looking, wide-mouthed creature with bewildered hair and face." He "looked so like a submissive dog that one might have thought he could be left to run free on the surrounding hills and would only need to be whistled for when the execution was to begin" (140). The prisoner is described here as a "creature" and compared to a dog that is incapable of understanding the situation, yet eager to please. There is dark comedy in this description from a narrator willing to trivialize a situation in which a human being is about to die. The dog image suits well the threat, "I'll eat you alive."

The officer never doubts the validity of his perspective. He does not question his devotion to the old Commandant, the apparatus or its role in the life of the colony. He says proudly, "My guiding principle is this: Guilt is never to be doubted" (145). Eager to be understood, he explains to his visitor the details of the machine's operation: "You see," said the officer, "there are two kinds of needles arranged in multiple patterns. Each long needle has a short one beside it. The long needle does the writing, and the short needle sprays a jet of water to wash away the blood and keep the inscription clear" (147). The officer wants what seems obvious to him to be clear to others. It is important to him that the inscription on the victim's body be readable, so that this guilt can be understood by all. The officer asks his listener, "Is that quite clear?" (146) or "Can you follow it?" (149). He is desperate for his guest to appreciate the truth and beauty of the old Commandant's vision, because at this moment there are "no longer any open adherents in our colony. I am its sole advocate" (153). His goal is to protect and pass on his reverence for the "enlightenment" he sees in the machine's victims in the sixth hour of their ordeal. He explains, "It begins around the eyes. From there it radiates" (150). In this encounter between the officer and his reluctant listener, the officer's objective is to inspire his guest to share his veneration for the Old Commandant's vision, so that it can be saved from extinction.

## THE NEUTRAL OBSERVER

Try as he may, the officer's listener can understand neither the ornate script the machine is designed to produce, nor the system of justice it enacts. Always giving readers a little less information than they need, Kakfa's narrator explains, "The explorer[10] considered the Harrow with a frown. The explanation of the judicial procedure had not satisfied him. He had to remind himself that this was in any case a penal colony where extraordinary measures were needed and that military discipline must be enforced to the last" (146). Here, the traveler strains to maintain his neutrality ("He had to remind himself"). He is calm and reasonable, a prime specimen of European Enlightenment skepticism,[11] but also ambivalent, as he argues with himself. He weighs the shortcomings of a judicial system lacking in due process against the special challenges of a penal colony in the middle of nowhere, much as today we debate the relative merits of the Geneva Conventions and the need for torture. The traveler thinks of the officer's mind as "narrow," but he also admires the man's devotion to duty, and his own ambivalence paralyzes him.

> The explorer[12] thought to himself: It's always a ticklish matter to intervene decisively in other people's affairs. He was neither a member of the penal colony nor a citizen of the state to which it belonged. Were he to denounce this execution or actually to try to stop it, they could say to him: You are a foreigner, mind your own business. . . . He traveled only as an observer, with no intention at all of altering other people's methods of administering justice. Yet here he found himself strongly tempted. (151)

This description of the traveler's qualms about sticking his nose in other people's business lacks affect, as if the "ticklish matter" were whether a host should invite embarrassing guests to a dinner party, rather than whether a man should be tortured and executed. Yet the grounds for the traveler's uneasiness—that he is not a member of the colony or the state that runs it— are just the concerns many people would ponder in a decision whether or not to butt into someone else's business. The rationality of his analysis is exemplary. Even so, as readers witness the traveler failing to stop a process that amounts to torture and murder, his combination of reasonableness and triviality in the face of horror builds in them an intense desire to do something. The traveler's excuse for inaction is that he is an observer, visiting the penal colony only briefly, to study, not to alter, their mode of administering justice. The very banality of this argument, and the fact that he is nevertheless "strongly tempted" to intervene, yet does nothing, makes readers want to leave the hypothetical corner where Kafka imagines them "crouching forgotten" and crash right into the text to "participate all the more intensely in what is happening there."

Meanwhile, committed as he is to his fanatic zeal, the officer is not incapable of imagining his listener's European perspective.[13] He tells him, "You might [say] something like this . . . 'In our country the prisoner is interrogated before he is sentenced,' or 'We haven't used torture since the Middle Ages'" (155–56). The officer is not unaware that an outsider would find the penal colony's execution process at least perplexing, if not repugnant. Still, he is confident that in the course of actually witnessing an execution the traveler will be won over to the campaign to prevent the new Commandant from abandoning tradition. But the traveler is not won over. At first he hangs on to his neutrality, crying out, "It's quite impossible. I can neither help nor hinder you" (157). By taking this stand, he tries to impose order on bizarre events he cannot control, but the officer keeps pressing him for support. The narrator describes the traveler's moment of crisis: "He was fundamentally honorable and unafraid. And yet now, facing the soldier and the condemned man, he did hesitate. . . . At last, however, he said, as he had to, "No" (159). The traveler, "fundamentally honorable," delivers to the officer his verdict, "I do not approve of your procedure." In fact, he has been pondering "whether it would be my duty to intervene and whether my intervention would have the slightest chance of success." He makes no effort to actually stop the execution-in-process, softening the blow of his disapproval by adding, "Your sincere conviction has touched me." He warns, though, that tomorrow he will have to "tell the Commandant what I think of the procedure, certainly, but not at a public conference, only in private" (160).

During the officer's plea, the initial stages of the execution have been proceeding, with the stripped prisoner lying in the apparatus beneath needles that are lightly grazing his body. Seeing the collapse of his last great hope, which was to enlist this traveler as an ally, the officer concludes, "Then the time has come" (160). He frees the clueless prisoner and resets the Designer to inscribe a new message: "BE JUST!" He undresses and prepares to take the condemned man's place beneath the needles:

> Now he stood naked there. The explorer[14] bit his lips and said nothing. He knew very well what was going to happen, but he had no right to obstruct the officer in anything. If the judicial procedure which the officer cherished were really so near its end—possibly as a result of his own intervention, as to which he felt himself pledged—then the officer was doing the right thing; in his place the explorer[15] would not have acted otherwise. (163)

Channeling the traveler's thoughts in free indirect style, the narrator conveys the man's commitment to neutrality and fairness, along with his respect for the officer's strength of conviction, which once again paralyze him. He tells himself that in the officer's place he would not have acted differently. With this truism he lets himself off the hook. In his mind the pledge to speak tomorrow with the new Commandant becomes a justification for not intervening at this moment. A hypothetical future activity that will not come to pass becomes his badge of honor. The traveler can feel good about himself. But a reader might wonder, "Would any sane person EVER be in the officer's place?" At this moment a reader "crouching forgotten in the corner of the room" is pressured most intensely to find a way to "participate," to make up somehow for the traveler's lack of action. As the officer's self-imposed execution unfolds, the traveler comes face-to-face with the horror of his own commitment to neutrality, which he maintains by being "determined not to lift a finger," yet resolving "to stay till the end" (164). At the same time, readers come face-to-face with all the moral responsibilities Kafka's traveler fails to accept.

## THE "CROUCHING READER"

The detachment of a narrator who largely but not consistently sees what the traveler sees, leaves readers on their own to supply a missing human connection. It is as if in the absence of a sufficient reaction to injustice and torture, readers are pressured to make up the deficit. In the face of indifference, we are tempted to intervene, even as (perhaps because) this lack of empathy is presented as the most normal of possible reactions to an obviously abnormal situation. Ten years before he wrote this story, Kafka said in a letter to Oskar Pollak, "A book must be the ax for the frozen sea inside us."[16] "In the Penal Colony" can be seen as a meditation on that metaphor. A frozen sea is cold and vast, and if it is inside us rather than outside us, it must be a sea of emotion, or potential emotion. The implication is that in our normal lives, like the traveler and the narrator, we are numb to the suffering around us. Our indifference is so vast, so cold, and so internal, that it freezes the very core of our shared humanity. This image of immobility, even unto a kind of spiritual death, is so strong that only the violence of a terrible jolt can break through. This story and its details are that jolt. In it, Kakfa goads his readers "crouching in the corner" to feel what his characters and narrator fail to feel.

As the traveler stands paralyzed by his ambivalence before the officer's decision to take the condemned man's place, suddenly there are problems with the aging apparatus. Wheels begin to fall off and roll onto the sand, and the traveler realizes that "the machine was obviously going to pieces" (165). Instead of delicate writing, the Harrow begins jabbing: "The explorer[17] wanted to do something, if possible, to bring the whole machine to a standstill, for this was no exquisite torture such as the officer desired, this was plain murder" (165). Before the traveler can "do something," the officer's body lies hanging suspended from the apparatus:

> It was as it had been in life; no sign was visible of the promised redemption; what the others had found in the machine the officer had not found; the lips were firmly pressed together, the eyes were open, with the same expression as in life, the look was calm and convinced, through the forehead went the point of the great iron spike. (166)

Channeling the traveler's experience of this execution, colored by his memory of the officer's explanations, the narrator dwells on what is visible to the traveler: no evidence for the officer's claim of the "enlightenment" that "the others had found, " and that came even "to the most dull-witted." That "redemption" is nowhere to be seen in the officer's face, though his singlemindedness, "calm and convinced," is apparent, even in death.

The narrator seems blind to the corpse's humanity, referring to its features without the personal pronoun, as "die Lippen," "die Augen," "die Stirn,"[18] or "the lips," "the eyes," "the forehead" (166). Nor does he describe the traveler's reaction to this trauma. Instead, there is a break in the story—a blank space on the page that falls where the traveler's reaction to this gruesome scene might have been. The promised meeting with the new Commandant also does not take place. What does happen is that the condemned man and the soldier who was guarding him lead the traveler to the teahouse where the old Commandant lies buried. From there the traveler beats a hasty retreat to the ferryboat at the dock, which will carry him back to his steamer. The condemned man and the soldier follow him down the stairs to the ferry. The narrator, channeling the traveler, is uncertain of the explanation for their decision to follow. He can only hazard a guess: "Probably they wanted to force him at the last minute to take them with him" (167). The story ends with the traveler's escape: "They could have jumped into the boat, but the explorer[19] lifted a heavy knotted rope from the floor boards, threatened them with it, and so kept them from attempting the leap" (167). This conclusion raises more questions than it answers. In a penal colony where there are swords, whips, chains, and executions, would a threat with a coil of rope stop a soldier? Why does the traveler try to prevent the condemned man and soldier from following him onto the ferry? Why does he not honor his pledge to the officer to speak with the new Commandant? Why is he so eager to escape?

Unsatisfied with this ending, which Kafka called "botched,"[20] the author experimented by revising it in several diary entries three years after he created the story and two years before he agreed to publish it. The entry for August 7, 1917, focuses on the moment just after the officer's self-execution, in which blank space stands where the traveler's reaction to the officer's death might otherwise be. In this entry, Kafka fills that gap by having the traveler pass judgment on himself: "I am a cur if I allow that to happen." The traveler then proceeds to "run around on all fours," dog-like, literalizing the metaphor he just used—the same metaphor that described the condemned man in the opening paragraph of the tale.[21] The next day's diary entry shows Kafka again revising this post-suicide moment. Now he has the traveler ask himself, "Who can penetrate this confusion?"[22] This question is both an exasperated call for help and an indirect evasion of responsibility, as if to say, "If I am to blame, anyone would be!" Kafka tries once more the following day with a diary entry in which the traveler collapses in fatigue after the officer's death and only imagines, rather than makes, his escape. In this third attempt to fix the "botched" ending, the past conditional "would have" emphasizes that what is being described is imagined not as a future possibility that might actually occur, but as a future possibility that has already been determined not to occur. In the traveler's mind, it is already finalized as impossible, even as he imagines it. In this reverie the executed officer reappears, complete with spike through his forehead, and he exposes the traveler's lie by pointing out that the condemned man is alive and well, carrying the traveler's bags.

> [The traveler] would have climbed aboard [his ship], except that from the ladder he would have once more denounced the officer for the horrible execution of the condemned man. "I'll tell them of it at home," he would have said, raising his voice so that the captain and the sailors bending in curiosity over the rail might hear him.[23]

Then the officer bends the truth himself: "I was executed, as you commanded."[24] Here, the officer casts blame that the traveler himself seems to feel in the August 7 diary entry, where he condemns himself as a cur, and in the August 8 entry, where he wonders who could have handled the situation any better. Kafka returns to the question of guilt, by having the officer accuse the traveler of commanding the execution, which he did not do (although, in the published tale the condemned man thought he did).

These diary entries all attempt to fill the lacuna left in the published version, where the traveler's reaction to the officer's death might otherwise be. Although Kafka chose not to incorporate any of these alternative endings, they reveal effort after effort to fill this gap with the traveler's meditations on his responsibility for the execution. The August 7 revision, where he directly blames himself, gives way by August 9 to a fantasy of unmasking, in which his desire to save face before the sailors on his ship (and later before every- one back home)—suggesting indirectly the guilt expressed in the August 7 revision—is crushed by the officer's appearance to point out the good health of the condemned man. Here the traveler's fantasy of self-justification incor- porates also the officer's contradicting restatement of an idea that in the published story is delegitimized as the condemned man's misunderstand- ing—that the traveler, not the officer himself, is responsible for the officer's execution. The recasting of the traveler's guilt as expressed August 7, be- neath complicated layerings of the desire to look good and the frustration of that desire, show that the traveler's reaction to the officer's suicide was for Kafka a provocative piece of unfinished business. That he ultimately decided against publishing any of these revisions, all of which would have given readers some explanation of the traveler's state of mind after the officer's death, shows that Kafka chose to retain his "botched" ending. He chose to leave readers on their own, "crouching forgotten in the corner," to draw conclusions about the moral choices they witness the traveler making or failing to make.

This withholding of information about the traveler's state of mind is particularly interesting in light of Kafka's earlier statements in his diary, December 1911, about what he considered to be the proper role of a reader:

> If one patiently submits to a book . . . one suffers oneself to be drawn away . . .
> by the concentrated otherness of the person writing and lets oneself be made
> into his counterpart. Thus it is no longer remarkable, when one is brought back
> to oneself by the closing of the book, that one feels better for the excursion and
> the recreation, and, with a clearer head, remains behind in one's own being,
> which has been newly discovered, newly shaken up and seen for a moment
> from the distance. [25]

Clayton Kolb argues that "in the theory of reading implicit here, the reader does not act upon the text, but rather the text takes the initiative and acts upon the reader. The reader submits." Thus "reading is understood to be the passive reception of an aggressive and powerful text."[26] According to Kolb, this passivity is congruent with the image of the reader in Kafka's famous letter to Oskar Pollak in 1904:

I think we ought to read only the kind of books that wound and stab us. If the book we're reading doesn't wake us up with a blow on the head, what are we reading for? . . . We need the books that affect us like a disaster, that grieve us deeply, like the death of someone we loved more than ourselves, like being banished into forests far from everyone, like a suicide. A book must be the axe for the frozen sea inside us. [27]

Kolb notes the violence of Kafka's images and the passivity of the reader who undergoes this violence: "Ultimately the book should plunge deep into the psychic interior, where its sharp edge can hack open something that has been frozen shut." Kolb connects this violence to the plot of "In the Penal Colony," which he reads as a story about the processes of reading and writing: "The text must stab the reader to succeed, an image that is acted out with brutal precision by the Old Commandant's machine. . . . The book as axe hews apart the present structure of the self both to make an entry for itself and to make the reader into a matrix upon which it can impose its own form" (73).

Kolb concludes that "In the Penal Colony" illustrates Kafka's ideas about the power of a text to impose itself on a passive reader. These conclusions about Kafka's concept of reading as passivity are open to debate, however. By examining the dialogic aspects of a reader's role, as described by Kafka, we can see that it is not at all passive. To be sure, phrases like "patiently submits" and "lets oneself be made" suggest passivity, and words like "wound," "stab," "blow," and "axe" certainly sound violent. But these words and phrases appear within a context that modifies their effects. A reader who undergoes the violence Kafka describes "is brought back to oneself . . . with a clearer head." A reader "remains behind in one's own being, which has been newly discovered, newly shaken up and seen for a moment from the distance." The experience here described involves seeing actively from a new perspective, not merely reacting passively with submission, because, according to Kolb, "submission is all the reader needs to do."[28] The blow on the head is meant to "wake us up," the images of disaster, grief, banishment, and suicide, to "grieve us deeply." The emphasis is not on submission but on the feelings awakened—feelings of empathy that might normally be elicited only by disaster or the loss of those we love most. This empathy is anything but passive or submissive.

A similar state of mind is described by Bakhtin variously as "active empathizing," "sympathetic understanding," or "participative thinking."[29] Confronting a sufferer, he argues, "I put myself in *his* place. . . . I penetrate him and almost merge or become one with him." But "my projection of myself into him must be followed by a *return* into myself," lest I be absorbed in his pain instead of being able to offer help.[30] To Bakhtin, a failure to "return into myself" would be pathological. For instance, the officer's complete identification with the old Commandant and his apparatus would constitute a pathological failure to maintain his own separate identity. Bakhtin advocates instead cultivating the mobility to see from the perspective of someone else, to navigate the epistemological layers of that person's experience, while retaining the ability to avoid passively disappearing into it, so that we can return to ourselves and take responsibility for our actions among others. This process of being "drawn away" into another world, and then returning from it, is described by Kafka in the letter and diary entry above. Empathy for human suffering, which is Bakhtin's focus, becomes in Kafka's hands a metaphor for the relationship between a reader and a book: "We need books that . . . grieve us deeply, like the death of someone we loved more than ourselves." The book affects us as if we were experiencing the death of a loved one, the isolation of banishment, the despair of suicide. For Kafka, as for Bakhtin, the experience must not end with one "drawn away." Rather, a reader closes the book and "is brought back to oneself. . . . One remains behind in one's own being," but that being is enlarged. Just as for Bakhtin the experience of empathy leaves one more able to see things from other perspectives, for Kafka the experience of reading—for many of the same reasons—leaves one more awake, with a clearer head, "newly shaken up," seeing "for a moment from the distance." "In the Penal Colony" gives readers that experience.

## READING "IN THE PENAL COLONY" FOR AND WITH DIALOGIC FREEDOM

I began this chapter by claiming that if we imagine dialogic freedom on a continuum from zero to ten, with zero representing the choices of a prisoner chained and gagged, and ten representing the situation of one who perfectly negotiates multiple perspectives, balancing the need for a unified explanation with the chaos of reality, "In the Penal Colony" explores the end of the scale closest to zero. We learn early on that the condemned man and the soldier guarding him do not speak French, the language of choice between the officer and the traveler. Thus, from the start the condemned man and the soldier are not part of the intended audience for the officer's enthusiastic explanations of the ins and outs of the apparatus, the tensions between the old and new Commandants, and the history of punishment on the island. If dialogic freedom involves listening and being heard, the condemned man and the soldier guarding him enjoy only the smallest modicum of it, which is furnished by their limited interchanges with each other in the local dialect. For instance, after the condemned man is set free and allowed to put his clothes back on, "The soldier and the condemned man were now busy together. . . . Both he and the soldier could not help guffawing, for the garments were of course slit up behind" (162). This slapstick routine is presented as a continuation of the trivializing and detached observations of the narrator about the "submissive dog" at the beginning of the story. Meanwhile, these interchanges between soldier and condemned man, disconnected from the decisions being made by the officer and the traveler, are not part of the two-sided act of deciding if, how, and when the execution should proceed.

Though the condemned man and the soldier can communicate with each other, that communication is presented as inconsequential, and they are in any case at the mercy of commands from the officer. These commands take the form of rudimentary sign language that can easily be misunderstood. When the officer takes the condemned man's place, for example, the prisoner concludes that the traveler must have intervened on his behalf to free him from the apparatus and to punish the officer for trying to execute him. No one bothers to explain the truth of the situation to him, so he is left to drift with this erroneous perspective (which, in any case, has a grain of truth—since the traveler's failure to intervene leads to the officer's death). Neither the traveler nor the officer considers the condemned man or the soldier worthy of more than minimal attention. Thus, at the conclusion of the story, communication is once again reduced to sign language, when the traveler threatens them with the "heavy knotted rope." There is no indication that he understands why they "probably" want to join his escape, or whether they understand why he blocks that effort. Only in the narrowest sense can we say that the perspectives of the French speakers and the non–French speakers in this story have overlapped. Though they respond (often mistakenly) to each other's gestures, they do not share an experience within which dialogic freedom is possible. The relationship between the condemned man and the soldier who guards him offers an alternative, though limited, avenue for dialogic freedom, but it is so trivialized by the narrator and circumscribed by control from above, that on a scale of zero to ten this freedom registers near zero. Furthermore, as long as the condemned man is gagged and bound beneath the machine, he is quite literally prevented from engaging in dialogue or activity. For him, communication is reduced to the involuntary act of vomiting.

The relationship between the traveler and the officer holds the promise of greater dialogic freedom. They speak the same language, and though their perspectives are radically different, each can imagine the attractions of the other's. Both are called upon to make decisions and take action based on their own thoughts, their responses to each other—anticipated, invited, ignored, satisfied, disappointed, or missing—and the execution process at hand. The officer's perspective is tightly unified by his fanatical devotion to the old Commandant's vision of guilt, torture, technology, and enlightenment. The tradition established by the old Commandant is the officer's superaddressee, to which he feels answerable above all else. Though the diagrams of the machine he carries with him can be read only by him, his faith in the old Commandant's system gives him the confidence to conclude that he can make everything clear to the explorer, answer all his questions, and convert him to his religion. The resistance he has met from the new Commandant serves only to energize him to try harder to enlist the traveler as his ally. At one point he gets so worked up in his fantasy of tomorrow's meeting between the traveler and the new Commandant that he urges, "Don't put any restraint on yourself when you make your speech, publish the truth aloud, lean over the front of the box, shout, yes indeed, shout your verdict, your unshakable conviction, at the Commandant" (159). Here words like "truth," "verdict," and "unshakable conviction" emphasize the settled nature of the officer's thinking. In his devotion to the old Commandant, he has committed himself to a single unified, centripetal way of knowing the world, and he is content to exist within the boundaries of this narrow epistemological layer.

In his certainty, the officer resembles the Grand Inquisitor before Christ kisses him. Like the Grand Inquisitor he has a positive liberty vision of enlightenment as something that few are capable of grasping. Both he and the Grand Inquisitor would argue that only someone who fully understands and appreciates the correct perspective can be truly free. Like the Grand Inquisitor, he is completely devoted to his vision, willing to commit violence in its name, and eager to defend it. Both, too, are inspired to their most strenuous persuasive efforts by listeners who fail to be persuaded. Just as Christ's silence coauthors the Grand Inquisitor's diatribe against freedom, inspiring greater efforts the longer that silence persists, the traveler's sustained neutrality coauthors the officer's increasingly frantic efforts to convert him.

That the officer's enlightenment is a projection of his own delusions becomes explicit when no sign of it is visible in his face after the "great iron spike" has pierced his forehead, leaving him with the "same expression as in life," which is "calm and convinced." True, the narrator leaves some wiggle room when he explains that "no sign was visible of the promised redemption," as if to imply that it was possible that the officer achieved the expected enlightenment, invisibly and unverifiably. The stronger implication, however, is that there never was any such enlightenment, and that the officer has failed to achieve even the minimal insight that his ideal was a delusion. He dies apparently "calm and convinced," holding onto the unified vision that has given his life purpose. In terms of dialogic freedom, he is a prisoner of that vision. He is unable to navigate among the multiple ways of knowing that could put his own fanaticism in perspective and eventually liberate him to examine it from afar. As he studies the inscriptions etched into the bodies of the victims of the apparatus, he may be able to decipher phrases like "HONOR THY SUPERIORS! " or "BE JUST!" but he remains incapable of becoming the reader that Kafka imagined in his diary, whose being could be "shaken up and seen for a moment from the distance."

This is not to say that the officer has been totally blind to perspectives beyond his own. He has been able to imagine the reservations of the traveler and the new Commandant well enough to anticipate and attempt to disarm possible arguments made from their rival perspectives. For instance, after the felt gag is forced into the condemned man's mouth, the prisoner "in an irresistible access of nausea shut his eyes and vomited." Offended at the vomit "running all over the machine," the officer complains:

> Have I not tried for hours at a time to get the Commandant to understand that the prisoner must fast for a whole day before the execution. But our new, mild doctrine thinks otherwise. The Commandant's ladies stuff the man with sugar candy before he's led off. He has lived on stinking fish his whole life long and now he has to eat sugar candy! But it could still be possible, I should have nothing to say against it, but why won't they even get me a new felt gag, which I have been begging for the last three months. How should a man not feel sick when he takes a felt gag into his mouth which more than a hundred men have already slobbered and gnawed in their dying moments? (152)

This speech is impeccably logical, if you accept the officer's premises. It emphasizes how unreasonable it is to alter one's diet before a stressful event, or to break routines that have been a source of stability, or to fail to maintain or upgrade sensitive machinery. There is in the officer's argument a grudging awareness of the "mild doctrine" of the new Commandant that presents the condemned with small luxuries. The officer understands this reformist thinking well enough to see the need to argue against it. Inside his logic, though, lie ironies of which he is unaware—the gruesomeness of the torture he embraces, the perversity of thinking that candy somehow makes it milder, the shock value of the hundred victims, and the window onto class warfare. Furthermore, the officer himself is never influenced in the least by the "mild doctrine" to which he alludes. He handles the objections it raises as a surgeon would lift dead tissue from a wound. These objections are to be disposed of gingerly, with a kind of patient distaste, on the way to achieving what the officer would consider a healthy shared certainty. The objections of others do not in any way jeopardize the unified vision to which the officer has committed himself. To the extent that his logic and passion anticipate responses from the traveler, or respond to the traveler's words and actions, these coauthored responses nudge the officer away from zero on the continuum of dialogic freedom, but not very far.

While the traveler, as listener, coauthors the officer's determination to defend his way of life and eventually to take the condemned man's place, the officer coauthors the traveler's ambivalence. This ambivalence is the product of much more, however, than the officer's arguments and an execution in progress. As the traveler navigates the turbulent waters of different perspectives on the experience at hand, his attitude is more elastic than the officer's, and his ability to navigate the ways of knowing inhabited by others is proportionately greater. He brings with him an Enlightenment European's misgivings about procedures not practiced since the Middle Ages, a researcher's curiosity, a world traveler's experience, and a tourist's ignorance and open-mindedness about local customs. He understands how the new Commandant might want to modify current traditions in the penal colony, but he is also touched by the officer's "sincere conviction." As he listens to the officer's appeal, coauthoring it by giving the impression that he might eventually be persuaded, he navigates the tensions between the perspectives listed above, by committing himself to the role of the neutral observer. He will neither "help nor hinder." This decision seems cut-and-dried, but the traveler's neutrality is constantly under stress, inspiring the officer to intensify his appeal for help. The traveler is sympathetic enough to feel that he has "no right to obstruct the officer in anything," and that "in his place the explorer would not have acted otherwise" (163). Although he must decline to help the officer with the new Commandant, he empathizes with the officer's commitment to the execution process, if not with the process itself. Thus, there is an aspect of the officer's perspective—his zeal, sense of duty, willingness to make the ultimate sacrifice—that the traveler understands and respects. To the extent that the officer's appeals have touched him, the traveler becomes paralyzed by his own ambivalence toward possibilities that remain open-ended until the moment the officer dies.

The constant possibility that the traveler might decide to intervene creates great tension in the story. In fact, each decision to do nothing is as powerfully codetermined by a variety of factors—the traveler's values and experience, the execution in progress, the apparent lack of official and public support for it, and the officer's increasingly desperate appeals—as a decision to intervene would be. When the traveler pledges to the officer to speak the next day in private with the new Commandant, in order to express his reservations about the procedure, that pledge is a two-sided act that is really multi-sided. It is coauthored in part by the officer's appeals for help, in part by the traveler's values, in part by his anticipated reception from the new Commandant, and in part by his experience of witnessing an execution. When the traveler stands paralyzed, about to act but failing to act, as the machine drives a spike through the officer's forehead, both his readiness and his paralysis are coauthored by the officer's appeal to him to respect the execution process. Even when the traveler flees the island, holding up the coil of heavy rope to block the soldier and condemned man from joining him, that action is codetermined, not just by his pursuers, but by his own unsettled emotional reactions, by the officer who has subjected him to an experience he now must flee, and by the new Commandant he has chosen not to face. In each of these instances, the traveler engages in multi-sided decisions, which involve deliberation from multiple perspectives, within a field of forces for unity and chaos. His actions suggest a level of dialogic freedom far beyond the officer's, which is circumscribed entirely by his fanaticism.

The complexities of the traveler's feelings of answerability, only suggested by his cryptic actions at the conclusion of the published tale, are spelled out more clearly in the diary entries where Kafka rethought his "botched" ending. In the entry from August 7, 1917, the traveler passes judgment on himself as a "cur if I allow that to happen." He holds himself accountable to his superaddressee, a moral system that requires a bystander to intervene to prevent a suicide. This answerability lasts but a moment, however. The traveler in this diary entry escapes responsibility by running around on all fours, dog-like, as if he were no longer human and thus not accountable to human standards of behavior. Yet even in this dog-like state he cannot escape intermittent awareness of his desperate situation: "From time to time . . . he leaped erect, shook the fit off, so to speak, threw his arms around one of the men [sent by the new Commandant to fetch him] and tearfully exclaimed, 'Why does this happen to me!'" (178). Unlike in the published version, here the new Commandant dispatches representatives to extricate the traveler from the execution, and the traveler sheds tears, throwing his arms around one of his saviors. This revision process reveals the author's struggle to find the right words to describe the traveler's state of mind as the officer self-destructs.

Kafka's August 9, 1917, diary entry tests out another possibility: the traveler's fantasy of what he might do but does not. He imagines denouncing the execution before addressees that include sailors on board his ship and listeners back home. These imagined audiences, before whom he wants to revise history and exonerate himself for doing what he in fact failed to do— denounce the execution—coauthor his thoughts by inspiring him to try to look good in their eyes. When this fantasy of self-exoneration is punctured by the arrival of the dead officer, who exposes the traveler as a liar, Kafka adds one more addressee, the officer, before whom the traveler feels inadequate. The officer's accusation is made all the more forcefully, because the condemned man, not at all dead, is now serving as the traveler's porter, while the officer himself still sports a lethal spike through the middle of his forehead. In this fantasy, the traveler considers himself answerable to the officer, the sailors, and the people back home. Above all, however, he is answerable in this fantasy to two irreconcilable superaddresees: his sense of responsibility to take action in a difficult situation, and the rational neutrality to which he has already committed himself.

In rejecting the revisions contained in these diary entries, all of which dramatize the coauthorship of various addressessees and superaddressees to whom the traveler feels answerable in the aftermath of the officer's death, Kakfa chose instead to strand readers on a blank gap on the page where there is no text at all. Whatever the traveler's thoughts are, they are withheld.

Instead of entering the confessional or fantasy modes experimented with in these diary entries, the traveler in the published version of the tale escapes without explanation. Officially he acts out his expressed policy not to meddle in the affairs of a foreign colony, a policy that has provided a framework of neutrality to justify his actions. This framework, unlike the officer's fanaticism, does not confine the traveler within one narrow way of knowing the world. It does, however, serve for him the same function of unifying his perspective enough so that he can take action. As he makes his escape, it allows him to insulate himself from other perspectives that might require him to embrace a different course of action, perspectives that might break through the frozen sea within him.

Kafka's decision not to include in his published story any of the diary entries chronicling the traveler's feelings of guilt, confusion, or desperation increases the pressure on a reader of "In the Penal Colony" to feel what it is like to crouch "forgotten in a corner of the room where he can participate all the more intensely in what is happening there." Witnessing the traveler's meditations on neutrality and his (in)actions in the face of a grotesque, unjust, and insane execution, readers are left to confront the moral questions dodged by both the traveler and the narrator, supplying the missing human response that is the other side of the two-sided act of intervention. Precisely because the traveler does nothing to stop the officer's suicide, readers must face both the attractions and the shallowness of the traveler's self-justifications. Precisely because the narrator can say, "in his place the explorer would not have done otherwise," readers are led to imagine making some other choice. "In the Penal Colony" shines a harsh light on the moral relativism of a traveler who intends to be a neutral observer in another culture, and it challenges readers to do a better job of deciding on a course of action within a context of other human beings. It is the hypothetical reader, not the traveler, who is "brought back" to himself or herself "by the closing of the book" to "remain behind in one's own being, which has been newly discovered, newly shaken up and seen for a moment from the distance." It is the hypothetical reader, not the traveler, who experiences the greatest possibility for dialogic freedom.

Kafka has the officer present his grotesque perspective as persuasively as he can, as if to invite readers not just to recoil in horror, but to really think that perspective through and see from inside it before they recoil in horror. Kafka invites readers also to examine the impulse toward neutrality and the attractiveness of its rationales for inaction, as if to invite us to share the traveler's route for as long as we possibly can, before the axe breaks through the frozen sea within us. By abandoning us to this experience in the hands of a curiously detached narrator, who generally channels the traveler's gaze but fails to show the characters in the story—even the traveler—the empathy we would consider only human, Kafka leaves readers to fill that vacuum and confront the neglected moral issues. This is of course a very hypothetical situation for a reader to be in, in that we cannot really enter the story, coauthor speech and action, or redirect its plot. Yet at the end of the tale, as the unresolved issues of "In the Penal Colony" continue to rattle in our heads, we remain behind, "shaken up," our "being . . . seen for a moment from the distance," yearning for a dialogic freedom that is inaccessible to its characters.

Thus it is that the combination of perspectives that seems necessary to reacting adequately to the events within Kafka's story can be assembled nowhere except within a potential reader's mind. As we squirm before the explorer's inaction, we bring our own superaddressees (gods, values about right and wrong, the law, traditions of reading and thinking about literature) to the reading experience. These superaddressees help each of us unify our individual orientations as we witness the contradictory perspectives of the officer, the explorer, the narrator, and the new Commandant. Confronted by the officer's superaddressee, which is the vision created by the old Commandant, and the traveler's superaddressee, which is a Western European tradition of rational neutrality—both of which seem inadequate—we are forced to dig deep within our own values to supply a moral orientation that otherwise seems absent. We want the explorer to save the officer from himself and to have his chat with the new Commandant. Instead, we watch him escape, as if his most important goal were to forget what has just happened. If the condemned man and the prisoner can be prevented from following him onto his steamer, he will not need to make explanations to anyone or rethink his own role in the officer's suicide. Better to pretend that it did not happen. Just such an impulse must have come over the soldiers and agents at Abu Ghraib who put the crucified body of Manadel al-Jamadi on ice, then inserted an IV, "put the body on a stretcher, and took it out of the prison as if Jamadi were merely ill."[31] There are things we would rather not think about.

"In the Penal Colony" can be seen as a story that exercises in readers the mental and moral muscles needed to balance the need for unified explanation with the chaos of reality, as they expand their own capacity for dialogic freedom. While the characters in the story are limited to one or another perspective, or only dimly or defensively aware of alternative perspectives, readers can see from multiple perspectives. We can see the degree to which characters' horizons overlap or fail to overlap. We can see the machine that "works all by itself" with an autonomy that erases two-sidedness from the equation. We can see the effort it takes to hold on to neutrality in the face of horror, and we are tempted to admire the zeal of the officer, the professionalism of the eminent traveler, and the ironic detachment of the narrator. Yet, in the end, we are charged up with the desire to intervene where the traveler has not intervened, to puncture the officer's delusions, and to shake the narrator by the scruff of the neck. We can never know if any one of us would be more up to the challenges of a visit to this execution site than Kafka's traveler was, but reading "In the Penal Colony" leaves us wishing that we were. In that sense his story inspires us to try to locate ourselves on the continuum of dialogic freedom nearer to ten than to zero.

## NOTES

1. Quoted in Clayton Kolb, *Kafka's Rhetoric: The Passion of Reading* (Ithaca, NY: Cornell University Press, 1989). 86. Kolb concludes that Kafka's "stories are meant to engage the reader in the problematic of reading. . . . They are meant to put the reader in a torture machine and stretch him out on the rack of this tough word" (107).

2. American prison in Cuba for suspected terrorists.

3. According to Seymour Hersh, "A fifty-three-page report . . . by Major General Antonio M. Taguba . . . found that between October and December of 2003 there were numerous instances of 'sadistic, blatant, and wanton criminal abuses' at Abu Ghraib." "Torture at Abu Ghraib," *New Yorker*, May 10, 2004.

4. Franz Kafka, "In the Penal Colony," in *Franz Kafka: The Complete Stories*, ed. Nahum Glatzer; trans. Willa Muir and Edwin Muir; foreword by John Updike (New York: Schocken, 1971), 156. Citations in English to "In the Penal Colony" are to this text.

5. The traveler is introduced in the opening sentence of the German text as "dem Forschungsreisenden" (the explorer). "In der Strafkolonie," in *Erzählungen* (Berlin: Schocken Verlag, 1946), 157. In the English version I quote, translators Willa and Edwin Muir consistently refer to the traveler as "the explorer," even though throughout the German edition he is almost always referred to as the "Reisende" (traveler). One could argue that Kakfa meant "Reisende," which is embedded in the longer word "Forschungsreisende" to be shorthand for the longer word, and that "Forschung" (research) is what an explorer (rather than a mere traveler) would do. On the other hand, the more general term "Reisende" (traveler) is almost always the term Kafka uses, implying for this character a much less deliberate purpose, as if he has blundered into an execution process that he has no real interest in witnessing. In any case, I follow the practice of more recent readers like Clayton Kolb, who refers to the officer's reluctant listener as the traveler, rather than the explorer (Kolb, *Rhetoric*, 96). In my quotations from the Muir translation, I indicate where "Reisende" in the original German has been translated "explorer" rather than "traveler."

6. See Allen Thiher, *Frank Kafka: A Study of the Short Fiction* (Boston: Twayne, 1990), 51.

7. According to Roy Pascal, Kafka's "liking for fable and parable" invites us to look for meaning "even if the lessons or 'morals' that are to be drawn from these fables are anything but simple. . . . One suspects that many of Kafka's stories are not amenable to a precise and definable meaning." *Kafka's Narrators: A Study of His Stories and Sketches* (Cambridge, UK: Cambridge University Press, 1982), 18.

8. Richard Gray summarizes "the plethora of diverse interpretations" of this story, dividing them into the abstract allegorical, which "fall into two main groups: those that interpret the text along various Judeo-Christian lines" and those that "view the text as a demonstration of existential guilt"; and the literal, which ground the text in contemporary history, including Clayton Kolb's interpretation of the story as "Kafka's reflections on his own writing practice." "Disjunctive Signs: Semiotics, Aesthetics, and Failed Mediation in 'In der Strafkolonie,'" in *A Companion to the Works of Franz Kafka*, ed. James Rolleston (Rochester, NY: Camden House, 2002), 213–16.

9. Gray, "Disjunctive Signs," 218.

10. "Der Reisende" (traveler), *Erzählungen*, 157.

11. See Thiher, *Study of the Short Fiction*, 58.

12. "Der Reisende" (traveler), *Erzählungen*, 162.

13. Thiher argues that in the penal colony Kafka's traveler "must enter into a cultural maze from which he is excluded by his Enlightenment skepticism" (Thiher, *Study of the Short Fiction*, 58).

14. "Der Reisende" (traveler), *Erzählungen*, 173.

15. "Der Reisende" (traveler), *Erzählungen*, 173.

16. Franz Kafka, "Letter to Oskar Pollak, January 27, 1904," in *Letters to Friends, Family, and Editors*, trans. Richard Winston and Clara Winston (New York: Schocken, 1977), 16.

17. "Der Reisende" (traveler), *Erzählungen*, 175.

18. Kafka, "In der Strafkolonie," *Erzählungen*, 176.

19. "Der Reisende" (traveler), *Erzählungen*, 177.

20. Gray, "Disjunctive Signs," 216.

21. Franz Kafka, August 7, 1917, *The Diaries of Franz Kafka 1914–1923*, ed. Max Brod; trans. Martin Greenberg (New York: Schocken, 1949), 178.

22. Kafka, August 8, 1917, *Diaries 1914–1923*, 178.

23. Kafka, August 9, 1917, *Diaries 1914–1923*, 180.

24. Kafka, August 9, 1917, *Diaries 1914–1923*, 180–81.

25. Kafka, *The Diaries of Franz Kafka, 1910–1913*, ed. Max Brod; trans. Joseph Kresh (New York: Schocken, 1948), 173–74.

26. Kolb, *Kafka's Rhetoric*, 74.

27. Kafka, *Letters*, 16.

28. Kolb, *Kafka's Rhetoric*, 74.

29. See chapter 1.

30. Mikhail Bakhtin, "Author and Hero in Aesthetic Activity," in *Art and Answerability: Early Philosophical Essays by M. M. Bakhtin*, ed. Michael Holquist and Vadim Liapunov; trans. Vadim Liapunov (Austin: University of Texas Press, 1990), 25–26.

31. Jane Mayer, "A Deadly Interrogation: Can the CIA Legally Kill a Prisoner?" *New Yorker*, November 14, 2005, 50.

## Chapter Nine

# Freedom under Impossible Conditions in *Beloved*

Dialogic freedom: a two-sided act, chosen within a field of unifying and fragmenting forces *along a continuum of minimal to maximal layers of knowing that are never final.*

If Kafka's "In the Penal Colony" dwells on failures of dialogic freedom under bizarre circumstances, Toni Morrison's *Beloved* celebrates the resilience of dialogic freedom under conditions almost guaranteed to destroy it.[1] In the process it explores opposite ends of a *continuum of minimal to maximal layers of knowing that are never final.* At one end of the continuum is Beloved, trapped in one narrow epistemological layer of need; at the other end is Sixo, who expands the possibilities of freedom for himself and for others. This novel presents multiple perspectives on one central choice: an escaped slave mother's infanticide. The most cryptic passages are snatches of conversation between that mother, Sethe, and what may be the ghost of her murdered daughter, Beloved. As they struggle to communicate, the mother trying to make up for the past, the daughter refusing to be consoled, their dialogic freedom nearly evaporates. The end of the novel holds hope that Sethe can regain the ability to navigate the ways of knowing of others. It also shows that in the open-endedness of her situation she codetermines the expansion of dialogic freedom for Paul D, the last of the Sweet Home men, and for the community that once failed her. Morrison seems to be saying that although we are freer the more we can see from the perspectives of others, this expansion of possibilities entails both dangers and limits. Dialogic freedom, though surprisingly robust, can also be destroyed.

In 1856, the year after "Benito Cereno" appeared in *Putnam* magazine, Herman Melville published it as one of his *Piazza Tales*. That was the same year twenty-two-year-old Margaret Garner killed her three-year-old daughter and attempted to kill her other three children. The *Cincinnati Daily Enquirer* reported on its front page, "A party of slaves had made a stampede from Kentucky to this side of the river." When their owners caught up with them in a house in Cincinnati, they found a "deed of horror":

> Weltering in its blood, the throat having been cut from ear to ear and the head almost severed from the body, upon the floor lay one of the children of the young couple, a girl three years old, while in the back room, crouched beneath the bed, two more of the children, boys of two and five years, were moaning, the one having received two gashes in its throat, the other a cut upon the head. As the party entered the room the mother was seen wielding a heavy shovel, and before she could be secured she inflicted a heavy blow upon the face of the infant, which was lying upon the floor. . . . The mother of the children is a good-looking hearty negress, while her husband bears the appearance of having been well cared for. [2]

In her Pulitzer Prize–winning novel *Beloved*, Toni Morrison works with this raw material, as Melville had worked with the 1817 *Narrative* of Amasa Delano, to refashion history as fiction. Retaining some elements, altering others, Morrison does what Melville did not try to do: she takes us inside the mind of the slave who has decided that slavery is intolerable.

Where Melville confined himself to the surface of Babo's words and deeds, Morrison makes us see from inside the mind of her main character, Sethe, who could not bear to let her children grow up slaves. She tried to put her babies "where they'd be safe," [3] and the author means to make us understand that decision. This is not an easy task. Much of Morrison's novel is devoted to the multiplicity of perspectives from which Sethe's desperate act is viewed by various characters. In the process of bringing us closer to understanding how a loving mother might kill her child, Morrison examines the complexities of dialogic freedom. Like Melville, she shows how racism undermines it for both racist and victim. She also demonstrates how under the most difficult circumstances human beings manage to nurture the conditions that make dialogic freedom possible. Where Kafka and Melville focused on what limits these possibilities, Morrison shows how opportunities for dialogic freedom can be created almost out of thin air.

## UNDERMINING DIALOGIC FREEDOM

If dialogic freedom involves deliberation from multiple perspectives, racism, which prevents people from empathizing with others enough to see from their perspectives, undermines this capacity. The racism that Melville explores in "Benito Cereno" is also present in *Beloved*, in owners who use and abuse slaves, in Abolitionists who seek to free them, and in a white girl who does not think to question the status quo. Near the end of the novel, a decade after the Civil War has ended slavery, Edward Bodwin, former Abolitionist, makes his way toward Sethe's house to pick up her daughter Denver, who is to start work in his kitchen. Eighteen years earlier the infant Denver had been spared death when her mother swung her by her heels but missed the post she was aiming at. While Bodwin drives his cart, he muses on the heady days of the movement, the "old days of letters, petitions, meetings, debates, recruitment, quarrels, rescue and downright sedition." He remembers especially that day when "a slavewoman . . . got herself in a world of trouble. The Society managed to turn infanticide and the cry of savagery around, building a further case for abolishing slavery" (260). Morrison's narrator drops this nugget without explanation, leaving it to readers to imagine the "case for abolishing slavery" built by Abolitionists out of "the cry of savagery." That case might go something like this: "Slavery dehumanizes people so much that it reduces the mother to a savage who kills her own child." Bodwin, who has more than once come to the rescue of this former slave's family, providing housing and work, both before and after the murder, thinks he understands what drove Sethe to kill one child and attempt to kill three more. But his racist perspective is "debilitating to his judgment of what is actually at hand,"[4] just as Amasa Delano's was in "Benito Cereno."

Morrison captures this debilitated judgment in a figurine on a shelf in the Bodwins' kitchen, "a blackboy's mouth full of money":

> His head was thrown back farther than a head could go, his hands were shoved in his pockets. Bulging like moons, two eyes were all the face he had above the gaping red mouth. His hair was a cluster of raised, widely spaced dots made of nail heads. And he was on his knees. His mouth, wide as a cup, held coins needed to pay for a delivery or some other small service, but could just as well have held buttons, pins, or crab-apple jelly. Painted across the pedestal he knelt on were the words, "At Yo Service." (255)

As former Abolitionists, impassioned enough to risk their lives to end slavery, the Bodwins nevertheless keep in their kitchen this symbol of degradation. The lethal pose, "head thrown back farther than a head could go," renders permanent the agony of the figurine's kneeling position. The mouth that should be used for speech is reduced instead to a receptacle for jelly, or whatever else the master has in mind, while hands meant for holding are rendered useless, stuffed in pockets. Rather than scream out in pain, the kneeling figure welcomes his fate with the motto "At Yo Service." His slogan, unutterable by a mouth filled with coins, yet carved below his figure, forces him to express the compliance of the happy slave imagined by Amasa Delano and staged for his benefit by Babo. The mere fact that Bodwin and his sister can stand to look at this ceramic image day after day, year after year, continuing to exploit the gaping mouth as a coin-holder, says volumes about their inability to free themselves of a racist perspective that regards slaves as less than human. While the figurine embodies the slave's torture and dehumanization, the racism that the figurine reflects limits the Bodwins' ability to imagine the perspectives of the people they think of themselves as helping. Thus, even as it embodies a slave's degradation, this figurine becomes a symbol of the Bodwins' diminished dialogic freedom.

The Bodwins are not the only whites with debilitated judgment in *Beloved*. Like Alexandro Aranda in "Benito Cereno," Mr. Garner, who owns the farm in Sweet Home, Kentucky, where three of Sethe's four children are born, prides himself on his enlightenment. He allows his slaves to hunt with guns and to earn money on weekends. He allows them to "buy a mother, choose a horse or a wife, handle guns, even learn reading if they wanted to." He goes so far as to encourage them to correct him, "even defy him" (125). He boasts to his gambling buddies, "Y'all got boys. . . . My niggers is men every one of them. Bought em thataway, raised em thataway" (10). Garner's treatment of his slaves lets him lord it over other plantation owners, showing them that a "real Kentuckian" is someone "tough enough and smart enough to make and call his own niggers men" (11). One of Garner's proudest moments comes when he delivers Baby Suggs into freedom, bought and mostly paid for by her son, Halle. Reviewing his own exemplary behavior, Garner asks her, "Did I let Halle buy you or not?" She answers "Yes sir, you did," but she also thinks to herself, "But you got my boy and I'm all broke down. You be renting him out to pay for me way after I'm gone to Glory." In his narcissism, Garner grants more humanity to his slaves than the figurine on the Bodwins' kitchen shelf allows, but his judgment is no less debilitated. Regarding human dignity as something to be bestowed by him, a reflection of his worth rather than theirs, prevents Garner from seeing his slaves as anything more than an extension of his own ego. It prevents him from questioning the legitimacy of owning them, or from anticipating their fate should something happen to him.

The fragility of their lives under Garner's watch becomes apparent when he suddenly dies and his widow needs to sell a slave to make ends meet. The exceptional circumstances permitted at Sweet Home come to an abrupt end for that slave and for the brothers he must leave behind, as they learn in an instant that their lives depend on one man staying healthy. Then, before Halle can begin to work the endless Sundays it will take to buy freedom for his wife, Sethe, their three children, and himself, Garner's brother-in-law, Schoolteacher, arrives to take over the farm and reeducate its slaves. Schoolteacher forbids both freelance work and carrying guns: "The information they offered he called backtalk and developed a variety of corrections" (11). His new regime is definitely a turn for the worse for the slaves, and Schoolteacher understands what slave-owner Alexandro Aranda in "Benito Cereno" had failed to grasp: that slavery is a state of war. He steps up surveillance, and when the slaves attempt to escape, he executes some, shackles others, and allows his nephews to beat and sexually assault the six-months-pregnant Sethe. When she amazes them by managing to escape afterwards, School-teacher does not hesitate to assemble the forces necessary to track her down. Like Bodwin's paternalism and Garner's narcissism, Schoolteacher's calm contempt reflects a debilitated judgment that blinds him to the slaves' humanity. When he teaches his nephews to make lists of Sethe's features, "her human characteristics on the left; her animal ones on the right" (193), he bequeaths to a new generation his damaged and damaging perspective.

## CREATING DIALOGIC FREEDOM

After she escapes from Sweet Home, Sethe runs until she drops. Her swollen feet cut and blistered raw, her back scored with welts, her hands and knees bloody from the last effort to crawl, she is ready to give up on life when she is discovered by the most important white character in the novel: Amy Denver. A runaway indentured servant on her way to Boston to buy velvet, Amy is "the raggediest-looking trash you ever saw," according to Sethe. On the surface she is an ill-chosen savior, whose first words are, "Look there. A nigger. If that don't beat all" (32). Readers are not led to expect much from Amy, but Sethe is desperate: "Below her bloody knees, there was no feeling at all; her chest was two cushions of pins. It was the voice full of velvet and Boston and good things to eat that urged her along and made her think that maybe she wasn't, after all, just the crawling graveyard for a six-month baby's last hours" (34). The white teenager sounds hilariously callous as she gathers leaves to prop up Sethe's feet, saying to her, "'I know a woman had her feet cut off they was so swole.' And she made sawing gestures with the blade of her hand across Sethe's ankles. 'Zzz Zzz Zzz Zzz.'" Yet Amy Denver turns out to have a gift for "sick things." She gathers antibiotic moss to put on Sethe's ravaged back, and she says to her, "Make you a bet. You make it through the night, you make it all the way." Then she warns her, "Don't up and die on me in the night, you hear? I don't want to see your ugly black face hankering over me. If you do die, just go off somewhere where I can't see you, hear?" (82).

In her ministrations to Sethe, the racism that peppers Amy's speech is trumped by the raw experience of confronting a pregnant woman barely alive, so that what was debilitating to the judgments of the Bodwins, the Garners, and Schoolteacher, becomes curiously comic from the mouth of this white girl who is also running from a master's lash. Miraculously, Sethe makes it through the night, but on the bank of the Ohio River, her water breaks and she goes into premature labor. Amy's reaction is to yell, "Stop that right now. . . . You the dumbest thing on this here earth" (83). There is no going back, though, and in a chaos of blood and pulling, instead of a pregnant slave dying in the underbrush, a baby is born:

> A pateroller passing would have sniggered to see two throw-away people, two lawless outlaws—a slave and a barefoot whitewoman with unpinned hair— wrapping a ten-minute-old baby in the rags they wore. But no pateroller came and no preacher. The water sucked and swallowed itself beneath them. There was nothing to disturb them at their work. So they did it appropriately and well. (85)

Without sentimentality, and without casting Amy Denver as the exceptional, race-blind white, Morrison tracks the responses of two young women to the situation they find themselves in, showing how these "throw-away people" go about doing a job "appropriately and well."

Amy has no intention of helping Sethe, and Sethe does not expect her help. Despite these attitudes and the improbability of success, Amy and Sethe coauthor each other's words and actions that lead to creating new life. In their encounter, Morrison seems to suggest that though racism undermines the racist's judgment and victimizes others, circumstances that place people face-to-face with their humanity, and their material needs for food, shelter, and human contact, can temporarily blunt racism's corrosive effects. Amy does not stick around long after the baby is born, not willing to "be caught dead in daylight on a busy river with a runaway" (85). Yet, the parentheses within which she and Sethe coauthor each other's possibilities and the birth of a baby give readers hope that the immediacy of human experience can reduce the corrosive power of racism and make possible the two-sided acts that constitute dialogic freedom. Amy and Sethe may not understand every-thing about each other's perspectives, but together they impose unity on the chaos of their own suffering and flight. Together they share survival and childbirth in a refuge they carve out within a field of forces harmful to them both. Sethe formally acknowledges Amy's coauthorship of the new infant by naming her Denver.

## BROTHER

Morrison's novel presents the emergence of dialogic freedom under the most unlikely circumstances, not just with two "throw-away" women, but on the plantation at Sweet Home. Before Sethe's escape, before her children are born, and before she even chooses Halle to marry, *Beloved* gives us a glimpse of how the slaves at Sweet Home create opportunities for dialogic freedom almost out of thin air. They carve out a public space at the edge of a field where there is a tree they call Brother. There they meet to sit and talk and eat potatoes cooked experimentally:

Indigo with a flame-red tongue, Sixo experimented with night-cooked potatoes, trying to pin down exactly when to put smoking-hot rocks in a hole,
potatoes on top, and cover the whole thing with twigs so that by the time they
broke for the meal, hitched the animals, left the field and got to Brother, the
potatoes would be at the peak of perfection. He might get up in the middle of
the night, go all the way out there, start the earth-over by starlight; or he would
make the stones less hot and put the next day's potatoes on them right after the
meal. He never got it right, but they ate those undercooked, overcooked, dried-
out or raw potatoes anyway, laughing, spitting, and giving him advice. (21)

Under impossible circumstances, these culinary activities create a town-hall
atmosphere of give and take. In the process, the slaves of Sweet Home
explore a ritual with endless variety, fueled by Sixo's audacity, creativity,
organizational skills, and humor. He is an instigator who is not afraid to be
laughed at, and the meal that is not a meal is nevertheless an intermission in
the life of slavery that illustrates how people who can be bought and sold still
manage to perpetuate brotherhood and joy. The gatherings at the foot of
Brother are a laboratory for dialogic freedom, where they engage in two-
sided acts of conversation, teasing, and advice that coauthor various schemes
for cooking potatoes and who knows what else. In the process, they entertain
each other by deliberating from multiple perspectives in a public arena that is
their own creation.

## THE CHAIN GANG

After Sixo, who before the advent of Schoolteacher spent many nights exploring the countryside beyond Sweet Home, learns about a group from the
Underground Railroad planning to escape north, and he persuades the other
slaves to seize this opportunity. It is a good plan, calling for them to listen for
a signal, then to meet in the cornfield by the creek. Some of them, including
Sethe's children, succeed in linking up with the escaping slaves. But the plot
is discovered, and most of the slaves are caught, some killed. Sixo dies
heroically and defiantly, laughing. In the case of Paul D, one of the men who
gathered at the foot of Brother to eat Sixo's undercooked potatoes, the escape
attempt leads to a chain gang in Alfred, Georgia. If the conditions for dialogic freedom were limited at Sweet Home, they are all but nonexistent on the
chain gang. Every morning forty-six men emerge from the solitary confinement of underground cages to stand in a trench running in front of them,
while they thread a chain through the loops in their leg irons. Then the guards
take their pleasure. "Occasionally a kneeling man chose a gunshot to the
head as the price, maybe, of taking a bit of foreskin with him to Jesus." Only
one black man is allowed to speak, and he shouts, "Hiii!," giving a mighty

yank on the chain, "the signal that let the prisoners rise up off their knees and dance two-step to the music of hand-forged iron" (108).

Eighty-six days into this purgatory, incessant, heavy rains bring work to a standstill: "It was decided to lock everybody down in the boxes till it either stopped raining or lightened up so a whiteman could walk, damnit, without flooding his gun and the dogs could quit shivering" (109). The slaves are chained together and left in their cages along the trench, where the water keeps rising, above their ankles, above the planks they sleep on. Suddenly mud oozes "under and through the bars," as the ditch caves in:

> It started like the chain-up but the difference was the power of the chain. One by one, from Hi Man back on down the line, they dove. Down through the mud under the bars, blind, groping. Some had sense enough to wrap their heads in shirts, cover their faces with rags, put on their shoes. Others just plunged, simply ducked down and pushed out, fighting up, reaching for air. Some lost direction, and their neighbors, feeling the confused pull of the chain, snatched them around. For one lost, all lost. The chain that held them would save them all or none, and Hi Man was the Delivery. They talked through that chain like Sam Morse and, Great God, they all came up. (110)

Men who have been deprived not only of freedom and dignity, but of language itself, find a way here to transmute the chain that enslaves them into an instrument of communication and escape. Diverse as their reactions are, some diving in the wrong direction, the steady yank from the chain pulls them all through. Chained together, they know that there will be no escaping alone. Either they all will make it or none will.

In terms of dialogic freedom, these slaves operate from multiple perspectives, some shared, some not. Unshared perspectives might involve the individual families they have been torn from, their various experiences of kind or unkind masters, and the educations they have gained in language and work. Their shared perspectives involve their lives as chained workers, prisoners in solitary confinement, sexual abuse victims, and people denied spoken language. Above all, they are men who want to live and be free. Even before the rain started they knew they had to be particularly careful, "for if one pitched and ran—all, all forty-six, would be yanked by the chain that bound them and no telling who or how many would be killed. A man could risk his own life, but not his brother's. So the eyes said, 'Steady now,' and 'Hang by me'" (109). Thus, a major shared value for these men is their sense of interdependence. It is this value, which they all feel answerable to, that coauthors their plunge down through the mud to freedom, as they "speak" and "listen" through the pull and resistance of the chain. The guards, the rain, and the institution of slavery also coauthor their act, which is a response to these factors. But the driving forces that keep their hopes alive involve answering to each other, to the families they will try to find, and to the values and experiences they share, as they coauthor their mutual decision to dive through the mud. Almost miraculously, from the brutality of the chain gang emerges the resourcefulness that uses slavery's tool, the chain, to promote freedom. Against all odds, these members of the chain gang take action within a field of forces that includes the chaos of mud, the guards' guns, the chain that unites them, and their common desire to escape. Under the most impossible conditions, members of a chain gang in Alfred, Georgia, nurture each other's opportunities for dialogic freedom.

## 124 BLUESTONE ROAD

Conditions for dialogic freedom merely glimpsed near Brother and on the chain gang are on full display at the house at 124 Bluestone Road in Cincinnati, rented by Edwin Bodwin to Sethe's mother-in-law, Baby Suggs. There, former and escaped slaves gather to glean news about lost kin and the issues of the day, while Baby Suggs, the childless matriarch bought into freedom by her slave son, presides over the comings and goings of an endless stream of refugees. Her kitchen becomes the public space where they debate the merits of the Settlement Fee, "catch news, taste oxtail soup, leave their children, cut out a skirt" (149). They discuss "the true meaning of the Fugitive Bill, . . . antislavery, manumission, skin voting, Republicans, Dred Scott, book learning, Sojourner's high-wheeled buggery, the Colored Ladies of Delaware, Ohio, and other weighty issues that held them in chairs, scraping the floorboards or pacing them in agony or exhilaration" (173). These encounters teem with two-sided acts that involve deliberation from multiple perspectives. Much of Morrison's novel is devoted to celebrating this community where people help each other understand the forces for unity and chaos in their world and work together to resist or shape those forces—a community that creates endless opportunities for dialogic freedom. At 124 Bluestone Road, every pair of shoes sewn for an escaped slave, every bowl of soup shared, every issue debated, enhances each participant's ability to see things from a variety of perspectives, make decisions, and coauthor effective action.

A pillar of this community is Stamp Paid, the clandestine agent who ferries escaped slaves, including Sethe and her infant daughter, across the Ohio River. From this community has also emerged an elaborate warning system for slaves on the run, so that ahead of the horses and carriages carrying white people with guns arrives the news that slave catchers are coming. This is the warning system that inexplicably breaks down the day after the giant feast at 124 Bluestone Road, with "twelve turkeys and tubs of strawberry mash," to celebrate Denver's birth, as well as Sethe's escape and reunion with the three children she sent ahead when she decided to stay behind to wait for Halle. Somehow, after a feast that seems to flaunt the good fortune of Baby Suggs's clan, one neighbor after another assumes that someone else must have warned the family that white men with guns were on the way. Thus Morrison presents the tragedy of infanticide not merely as an expression of Sethe's love, but as a failure of community. Neighbors who are answerable to Sethe, and to whom she is answerable, fail to get the message to her that would coauthor an escape that does not happen. Thus, the community that is a breeding ground for dialogic freedom is also the locus of its failure. In *Beloved*, Morrison is not content to blame everything on slavery and the racist views that perpetuate it. Her reality is more complicated, including a young white racist who saves the lives of an escaped slave and her baby, under impossible conditions, and a black community that fails to protect those same people, under conditions where their protection would have been routine.

## THE GHOST THAT MAY NOT BE A GHOST

The title character, Beloved, is the most enigmatic presence in Morrison's novel. It is not clear whether she is a human being or a ghost, and although she coauthors actions of Sethe and Denver, both of whom respond to her, she seems to answer to needs and forces beyond the grasp of anyone in the novel. It is never clear exactly who coauthors her actions, or to what degree she even chooses them. In fact, the novel gives two mutually exclusive explanations for the appearance of a young woman in the yard at 124 Bluestone Road, eighteen years after Sethe's baby's death. This not very coherent woman, sleeping and wheezing, wearing a new dress, her shoelaces untied, may be the baby's ghost come to life. This interpretation, which most readers of *Beloved* embrace, dominates the 1998 movie starring Oprah Winfrey and Danny Glover, which opens in a bath of red light created by the ghost. But there is another possibility. Two years after Morrison's novel appeared, Elizabeth House argued that the title character is not a ghost at all but rather a damaged victim of slavery, abandonment, and sexual abuse. [5] Examining the details of Beloved's stream-of-consciousness, House describes persuasively the step-by-step process by which the character has been enslaved in Africa, transported in the hold of a ship (where a father-figure dies and her mother abandons her by jumping overboard and committing suicide), taken captive by a white man who sexually abused her, then somehow freed. House argues that after Beloved shows up in Sethe's yard they form a bond, but that this bond is experienced differently by each, a product of their separate needs, Sethe's to make up for killing her daughter, Beloved's to find the mother who abandoned her. Thus the girl who calls herself by the name on the baby's tombstone may not be a ghost at all. Instead, she may be the victim of a white man who captured her as a child and sexually abused her for years until she managed to kill him and escape. Stamp Paid explains to Paul D, "Was a girl locked up in a house with a whiteman over by Deer Creek. Found him dead last summer and the girl gone. Maybe that's her. Folks say he had her in there since she was a pup" (235). The novel never clarifies which possibility explains Beloved's sudden appearance in Sethe's yard. She is definitely damaged goods, though, barely able to speak, infantile in her appetites, incapable of seeing from any perspective but her own.

In order to decipher Beloved's identity, a reader needs to make sense of the most difficult passage in the novel, her stream-of-conscious reverie that is all but impossible to follow:

> I see her take flowers away from the leaves she puts them in a round basket the leaves are not for her she fills the basket she opens the grass I would help her but the clouds are in the way how can I say things that are pictures I am not separate from her there is no place where I stop her face is my own and I want to be there in the place where her face is and to be looking at it too a hot thing (210)

This reverie continues with a description of crouching people packed so close together that "there is no room to tremble," including a dead man whose "teeth are pretty white points" (211). There are also "men without skin" who "bring us their morning water to drink" and who "are making loud noises":

> the bread is sea-colored I am too hungry to eat it the sun closes my eyes those able to die are in a pile I cannot find my man the one whose teeth I have loved a hot thing the little hill of dead people a hot thing the men without skin push them through with poles the woman is there with the face I want the face that is mine they fall into the sea which is the color of the bread she has nothing in her ears if I had the teeth of the man who died on my face I would bite the circle around her neck bite it away I know she does not like it (211)

Suddenly "the woman with my face is in the sea." Beloved adds, "they push my own man through they do not push the woman with my face through she goes in they do not push her she goes in" (212).

House argues that Morrison's title character is "simply a young woman who has herself suffered the horrors of slavery" (17). From Beloved's stream-of-consciousness House pieces together the following story:

> White slave traders, "men without skin," captured the girl and her mother as the older woman picked flowers in Africa. . . . She and her mother, along with many other Africans, were then put aboard an abysmally crowded slave ship, given little food and water, and in these inhuman conditions, many blacks died. To escape this living hell, Beloved's mother leaped into the ocean. (18)

With this outline in mind, the details of Beloved's disjointed speech fall into place. "She opens the grass" describes her mother falling down during the capture where "clouds" of gun smoke "are in the way." The child understands that her mother does not like the iron collar they put on her, "the circle" around her neck. In the crowded hold of the ship that transports them to America, "a hot thing" where slaves die, the white crew, who have given them urine to drink, push the bodies of dead slaves through portholes into a sea which is the same color as the moldy bread they give them to eat. The African man with filed teeth is one of those bodies. But the sight seared in Beloved's memory is of her mother ("her face is my own") choosing to commit suicide by jumping overboard rather than to continue in this living hell.

The possibility that Beloved is not a ghost at all, but rather a survivor of capture, transport, abandonment, imprisonment, and sexual abuse, explains much of her odd behavior and also resonates with the book's inscription, "Sixty Million and more," the number of people thought to have perished in the crossings that brought captured Africans to America. Sixty million people may have disappeared with barely a trace, but through the expression of Beloved's disjointed thoughts Morrison allows their voices to be imagined. Part Two of Morrison's novel begins, "124 was loud" (169). Inside the house is "a conflagration of hasty voices—loud, urgent, all speaking at once" (172). These are the voices that include the chaotic fragments of Beloved's reverie, through which Morrison allows us to piece together what might have happened to some of the sixty million and more. In Beloved Morrison also presents us with a person so damaged by watching her mother jump overboard, and by her captivity, that she might well fixate on Sethe as her lost mother, as she does when she says, "Sethe went into the sea" (214).

Sethe encourages Beloved to see her as her mother, because Sethe has just as strong a need to reconnect with her lost daughter as Beloved has to find her lost mother. Their mutual need is reinforced by Denver, who takes Beloved to be her lost sister. Thus the three women coauthor the narrative that Beloved is the ghost of the lost child. From this perspective it does not matter whether Beloved really is that ghost, since her presence haunts Sethe and Denver as if she were, even as it expresses the suffering of captured Africans silenced in the crossings. Through Beloved's reverie, Morrison presents these irreparable losses, as well as the consciousness of a person who is too damaged to recover from her injuries. When we take into consideration that Beloved cannot form a coherent picture of what she sees, and that she represents two mutually exclusive realities, it is not so surprising that her thoughts are presented in a way that stretches the very limits of a reader's ability to comprehend.

Whether Beloved is a ghost, as presented in the 1998 movie, or a person, as argued by House, once Sethe comes to regard her as her lost daughter, the relationship between them is so charged with reciprocal needs—Sethe's to make up for, and Beloved's to be made up to—that virtually every communication is forced to mean both what its speaker must say and what its listener must hear, whether or not these two sets of needs overlap enough to create a shared coherence. Everything Beloved says, sees, does, or experiences is an answer to the mother who abandoned her, which she takes Sethe to be. Beloved hungers obsessively for the identity, protection, and love long since absent and impossible now to make up for by the mother she thinks has returned. Everything she says anticipates the response of Sethe as that mother. With increasingly similar levels of obsession, Sethe, too, comes to answer only to Beloved. In everything she does, she anticipates Beloved's response as her reincarnated baby. Each is thus the superaddressee the other imagines as the perfect listener, yet both are inadequate to that role, unable to hear what is being said or to respond in the way being demanded. The narratives of Sethe and Beloved overlap just enough to perpetuate misunderstanding and to narrow rather than enlarge the sphere of activity for each character.

Beloved's narrative of the abandoned, molested child calls with unstoppable, finalizing, centripetal force, according to which Sethe, her rediscovered mother, is her only addressee, and their life together is reduced to one epistemological layer where Beloved experiences insatiable hunger and Sethe tries in vain to satisfy it. Despite her best efforts, Sethe is oblivious to this narrative of abandonment, immersed in her own narrative of desperate love. For both characters speech is a two-sided act, but the imagined perfect listener is not capable of listening. Each person is merely snatching from confused conversation the bits that can be absorbed into her own perspective. The conversation between Beloved and Sethe is thus the consequence of each one reducing life to a single, centripetal, unified, finalized, monologic epistemological layer. What they have in common is that at this moment they both inhabit an arena where, if there is any dialogic freedom at all, it is minimal.

Just after Beloved's confusing reverie about her capture, abandonment, and abuse, Morrison presents fragments of the mingled voices of Beloved and Sethe, which reflect their separate understandings. The speakers are not identified. Readers can identify them only by what they say and how they react to each other:

> Do you forgive me? Will you stay? You safe here now.
> Where are the men without skin?
> Out there. Way off.
> Can they get in here?
> No. They tried once, but I stopped them. They won't ever come back.
> One of them was in the house I was in. He hurt me.
> They can't hurt us no more. (215)

The first speaker is Sethe. She asks Beloved's forgiveness and implores her to stay, promising to keep her safe. Beloved responds by asking about the white men on the slave ship, about which Sethe knows nothing. Sethe takes Beloved's question to refer to Schoolteacher and the slave catchers. She assures Beloved that they can't get in the house at 124 Bluestone Road or hurt her any more. They got in once, but Sethe stopped them. Beloved, who knows nothing of this incident, responds with a comment about the man who held her captive. Sethe and Beloved are speaking to each other with promises and pleas, but they are also speaking past each other, because Sethe does not know about the girl held captive in the cabin by the river, and Beloved shows no sign of knowing what Sethe did to make her children safe. Thus, they coauthor each other's speech, but from uniquely different perspectives, without understanding what they are hearing or how they are being heard. Both Beloved and Sethe impose the unity of coherence on their conversation, but their unifying viewpoints are mutually exclusive.

Sethe is as committed to making up for the past as Beloved is to making her make up for the past, and this mutual need is strong enough to allow them to continue along their mutually exclusive paths, inhabiting their different ways of knowing, rarely intersecting. Thus these characters enter into conversations filled with misunderstandings that perpetuate the separate narratives in which they are trapped.

> Beloved accused her of leaving her behind. Of not being nice to her, not smiling at her. She said they were the same, had the same face, how could she have left her? And Sethe cried, saying she never did, never meant to—that she had to get them out, away, that she had the milk all the time and had the money too for the stone but not enough. That her plan was always that they would all be together on the other side, forever. Beloved wasn't interested. She said when she cried there was no one. That dead men lay on top of her. That she had nothing to eat. Ghosts without skin stuck their fingers in her and said beloved in the dark and bitch in the light. Sethe pleaded for forgiveness. (241–42)

Here two narratives swirl together like oil and water. Beloved is obsessed by her mother's shipboard suicide, "leaving her behind." This event is not part of Sethe's narrative, however, so she denies abandonment, saying "she never did." Sethe focuses instead on her rationale for killing the baby she was still carrying milk for in her breasts, the one she wanted to protect by taking her to "the other side," the one she provided a headstone for, in the only way she could, after there was no longer any need for milk. Because Sethe's counternarrative is not part of Beloved's story, Beloved is not interested in it, and she drifts back into memories of being on the ship, under piles of the dead, until white men, "ghosts without skin," select her to sexually abuse.

Talking past each other characterizes the dialogue between Sethe and Beloved and reflects the minimal possibilities of freedom in a totally determined world of need. Here the word is still a two-sided act, but instead of enriching each other's lives by putting their stories next to each other, Sethe and Beloved reduce each other to unheard voices, the condition Bakhtin most associates with despair. Their lack of freedom is particularly ironic, in that from a negative liberty perspective one could argue that at this point in the novel the inhabitants of 124 Bluestone Road are most free: from Sethe's job, from outsiders coming in the house, even from Denver, Sethe's other daughter, who is increasingly cut out of the games between her and Beloved. They can do as they please, and are thus free in that sense, but their desires go unheard by each other and unfulfilled. The most disturbing irony of their situation is that Beloved has lived the imprisonment and sexual abuse that Sethe saved her own daughter from by cutting her throat.

## DANGERS OF EMPATHY

Sethe's attempts to make things up to Beloved can be viewed in terms of Bakhtin's concept of empathy discussed in earlier chapters. According to him, this emotional identification with someone else is a good thing, within limits. It calls on us to "penetrate" the consciousness of another "and almost merge or become one with him from within." But he warns against "pure empathizing," "experiencing another's suffering as one's own," which he calls "pathological"—"an infection with another's suffering, and nothing more." To him "pure empathizing" creates a kind of emotional black hole that threatens to suck the observer into the helplessness of suffering itself, a process that is self-destructive. The important thing is to experience another's suffering "precisely as *his* suffering," so that my reaction is not "a cry of pain" but a "word of consolation or an act of assistance."[6] This more restrained capacity, which Bakhtin calls "sympathetic understanding" requires a "return into ourselves" (AH, 102). He explains, "I empathize actively into an individuality and, consequently, I do not lose myself completely nor my unique place outside it, even for a moment."[7]

Sethe's ministrations to Beloved are filled with empathy, as she showers her with love and tries to make up for her own desperate attempt to save her daughter from slavery. These ministrations are also filled with misunderstandings, as their mutually exclusive narratives swirl past each other. Eventually, her efforts to answer only to Beloved—to meet her unmeetable needs, closing out the rest of the world, including her other daughter—exhaust Sethe and take her to the verge of starvation. Certain that Beloved is her murdered daughter come back to life, she enters into what she takes to be Beloved's suffering, experiencing it as her own with a kind of "pure empathizing" that Bakhtin would consider pathological. Even though, if House's reading of the novel is correct, Sethe misjudges the true nature and sources of Beloved's suffering, she nevertheless gives herself up completely to her experience of it. Thus, she winds up "infected" by it, unable to help Beloved, not just because she has no understanding of the loss Beloved has suffered on the slave ship, but because she has no ability to "return" to herself. She is unable to "read" Beloved as Kafka would have a reader read a book, "brought back to oneself by the closing of the book . . . with a clearer head," remaining behind "in one's own being, which has been newly discovered, newly shaken up and seen for a moment from the distance."[8] By the time Sethe has lost her job, exhausted her meager savings, given Beloved all her food, and used up her last reserves of emotional energy trying to explain what cannot be explained, she has also lost her "unique place" outside Beloved's damaged world, confined, like Beloved, to one epistemological layer of need.

Beloved remains trapped within her narrow experience, until she disappears at the end of the novel. Sethe, however, has the potential to avoid this fate. She has the potential not to succumb to the "pure empathizing," which has reduced her dialogic freedom nearly to zero and has almost killed her. While Beloved was never part of a world that could be called political—because she either died or was enslaved as a baby—Sethe was once immersed in a world among other people, until she cut herself off from it. At Sweet Home, before Schoolteacher's arrival, she was part of a slave community that celebrated Sixo's failed culinary experiments with baked potatoes, and after Schoolteacher's arrival found a way to escape, debated the merits of the plan, and reached a decision to act. At 124 Bluestone Road, before the infanticide, Sethe led her life among ex-slaves who gathered in Baby Suggs's kitchen, which was both their university and their public square, where they discussed political issues and coauthored the choices that were most important. Baby Suggs's yard was where they celebrated Sethe's escape and Denver's birth by holding a public feast. This world of others coauthored Sethe's infanticide by failing to warn her that Schoolteacher was approaching. By shunning her afterwards, it then coauthored her retreat into a life of isolation. The crisis precipitated by Beloved's arrival, in which Sethe nearly disappears into "pure empathy," now presents an opportunity for this community, which had failed Sethe in the past, to find redemption in the present by reaching out to her with "sympathetic understanding."

## EXORCISM

Desperate to prevent her mother from starving, the eighteen-year-old Denver musters the courage to leave the yard at 124 Bluestone Road and seek help.

In response to her request for food, women who had shunned Sethe "when she got out of jail and made no gesture toward anybody, and lived as though she were alone" (256), begin by sending over a loaf of bread or a basket of eggs and end up banding together one day to exorcise the ghost that has all but killed Sethe. While Denver waits on the porch for Bodwin to pick her up for her new job, the women who failed long ago to warn Sethe about the slave catchers coming to get her, gather to approach her house:

> Some brought what they could and what they believed would work. Stuffed in apron pockets, strung around their necks, lying in the space between their breasts. Others brought Christian faith—as shield and sword. Most brought a little of both. They had no idea what they would do when they got there. They just started out, walked down Bluestone Road and came together at the agreed-upon time. The heat kept a few women who promised to go home. Others who believed the story didn't want any part of the confrontation and wouldn't have come no matter what the weather. And there were those like Lady Jones who didn't believe the story and hated the ignorance of those who did. (257)

This is a diverse group, some Christian, some not, some believing the story of the ghost, some not. With various explanations of what might be going on inside 124 Bluestone Road, they do not attempt to forge a consensus about what Beloved represents or who she is. They do not even have a plan about what they are going to do once they reach the house, or how to use their faith or their superstition as a "sword" or "shield" to protect Sethe or them from the presence that might or might not be a ghost. They just know that Sethe has suffered enough. Their shared desire to help Sethe re-consecrates as a public space the yard in front of 124 Bluestone Road. If dialogic freedom is a two-sided act that involves deliberation from multiple perspectives, within a field of forces for unity and chaos, this public exorcism is to be a multi-sided act, coauthored by Sethe, Beloved, and these women.

As they get closer to the house, the women see not the present but the past. They remember their younger selves at the feast that celebrated Denver's birth, where they ate catfish, German potato salad, and cobbler—where they "sat on the porch, ran down to the creek, teased the men, hoisted children on their hips or, if they were the children, straddled the legs of old men who held their little hands while giving them a horsey ride." They no longer feel "the envy that surfaced" the day after that feast. Coming to help the woman they have shunned for eighteen years, they are now reconnecting with themselves and the values they shared when Baby Suggs "laughed and skipped among them, urging more" (258). Maybe they remember the sermons Baby used to give in the clearing deep in the woods behind the house. This "unchurched preacher" had preached an unusual message:

> She did not tell them to clean up their lives or to go and sin no more. She did not tell them that they were the blessed of the earth, its inheriting meek or its glorybound pure. She told them that the only grace they could have was the grace they could imagine. That if they could not see it, they would not have it. (88)

Instead of urging them to endure their suffering and defer happy times to some future paradise, Baby Suggs urged them to manufacture their own grace right now, and above all "to love your heart. For this is the prize." To her, the most important thing was not a gift passively expected from God, but the "grace" actively imagined by every one of them, in the form of love.

As thirty women approach Sethe's house eighteen years after the event that caused Baby Suggs to give up preaching and lie down to die, they work together to create the grace that they can imagine. Praying, chanting, singing, they have come to exorcise the ghost. Sethe is busy breaking a lump of ice into chunks for Beloved, and she drops the ice pick into her apron as she goes with Beloved to the doorway, drawn by the women's voices, "a wave of sound wide enough to sound deep water and knock the pods off chestnut trees" (261). Denver is sitting on the steps. At this moment Edward Bodwin rides up in his cart. Suddenly Sethe is taken back eighteen years to the moment when Schoolteacher rode up and all she could think to do was put as many of her babies as possible where they would be safe forever from slavery. The same urge to protect them wells up in her now, but instead of picking up a saw to use on her daughter's throat, she grabs the ice pick in her pocket to use on Bodwin. When Sethe drops Beloved's hand to run at the man coming for her child, Beloved relives the abandonment she felt on the slave ship when her mother jumped overboard. At that moment she runs into the crowd and disappears like an exorcised ghost. Meanwhile, Sethe alters her old narrative even as she relives it, turning her violence not on her children, but on the white man coming to take one of them away. Fortunately for Bodwin, Denver and the women who have gathered in front of the house intervene. They grab Sethe before she can stab Bodwin, who, as oblivious as Amasa Delano on the *San Dominick*, does not even notice that she has tried to kill him.

Thus the community that once failed to coauthor Sethe's escape from Schoolteacher and the slave catchers coauthors her rescue. In the process they exorcise the spiritual ghost of their past failure to be there when Sethe needed them most. Yet, when Sethe experiences Bodwin's arrival to pick up Denver for work as the arrival of Schoolteacher to enslave her and her children, the women assembled in front of her house face a new imperative: not just to save Sethe or her children, but to save the white man who has come in her yard. To put it another way, caught in the midst of the paradigm shift that allows Sethe to turn her violence not on her child this time, but rather on the man she thinks has come to take her "best thing," the community that failed Sethe in the past, saves her now not by stopping the white man but by saving him and hence preventing Sethe from doing something that would land her in prison. When Sethe lunges at Bodwin, she exorcises the ghost of her past decision to turn her capacity for violence not on the slave catcher but on her children. When the community intervenes to prevent Sethe from stabbing Bodwin, they exorcise the ghost of their past failure to prevent the conditions that made Sethe's infanticide seem like the only option. In the confusion of bodies lunging and falling, different perspectives are experienced, among them Beloved reliving her abandonment by her mother, when Sethe runs from her, and Sethe reliving the loss of her daughter, when Beloved disappears. This second loss of Beloved, like Orpheus's second loss of Eurydice, is almost too much for her to bear. She takes to bed as Baby Suggs had, ready to die.

## RETURNING TO LIFE AMONG OTHER PEOPLE

After almost killing Bodwin—the abolitionist who rented 124 Bluestone Road to Baby Suggs, got Sethe out of jail after the murder, and eighteen years later offered Denver a job—Sethe collapses in the same bed where Baby Suggs, her mother-in-law, took ten years to die. She expects to follow the same path, because without Beloved she feels like she has lost her "best thing" (272). Paul D, Denver, and the community of ex-slaves who shunned her after the murder have other plans, though. Whereas Beloved's arena for knowing the world was reduced to one kind of obsessive miscommunication with Sethe, Sethe's arena is not so finalized. True, she has closed herself off in a world of "pure empathy" with Beloved, but now her surviving daughter and the community join forces to call her back to herself and to a life among other people. A desperate Denver reaches out for food, starting a trail of attention that leads to the job offer from Bodwin, an exorcism, and the return of Paul D, the last of the Sweet Home men, who had spent eighteen years tracking down Sethe, then abandoned her when he found out about the infanticide.

Paul D had left after he heard from Sethe's own lips what she had done. Stamp Paid, having decided that it was wrong for the last man from Sweet Home to be the only person in Cincinnati who was ignorant of Sethe's past, had presented Paul D with an old, faded clipping from the local newspaper. Unable to read the article and also certain that there must be some mistake, Paul D had shown the clipping to Sethe, eager for her to share a laugh at the error of it all. Instead, he heard for the first time what she had never told anyone else, the story of what happened that day:

> She was squatting in the garden and when she saw them coming and recognized schoolteacher's hat, she heard wings. Little hummingbirds. . . . And if she thought anything, it was No. No. Nonono. Simple. She just flew. Collected every bit of life she had made, all the parts of her that were precious and fine and beautiful, and carried, pushed, dragged them through the veil, out, away, over there where no one could hurt them. (163)

Paul D listens, but the man who has walked across five states just to find this woman, and who has made her feel loved, does not understand the explanation. The whole idea that she "talked about safety with a handsaw" is more than he can fathom. He tells her, "Your love is too thick," and "You got two feet, Sethe, not four" (165). He probably meant something like, "Surely there was another alternative!" His words come into the world already loaded with meaning, though, and what Sethe registers is a defection to the enemy. She hears the centripetal, finalizing voice of Schoolteacher, the slave catcher, who had his nephews list her animal and human characteristics. When Paul D counts her feet Sethe hears him affirming that all along Schoolteacher was right: she was less than human. When Paul D returns after Sethe's failed attack on Bodwin and after Beloved's disappearance, he finds a Sethe who has given up on life but not forgotten his remark. He asks, "Is it all right, Sethe, if I heat up some water?" She asks, "And count my feet?" He responds, "Rub your feet" (272). Here the layers of meaning stretch in several directions: to their previous conversion, in response to which Paul D is saying "I'm sorry"; to Sethe's first days at 124 Bluestone Road, when Baby Suggs, holy, bathed the feet that had been mangled in her escape, showering her with love that proved "the only grace they could have was the grace they could imagine" (88); and to Sethe's eighteen-year struggle to beat back the past and hold on to her sense of humanity.

Years after Baby Suggs, unable to "approve or condemn Sethe's rough choice" (180), had "proved herself a liar" (89) and traded her own gospel of hope and love for a desire to die, Sethe has elected the same path. Paul D resists, shouting, "Don't you die on me!" (271). Taking up fragments of Baby Suggs's sermon in the clearing, where she had said "Love your heart, for this is the prize" (89), and remembering that this is the woman who never mentioned or looked at his "neck jewelry," the woman he wants to "put his story next to," he tells Sethe, "You your best thing, Sethe. You are" (273). This simple phrase is rich with meaning. It acknowledges the love that led Sethe to kill her own child. It acknowledges her resourcefulness in escaping slavery and giving birth on the run. It acknowledges her tolerance for pain and her descent into Beloved's damaged world and the "pure empathy" that almost kills Sethe. It acknowledges the force of Baby Suggs's sermons in the clearing. It also acknowledges Paul D's survival of the chain gang, his other humiliations and losses, and his hope that, as the Thirty-Mile Woman did for

Sixo, she will help him "gather the pieces that I am" and "give them back to me in the right order" (272). Above all, this small phrase acknowledges the degree to which placing their stories next to each other will enlarge rather than narrow their choices, freeing them to confront the worst and embrace life. In Hannah Arendt's words, by telling Sethe she is her own "best thing," Paul D invokes the "freedom to call something into being which did not exist before."[9]

In terms of dialogic freedom, this conversation between Paul D and Sethe is the opposite of the cryptic exchange above between Beloved and Sethe. Whereas Beloved finalizes Sethe in a conversation where neither is truly heard, closing her off in a self-destructive world of pure suffering, Paul D opens possibilities for a Sethe who can now be heard. She no longer needs to beat back the past, to fear what he, or her dead mother-in-law, or her disappeared husband, Halle, or her surviving daughter, or the community, or she herself, might think of her rough choice. This is not because she has put the past behind her or succeeded in forgetting it, but because she can now hope to face it. All she says in response is "Me? Me?" but in that question she relinquishes the certainty and finality of death in favor of an open-endedness that holds hope for a future. As she and Paul D put their stories next to each other, coauthoring intersecting narratives, a rich range of centrifugal and centripetal forces will be unleashed by memories of Sweet Home, escape, misery, and the aftermath.

In this process the centripetal force for unification will take many forms, among them the epic saga of Sixo, who refused in the end to speak English and died laughing, the degrading image of a broken-down Halle with butter smeared on his face, and the conflation of Schoolteacher with Bodwin, which provoked Sethe to try to kill not her child, but the man she thought had come to take them both back to slavery. Each of these stories reflects an effort to unify the centrifugal elements of prosaic reality into a narrative, complete with various perspectives of speakers, addressees, and superaddressees. As these narratives and perspectives accumulate in the two-sided act of putting their stories next to each other, the layers of knowing open to Sethe and Paul D expand. In tension with their unifying efforts to create meaning together will be the centrifugal force of memories so damaging and intense that they can be overwhelming. Yet, when she puts her story next to his, and he puts his story next to hers, each will, in the telling, as Denver has done with her own birth story, unify chaotic material, while the other coauthors just by listening. In these stories Halle, Baby Suggs, Sethe's children, Paul's chain gang, and the community of ex-slaves all pull in different directions, as do the threads of history and culture that touch the storytellers, so that the tension between unifying and chaotic forces becomes a rich continuum of possibilities that are never final. Thus, the ending of *Beloved* celebrates Sethe's and Paul D's abilities to enlarge and maximize the layers of knowing within which they operate. In the process, it holds the hope and expectation that Sethe will reenter the larger community that has coauthored both her crisis and her survival. At the end of the novel, Sethe can hope once again to become one of those who take part in conversations, debates, and decisions within this renewed community. At the same time, the ending of the novel resonates with the horror of Beloved's lack of dialogic freedom, her inability to navigate beyond her own finalized perspective, even as she mysteriously disappears.

## READING WITH DIALOGIC FREEDOM

One of the most remarkable things about *Beloved* is the window it provides on imagining life as experienced by the victims of slavery. Whether what we see is people laughing about under- or over-cooked potatoes at the foot of Brother, men pulling each other through the oozing mud of the chain gang, two "throw-away women" making sure a child gets born, a community gathered around a kitchen table to discuss politics and life, captives subjected to the unspeakable horrors of the middle passage, the chaos of an exorcism, or the many attitudes various characters take toward Sethe's infanticide, Morrison enables readers of *Beloved* to imagine points of view that to twentieth- and twenty-first-century minds have been largely unimaginable. In *Beloved* Morrison gives readers an opportunity to see not just the debilitated judgment that traps Garner in his paternalistic narcissism, that causes the Bodwins to regard Sethe as savage, or that inspires Schoolteacher to try to recover his lost property, but also to see and feel what victims of slavery saw and felt. By allowing readers to experience sometimes contradictory, even mutually exclusive, perspectives on Sethe's infanticide, *Beloved* expands our ability to navigate among the ways of knowing entailed in each of these different perspectives, as fish navigate different layers of the sea. At times, as in the reveries of Sethe and Beloved, or during the exorcism of the ghost, characters coauthor and experience mutually exclusive realities that can be sorted out, if at all, only by the reader described by Kafka, "crouching forgotten in a corner of the room where he can participate all the more intensely in what is happening there."[10]

Furthermore, by giving us at the end of *Beloved* the experience of watching Paul D's perspective on Sethe's desperate act expand before our very eyes, Morrison allows us to witness dialogic freedom in the making. We share this process of expansion to the extent that we, like Paul D, find infanticide impossible to fathom; to the extent that we, like Baby Suggs, find it difficult to approve or condemn; and to the extent that we, like Sethe, cannot begin to imagine allowing our own children to be bought and sold. Thus Morrison coauthors her readers' expanding perspectives on one mother's desperation, as well as our willingness in general to try to think about shocking actions from other people's points of view, before we condemn them. In this state of mind we are ready to reread the front-page story about Margaret Garner from the 1856 *Cincinnati Daily Enquirer*. Morrison's invitation to rethink this crime makes us uneasy, and we get the sense that the author, too, is uneasy about it. Her novel ends not with Paul D and Sethe, but with Beloved, who remains a loose end, "disremembered and unaccounted for" (275). It is as if Morrison is saying that although we are freer to the extent that we can see things from others' perspectives, this expansion of perspectives will never be easy. We will encounter suffering we can neither comprehend nor make up for, and there will be perspectives that we can only strain to incompletely share. The more perspectives we are able to see from, however, the freer we will be to navigate the layers of knowing that enable us to coauthor decisions among other human beings. For Morrison, dialogic freedom is an open-ended process and an imperative, not a goal that can ever be finally achieved.

## NOTES

1. Much of the material from this discussion of *Beloved* appears in my article, "Dialogic Freedom: In the 'Sideshadow' of Bakhtin," *Modern Philology* 106, no. 4 (2009): 648–76, used by permission from the University of Chicago Press.

2. Cynthia Griffin Wolff, "Margaret Garner: A Cincinnati Story," *Massachusetts Review* 32, no. 3 (1991): 417–40.

3. Toni Morrison, *Beloved* (New York: Plume, 1987), 164. Citations to *Beloved* are to this text.

4. Elizabeth Hardwick, *Herman Melville* (New York: Viking, 2000), 106.

5. Elizabeth House, "Toni Morrison's Ghost: The Beloved Who Is Not Beloved," *Studies in American Fiction* 18 (1990): 17.

6. Mikhail Bakhtin, "Author and Hero in Aesthetic Activity," *Art and Answerability: Early Philosophical Essays by M. M. Bakhtin*, ed. Michael Holquist and Vadim Liapunov; tr. Vadim Liapunov (Austin: University of Texas Press, 1990), 26. Citations to "Author and Hero in Aesthetic Activity" are to this text, with the abbreviation AH.

7. Bakhtin, *Toward a Philosophy of the Act*, ed. Vadim Liapunov and Michael Holquist; tr Vadim Liapunov (Austin: University of Texas, 1993), 15.

8. Frank Kafka, *The Diaries of Franz Kafka: 1910–1913*, ed. Max Brod; trans. Joseph Kresh (New York: Schocken, 1948), 74.

9. Hannah Arendt, "What Is Freedom?" In *Between Past and Future: Eight Exercises in Political Thought*, 1954 (Reprint, New York: Viking Press, 1968), 151.

10. Franz Kafka, "Letter to Oscar Baum 1921," *Letters to Friends, Family, and Editors*, trans. Richard Winston and Clara Winston (New York: Schocken, 1977), 276.

## Chapter Ten

# Freedom under Construction in a Polarized World

> Dialogic freedom: A two-sided act, chosen within a field of unifying and fragmenting forces along a continuum of minimal to maximal layers of knowing that are never final.

In our attempts to ponder the many hot-button issues of our day, we each answer to multiple voices, real and imagined, the sheer number of which would lead to chaos if we tried to listen to all of them at once. In fact, on a daily basis we all engage in a sifting and focusing process, as we seek to balance the desire for unified explanations with the chaos of a world that resists our efforts at meaning making. In this process, we are constantly tempted to simplify and reject the alien perspectives of others. The problem is not that we disagree, but that we disagree dismissively, satisfied that we already know enough about our opponent's position. Like the racism explored by Melville and Morrison, this "polarism" prevents us from seeing what is happening before our eyes and interferes with our ability to choose well. Opponents often have little interest in understanding why someone else might believe differently, or how a good person might reach different conclusions. When we do make an effort to learn more about an opposing perspective, we do it more out of self-defense, or from a sense of fairness or generosity, than from any thought that our own views, which in any case are settled, might change. This polarized self-confidence has reached epidemic proportions, spread in sound bites, slogans, and various forms of propaganda, all of which undermine our ability to find common ground. Like racism, polarism victimizes those it dismisses as inferior, but it also limits the "polarist" to a narrow way of knowing in which the choices that can be coauthored are restricted to the choices that can be imagined. In that sense it undermines dialogic freedom. It accomplishes this effect invisibly, since a polarized perspective, like a racist perspective, is not likely to recognize itself as narrow.

This book has focused until now on how the concept of dialogic freedom can open new possibilities for reading and discussing literature. In this chapter, I argue that thinking about freedom from a dialogic perspective can also help us find better ways to confront the difficult issues that divide us today. There are plenty of hot-button topics that could illustrate this point, because in the twenty-first century more and more subjects have become almost impossible to discuss: gay marriage, the death penalty, gun control, embryonic stem-cell research, immigration, Islam, terrorism, torture, fiscal responsibility—even what constitutes an acceptable school lunch.[1] I focus here on the issue of abortion because it has been so controversial for so long and because it strikes a raw nerve for many, whether they are pro-life or pro-choice. This issue demonstrates well how viewing freedom as autonomy and enlightenment only exacerbates polarization, as both sides champion the desire to defend a right—to live or to choose—as the only enlightened perspective. The shared focus of pro-life and pro-choice advocates on rights and enlightenment leads to dysfunctional communications that obstruct opportunities for meaningful action. This chapter explores how both sides in the abortion debate promote polarization by thinking about freedom mainly in terms of autonomy and enlightenment, and how rethinking the issue from a dialogic perspective presents opportunities to break through the polar ice.

## RIGHTS AND ENLIGHTENMENT

Protecting freedom as autonomy has led to an obsession with rights. We see this in discussions not just about abortion, but about the right to terminate life, the right to carry a gun, the right to strike, the right to vote, the right to hold office, the right to marry, the right to smoke, the right to worship, and so on. Such thinking tracks expansions or contractions of rights, according to which people are seen as more or less free. The more rights we have, or the more significant these rights, the greater our freedom as autonomy. From a Millian "negative liberty" perspective, rights protect our freedom to do as we please, without interference from others, as long as we don't harm anyone else. This focus on rights helps simplify our thinking by reducing important questions to a matter of which rights are or are not protected, and by focusing on the legal arenas—courts and legislatures—where battles over rights are won and lost. In terms of gay marriage, we urge legislatures to grant gay people the right to marry, or we urge them to uphold the people's right to establish who can and cannot marry. On the issue of capital punishment, we urge courts to uphold an inmate's right to avoid cruel and unusual punishment, or we defend the people's right to impose lawful penalties. In battles waged in legislatures and courtrooms, where the emphasis is not on under-standing each other but on winning, this focus on rights as the guarantors of freedom creates constant pressure to attack enemies and gather support among friends—activities that promote polarization.

Protecting freedom as enlightenment does not in any way undermine this rights-based thinking. In fact, these two views of freedom work hand in hand as people are considered more or less free according to their level of emanci-pation from the illusions of unenlightened opponents who disagree about which rights should be protected. From a Platonic "positive liberty" perspec-tive, education becomes paramount, under the presumption that emancipa-tion comes to those who are exposed to the enlightened thinking of anyone who has escaped the cave of illusion to face the blinding light of Truth. Viewing freedom as enlightenment encourages people to regard education and religion not as opportunities for problem solving and discovery, but as conduits for the transmission of wisdom. In a polarized world, opposing political or religious organizations embrace conflicting visions of enlighten-ment and dismiss opponents as fools. The unholy alliance between rights-based and enlightenment-based views of freedom has led to a dead end, where Republicans and Democrats barely speak to each other, culture wars on campus thwart communication, and airwaves sputter with sound bites and slogans that substitute for thought.

The debate about abortion illustrates well how both sides can embrace views of freedom as autonomy and enlightenment, with polarizing conse-quences. To begin with, both sides focus on rights and presume that an enlightened person should value those rights. A pro-choice advocate supports the majority decision in Roe v. Wade, which protects a woman's right to choose. This advocate regards as enlightened those who reject paternalistic efforts to control women's reproductive decisions. A pro-life advocate seeks instead to protect the rights of unborn children and regards enlightened think-ing as the ability to recognize the sanctity of each potential child's life. If we examine the official publications of either camp, we see their mutual empha-sis on rights and enlightenment. When the National Organization for Women (NOW) was founded in 1966, its "Statement of Purpose" focused on rights: "The time has come to confront, with concrete action, the conditions that now prevent women from enjoying the equality of opportunity and freedom of choice which is their right, as individual Americans, and as human be-ings."[2] Here "freedom of choice," which is autonomy, becomes synonymous with the "right" to choose. A NOW letter from 2005 retains this focus, with an emphasis on abortion: "Now is the time we need to stand together to protect reproductive rights."[3] It calls for readers to support a filibuster to block the appointment to the U.S. Supreme Court of "right-wing fanatics" who threaten to "turn back over 35 years of progress for women's rights" (1). This letter presumes that the recipient is already one of the enlightened who appreciate the progress of the last 35 years, and that those who disagree are unenlightened reactionaries. A press release posted at the NOW website in 2013 referred to the "war on women waged by right-wing extremists," who champion legislation to curb abortions.[4] The implication is that no enlightened person would hold such "extremist" views or seek to limit "reproductive rights" that are "issues of life and death for women."[5]

The National Right to Life Committee (NRLC), formed in 1973 to protest the passage of Roe v. Wade, disagrees completely with NOW's positions on abortion but shares its focus on both rights and enlightenment. The very name of the organization puts rights front and center. Its mission statement explains its purpose, "to restore legal protection to innocent human life."[6] The phrase "innocent human life" implies that any enlightened person would recognize the innocence and humanity of unborn children. Restoring legal protection to these children presumes that such protections were once in place and that only in the unenlightened age post Roe v. Wade have they been stripped away. Commemorating in 2013 the fortieth anniversary of that ruling, NRLC president Carol Tobias said on the website's home page: "Our humanity is not defined by the atrocities that have been committed throughout history, but by the shining light of those who recognize injustice and refuse to be complicit through silence."[7] Here the implication is that any enlightened person would recognize "the shining light" of truth and speak out against the injustices and atrocities sanctioned by forty years of bad law. According to her, "Roe is an assault on the very foundation of our country—the principle that life is the most fundamental of all human rights." She links her organization's mission to the enlightened founding principles of our country, which according to her include the right to life as "the most fundamental of human rights."[8]

Though their goals are diametrically opposed, both the National Organization for Women and the National Right to Life Committee express their positions in terms of protecting rights, and both presume that their members share an enlightened perspective. Both organizations also aim to pass or obstruct legislation, and for both of them the prize will be won or lost in courtrooms, legislatures, or ballot boxes, where rights are protected or eroded. Indeed, in a 5–4 decision released on April 18, 2007, the U.S. Supreme Court upheld the Partial Birth Abortion Ban Act passed by Congress in 2003, alarming pro-choice advocates and encouraging pro-life advocates, that one day Roe v. Wade may be reversed.[9] The majority opinion, written by Justice Kennedy, held that the congressional act of 2003 does not impose "an undue burden on a woman's right to an abortion."[10] Kennedy also explained that "whether to have an abortion requires a difficult and painful moral decision which some women come to regret" (6). In a summary of her dissent, Justice Ginsburg took exception to what she regarded as Kennedy's paternalistic attitude toward women, which "reflects ancient notions about women's place in the family and under the Constitution—ideas that have long since been discredited."[11] She defended "the right to reproductive choice," objecting that in this decision "the court deprives women of the right to make an autonomous choice," chipping away at a "right declared again and again by this court."[12]

Here, both the majority opinion and the dissent focus on rights and enlightenment. Both specifically reference a woman's right to an abortion under Roe v. Wade, and implicit in the discussion about what a woman might come to regret are conflicting ideas about what constitutes an enlightened view of "women's place in the family and under the Constitution." While those who oppose this ruling lament the restrictions it imposes on a woman's right to choose, those who endorse it celebrate its defense of the rights of the unborn. The problem with this focus on winning or losing a struggle for rights, shared by opposing camps who both consider themselves enlightened—a problem reflected in both the majority opinion and the dissent—is that it undermines the dialogic freedom of both pro-choice and pro-life advocates, by encouraging people to be dismissive of the perspectives of others, to consider the important questions as already settled, and to be blind to potential common ground. Under these conditions, a pro-choice advocate might examine the views of a pro-life advocate, or vice versa, but when opponents in the abortion debate do this, the goal is more often than not to strengthen their own arguments by becoming more familiar with those of the opposition, not to reexamine the basis for their own thinking.

This tendency to dismiss contrary ideas is only exacerbated by what advocates on either side will find if they happen to visit each other's websites. At the NRLC website there are detailed reports on the legal battles about "partial-birth abortion."[13] Readers can also download graphic descriptions of "the pain of the unborn."[14] The language used in these descriptions is calculated to appeal to an enlightened pro-life advocate and to offend an unenlightened pro-choice advocate, who would resent the phrase "partial-birth abortion" as inflammatory and inaccurate, as well as the phrase "unborn humans," as opposed to "fetuses." In 2012 the home page of the NRLC website included the headline, "Obama and 168 House Members Defend Single-Sex Abortion," words calculated to fire up supporters and infuriate critics.[15] At the NOW website is similarly inflammatory material: detailed reports on legal battles about "health care providers" who are "targets of domestic terror," as well as information about "emergency contraception."[16] The murder of one such physician, Dr. George Tiller, at a Wichita church on May 31, 2009, is called "terrorism."[17] In 2012 the website called on women to sign up to "speak out against anti-abortion terrorism."[18] The repeated use of the word "terrorism" is calculated to appeal to enlightened pro-choice advocates and to offend unenlightened pro-life critics, who might resent equating violence against abortion clinics with terrorism, or using euphemisms like "emergency contraception." For both NOW and the NRLC, an opponent who visits the other side's website will come away angry, threatened, and more resolved than ever to pursue the relevant quest for rights. Hence both websites contribute to the polarization that undermines dialogic freedom.

No wonder, then, that by the time the fortieth anniversary of Roe v. Wade rolled around in 2012, both sides in the debate were more committed than ever to their efforts to prevail in courtrooms and legislatures. According to Emily Le Coz of the *Huffington Post*, during 2011, as that anniversary approached, sixty anti-abortion laws passed in twenty-four states.[19] The Guttmacher Institute calls 2011 "a year for the record books," because states passed 92 provisions to restrict access to abortions, "eclipsing the previous record of 34 in 2005."[20] Not too surprisingly, this flurry of legislation is interpreted differently by pro-life and pro-choice advocates. Mary Spaulding Balch, director of the NRLC department for state legislation, trumpeted the need to protect women from "circuit rider" abortion providers who touch down in a state to perform procedures, then take off as soon as they are done.[21] Jordon Goldberg, the state advocacy counsel for the Center for Reproductive Rights, disagreed, calling these laws "a seismic attack on reproductive rights" at a time when anti-government sentiment has come to dominate state legislatures.[22] A press release at the NOW website argues that 2013 is a "critical turning point. . . . Public support for Roe v. Wade is even stronger right now than it was just two years ago. The right wing's escalated attacks on women's access to reproductive health care have backfired."[23] Whatever the long-term prognosis for access to abortions in the United States, the large number of laws debated, passed, vetoed, or otherwise acted upon in state legislatures across the country forty years after Roe v. Wade indicates that the battle is far from over.

I do not mean to suggest that in this struggle no one seeks common ground between pro-choice and pro-life positions, but rather that these polarized positions do not encourage such efforts. If communication is to take place on this subject, it will happen in spite of, not because of, organizations devoted to rights and enlightenment, and the legislation they champion. One such effort can be glimpsed in a 2005 article from the Guttmacher Institute, "Reasons U.S. Women Have Abortions," which is cited by both NOW and NRLC websites as a good source of information. The mission of the Guttmacher Institute, "to protect the reproductive choices of all women and men in the United States and throughout the world,"[24] reflects the pro-choice orientation of NOW, but the National Right to Life Committee website nonetheless cites the article as a reliable source of information about the 22% reduction in U.S. abortions between 1987 and 2002.[25] The Guttmacher study goes beyond rights-based and enlightenment-based thinking to help people understand why each year 1.3 million women choose to end a pregnancy with abortion. Observing that "public discussion about abortion in the United States has generally focused on . . . who should be allowed to have abortions, under what circumstances,"[26] the authors lament the rights-oriented focus of current debate. They focus instead on the reasons why women have abortions. The article notes that although "the abortion rate declined by 22% between 1987 and 2002," abortions increased among non-whites (from 39% to 50%) and the poor (from 50% to 60%) during that same period (110). Of the 1,209 women responding to their written survey in 2004, 73% gave as a reason for abortion, "I can't afford a baby now" (112).

In addition to their written survey, the authors conducted interviews that gave thirty-eight women an opportunity to elaborate on their reasons for choosing abortion. One nineteen-year-old with three children said, "It's a sin to bring the child here and not be able to provide for it" (115). In the word "sin" we hear her religion, in the word "provide," we hear her poverty, both of which coauthor her decision, among other coauthors not here acknowledged (the father, friends, family). A twenty-two-year-old below the poverty line said, "I am alone with three kids, and they are all I have. It's hard . . . you can't get food, you know." A thirty-year-old with two children, also below the poverty line, said, "There is just no way I could be the wonderful parent to all three of them and still have enough left over to keep the house clean and make sure the bills are paid and I'm in bed on time so I can be at work on time. It's impossible" (117). In these interviews more than one-third of the women "volunteered that they had considered adoption and concluded that it was a morally unconscionable option because giving one's child away is wrong" (117). These statistics and narratives suggest that even with a falling abortion rate, financial pressures play a growing role in women's decisions to get abortions, racial inequities exacerbate these problems, and resistance to adoption is strong. The implication here is that some of the energy now spent on litigating to safeguard a woman's right to choose or an unborn's right to live might be better spent listening to the voices of the women who actually get abortions, trying to understand the forces for unity and chaos in their worlds, and promoting economic and social opportunities that expand the choices they can coauthor, including adoption.

To some extent this effort to hear women's voices and promote opportunity is already under way. Planned Parenthood's website offers information on adoption,[27] and the NRLC website describes 3,000 crisis pregnancy centers that provide counseling and temporary financial help to pregnant women to "obtain housing, maternity and baby clothes, baby equipment, pre- and post-natal medical care, legal assistance and financial support, information about adoption, and even advice on how a mother in school can continue her education."[28] The NRLC website also links to standupgirl.com, which offers testimonials from young women who have chosen to give birth rather than abort.[29] Though hardly nonpartisan, this website offers personal narratives that give flesh and blood to some of the statistics that dominate the abortion debate. Much more could be done to bring resources and energy to what appears to be a common desire among pro-choice and pro-life advocates, to give women a chance to learn more about adoption alternatives and to weigh the challenges of bringing a pregnancy to term against the consequences of deliberately ending it.

Recognizing the need to move beyond the polarized abortion debate, in 1989 Laura Chasin founded the Public Conversations Project, dedicated to "promoting constructive conversations and relationships among those who have differing values, world views, and positions related to divisive public issues." She and her colleagues developed a remarkable series of workshops where pro-life and pro-choice advocates could meet without rancor to seek common ground. At the center of these workshops were two questions for participants: "1) What events or other personal life experiences may have shaped your current views and feelings about abortion? and 2) Do you experience mixed feelings, value conflicts, uncertainties, or other dilemmas within your own perspective?"[30] The emphasis on personal experience and on the mixed feelings of participants was an open invitation to resist the temptations of polarization in favor of the complexities of reality and common ground. "Your current views" acknowledges the centripetal force of each unified perspective, while "mixed feelings, value conflicts, and uncertainties" acknowledges the centrifugal force of various religious and political values, not to mention the diversity of individual experiences moment by moment in a changing world. Rather than focusing on how to win a debate with an opponent, participants in these workshops sought to understand the opponent's thinking.

The success of this project in fostering a six-year conversation between pro-life and pro-choice advocates in Boston was recognized by the *Boston Globe* in 2001, in "Talking to the Enemy,"[31] and in the November 2005 issue of *O, The Oprah Magazine* in "Us and Them."[32] The Common Ground Network for Life and Choice, founded by Adrienne Kaufmann, has created a manual for leading such discussions, distributed by the National Association of Community Mediation.[33] By 2013 the Public Conversations Project had branched out into conversations about "partisan politics, homosexuality in faith communities, the Israel/Palestine conflict, environmental divides, postgenocide reconciliation, labor standards in the developing world, and racial, cultural, and economic divides at nonprofits and academic institutions," and to leadership training programs for thousands of people in more than fifteen countries.[34] The successes of these projects indicate that polarization can be challenged as participants seek to understand better each other's conflicting perspectives. Yet, as long as the abortion debate focuses on legislation about the conflict between rights of women to choose and rights of unborn babies to live, as long as the gay marriage debate focuses on the conflict between rights of homosexuals to marry and the rights of citizens to pass laws about who can marry, as long as the capital punishment debate focuses on the conflict between rights of prisoners to avoid cruel and unusual punishment and the rights of citizens to enforce legal penalties, we will be saddled with the winning and losing that simplifies and demonizes the enemy. As long as the pro-life and pro-choice camps dismiss each other as unenlightened, as long as an advocate of gay marriage spurns homophobic bigots, while opponents of gay marriage disdain those who fail to respect the sanctity of marriage, as long as opponents of capital punishment consider it barbaric, while defenders consider it the law of the land, proponents of these various positions will continue to dedicate themselves to defending their rights, spreading enlightenment, and nurturing divisiveness.

## CONCLUSION

The paradigm shift that is called for is not just to tolerate or understand an opponent—as an act of generosity, or as a way to anticipate objections—but to regard understanding an opponent's perspective as essential to my own freedom. I may think my opponent's position is as insane as the officer's in Kafka's penal colony or the Grand Inquisitor's in Dostoevsky's *Brothers Karamazov*. I may think my opponent is as hard of listening as either Portia or Shylock in *The Merchant of Venice*. I may think my opponent's position is as dangerous as Francesca's in the *Inferno* or Satan's in *Paradise Lost*. I may think my opponent is as unenlightened as Amasa Delano in "Benito Cereno" or Edward Bodwin in *Beloved*. I may think the conditions for conversation have not yet arrived, and that I must wait until they do, biding my time, taking a neutral position on controversial topics, as does Kafka's traveler. If in the fictitious world of the penal colony the consequences of neutrality are horrifying, how much more is at stake in the conflicts in our all-too-real polarized world? These conflicts call on us with increasing urgency to do something before it is too late. They call on us to try to see as our enemy sees, and to think as our enemy thinks, not for the purpose of staying one step ahead, or to be generous, or to drown in a sea of relativism, but to deepen the dimensions of our own humanity, to sharpen our ears for hearing and our minds for judging, so that we can navigate the layers of meaning around and within us and judge best which voices to listen to, as we coauthor among other human beings the decisions that count.

Our dialogic imperative is a call to action that is not easy. But this sort of thing has never been easy. We would be wrong to think that somehow the Trojan king Priam's success at convincing Achilles to release Hector's body for burial was easier to accomplish than it would be to coauthor decisions together today. How likely was it that an old man, without bodyguards or a military escort, would be able to clatter in his wagon past sentries, beyond enemy lines, all the way to their headquarters? It was so unlikely that Homer needed to bring in the god Mercury as escort, as if to say, "This could never happen in real life. It would take a miracle!" Then the god disappears, and Priam is on his own to make the argument about fathers and children that reaches Achilles, though each moment threatens an explosion of the warrior's murderous rage. Even millennia later, as we read about this encounter between an old man and his enemy, Homer makes us register moment by moment the open-ended possibility that Priam will ignite the anger of Achilles, and the warrior will snap his neck. Until Priam has escaped with his son's corpse, we are not sure he will succeed. There is nothing easy about what he accomplishes in his mission to the enemy's tent. In fact, the difficulty of it, and Priam's resourcefulness and determination in the face of such difficulty, are what make his reckless journey, which his wife begs him not to undertake, heroic. That he could so enter into Achilles' thinking as to persuade him to imagine his own father's grief, should Achilles die, requires not just that Priam project himself into the enemy's consciousness, but that Priam at that same moment contain his own anger and grief in the presence of the man who has dragged Priam's dead son by the heels, round and round the battlefield. This moment of personal experience shared between enemies requires courage from both men as they meet the challenge of coauthoring each other's decisions.

The conflicts within our polarized world call for us to show no less courage than is shown by Priam and Achilles, in order to see from each other's alien perspectives and contain our own anger and hurt, so that we can coauthor the actions that need to be taken. In *Beloved*, Morrison gives us a model for imagining how we might go about meeting this challenge, when she presents as the central event of her novel an action that is universally condemned—a mother killing her own child. She presents Sethe's infanticide from so many perspectives that we begin to understand how a good person might do such a thing. This realization does not turn readers into advocates of infanticide, as if the solution to polarization were to embrace the opponent's perspective. It makes us think twice, though, about condemning this infanticide and the person who commits it. Bringing a reader to this realization is not a simple process. Carefully, Morrison manages our reactions by presenting the condemnations not just of Abolitionists, who saw Sethe's infanticide as a reversion to savagery, but of the black community Sethe never explains herself to, and of the lover Sethe tries but fails to explain herself to. Morrison also presents the reactions of Sethe's sons who flee, her daughter who stays behind, and the enigmatic ghost-figure, Beloved. Her reaction to Sethe may be the response not of a ghost, but of a young woman who has suffered the life worse than death that Sethe wanted to spare her dead daughter. Perhaps the fiercest and most problematic reaction to Sethe's infanticide comes from the grandmother, who can neither condone nor condemn her action and instead lies down to die. To bring a reader the experience of seeing Sethe's desperate solution from Sethe's perspective, Morrison must present it also from all these other perspectives.

Morrison shows us just how much is at stake when Paul D returns to Sethe's house not to count her feet but to rub them. Since Sethe has given up on living and is about to die, as Baby Suggs did, Paul D's ability to see things now from Sethe's perspective, as well as his own and the community's, has become literally a matter of life and death. To not intervene would be to watch her die, even as Kafka's traveler watched the officer die. To not intervene would also be to forgo an opportunity to coauthor a life together. The conclusion of Morrison's novel celebrates not just the possibility that Sethe will survive but that she can be for Paul D what the Thirty-Mile Woman was for Sixo, who had said, "She is a friend of my mind. She gather me, man. The pieces I am, she gather them and give them back to me in all the right order."[35] Paul's effort to see things from Sethe's perspective will benefit not just Sethe, who, unlike Shylock, can now be heard. It will benefit Paul D, who will be better able to make sense of himself in the world. None of this would be possible without Paul D engaging in the strenuous process of working himself through the various perspectives on the unthinkable.

Like Paul D, we are all called upon to think about the unthinkable from the perspectives of those who resort to it, whether that action involves executing a murderer, aborting a life, cloning an embryonic stem cell, terminating the suffering of a dying person, invading a country, bombing a school, or taking some other action that is defended by some and condemned by others. This does not mean that we need to stop thinking about these issues from perspectives we consider reasonable and ethical. Cultivating dialogic freedom involves not replacing one set of beliefs with another, but rather negotiating the multiple voices within and outside us, calling to us with one value or another, with one recommendation or another, with reinforcing or conflicting mandates, as we expand our capacity to navigate alien ways of knowing. Dialogic freedom also involves nurturing the capacity to hear new voices and evaluate their appeal. Yet it is not a panacea. Dante warns that not all voices are to be trusted—that empathy in fact can lead us astray. Morrison expands that warning to include the "pure" empathy that almost kills Sethe as she comes to answer only to Beloved's unfulfillable needs. Milton expands that warning to present the deceptive empathy of Satan, who seems to understand all perspectives, and who manipulates others by coauthoring action to get what he wants. Dostoevsky warns that the ability to see from multiple perspectives can lead to the despair of the Grand Inquisitor, locked in conflict between his intellectual beliefs, which challenge moral freedom, and his heart, where Christ's kiss glows. The challenge of dialogic freedom is not to achieve enlightenment, nor to see from all perspectives, but to cultivate the courage to balance the chaos of the world with the necessity to make meaning and take action among other people. In the continuum between the chaos of relativism and the unity of polarism, we need to locate ourselves in a position where we resist these extremes in favor of the hard work of coauthoring action together.

The preceding chapters have presented dialogic freedom not as a new concept but as a new way of thinking about a constellation of activities that have characterized the two-sidedness of human decisions throughout history. I have used literature, from ancient Greece to modern America, to examine how dialogic freedom operates to enrich the decision-making lives of people under a wide range of circumstances. Homer's *Iliad* shows how pleading for the release of a son's corpse hinges on a Trojan king's ability to persuade a volatile warrior to think about his own father. Dante's *Inferno* shows how decision making involves a multitude of voices that we answer to, and that it is a matter of life and death that we not shut out the wrong voices. Shakespeare's *Merchant of Venice* shows what happens when a person's need to be heard elicits only deafness from others. Milton's *Paradise Lost* presents the dark side of dialogic freedom in the virtuosity of Satan, who can always say what his listener most needs to hear. Melville's "Benito Cereno" explores how racism debilitates the judgment of racists in ways that can be exploited by slaves. Dostoevsky's "Grand Inquisitor" explores the dialogic power even of silence, as well as what happens when an advocate of a unified, finalized perspective is unable to jettison another mutually exclusive way of thinking. Kafka's "In the Penal Colony" goads readers to reexamine comforting bromides about neutrality and to want to intervene in an inhuman situation. Morrison's *Beloved* presents the emergence of dialogic freedom under the most impossible conditions. These works all illuminate aspects of dialogic freedom and explore the complexity of its operations, emphasizing that we need not wait for conditions to be right for its emergence. Indeed, the two-sidedness of life among others makes dialogic freedom a constant possibility and an imperative, for better and worse.

Like the characters making decisions in these works of literature, we each answer to many voices, real and imagined: from family, friends, lovers, religions, traditions, communities, nationalities, hobbies, professions, travels, mistakes, triumphs, losses, and so on. The sheer number of these voices would lead to chaos if we tried to listen to all of them all the time. To call decision making two-sided is to speak in shorthand about a situation that is really multi-sided. Like these literary characters, we engage in a sifting and focusing process that lets us listen to one voice more than another, or balance diverse voices. This process is essential to our efforts to unify our thinking enough to take action on a daily basis in a world that can never be fully taken in or understood. The quest for unity is a challenge to manage, however. If we are insufficiently able to unify our thinking, like Kafka's traveler we become reluctant to settle on a course of action. If we are too ready to unify our thinking, like Melville's Amasa Delano we wind up filtering out essential aspects of reality. If the ways in which we unify our thinking make it impossible to share significant common ground with others, as is the case with Shylock or Portia, we may share a common vocabulary but not register the same words in the same way, undermining communication. If we unify our thinking in a way that leaves no room for an unavoidable reality that defies our paradigm, as in the case of Dostoevsky's Grand Inquisitor, we may wind up in despair. Seeking the right balance between the chaos of the world and our own need to make meaning in it can be exhausting. Hence the appeal of polarization, which eliminates chaotic complexity in favor of reassuring, confident, unified, finalized, dismissive belief. I have tried to show how polarization undermines communication between opponents in the abortion debate. If we are to move beyond name calling on this issue and on so many others, we need to move beyond viewing freedom mainly in terms of rights and enlightenment. If we think of freedom instead as something we coauthor among others, we can reduce the attractions of polarization and make it a lifelong project to try to find the right balance between our need for unified thinking and our recognition of the complexities of a chaotic world.

I hope others will join in this project to test, develop, and flesh out the concept of dialogic freedom. Although I have explored it with the help of literature, arguing in favor of protocols of reading both for and with dialogic freedom, this concept is not finally an idea confined to literature. The world we inhabit is neither an epic nor a novel. Yet in it we must become better readers of ourselves, each other, and the experiences of daily life, if we want to become more free. Though many might argue that our universe has a well-defined plot shaped by the Author of All, I would argue with Milton that even if this is true, any cosmic Author worth believing in would insist on human responsibility for the decisions that alter this world. Thus, we must take responsibility for planning the shape dialogic freedom takes in our lives. We must take responsibility for settling for less of it or struggling for more of it, using it or abusing it, according to the choices we coauthor among other human beings. That those choices are themselves products of our ability to think from multiple perspectives, within a field of forces for unity and chaos, means only that we are responsible for trying to create the conditions that will enhance our opportunities for understanding the perspectives of others. Our goal should be not merely to rectify injustices of the past or include others in the decision-making process. Our goal should be to enrich everyone's exposure to the multiplicity of voices we need to hear in order to cultivate the ability to navigate the ways of knowing inhabited by others and to coauthor decisions with them. Including others in the conversation enhances not just the dialogic freedom of the formerly excluded, but the dialogic freedom of the formerly excluding. If instead of cultivating this possibility we continue to settle for the polarizing echo chambers of mutually dismissive enemies, we condemn ourselves to a perpetual war of all against all, in a shrinking arena for dialogic freedom.

## NOTES

1. Jerusha Klemperer tracks the controversy surrounding the Child Nutrition Act debated by Congress in 2010, with regard to issues of childhood obesity. The *Slow Food USA Blog*, updated February 4, 2010, http://www.slowfoodusa.org/index.php/slow_food/blog_post/school_lunch_debate_picking_up_speed/. The act was passed and signed into law by President Obama on December 13, 2010, as the Hunger-Free Act of 2010, which set new standards to improve the quality of school lunches.

2. "The National Organization for Women's 1966 Statement of Purpose," National Organization for Women, accessed June 12, 3013, http://www.now.org/history/purpos66.html.

3. Kim Gandy, "Letter to Supporters," National Organization for Women, December 22, 2005.

4. Terry O'Neill, "NOW Cheers Obama-Biden Win Delivered by Women Voters, Calls for Unconditional End to War on Women, Statement of NOW President Terry O'Neill," National Organization for Women, updated November 6, 2012, http://now.org/press/11-12/11-06.html.

5. "NOW and Abortion Rights/ Reproductive Justice," National Organization for Women, accessed June 12, 2013, http://www.now.org/issues/abortion/.

6. "Mission Statement," National Right to Life, accessed June 12, 2013, http://www.nrlc.org/missionstatement.htm.

7. Carol Tobias, National Right to Life Committee, accessed May 10, 2011, http://www.nrlc.org/.

8. Carol Tobias, "Roe v. Wade: 40 Years Too Many," National Right to Life Committee, updated January 22, 2013, http://www.nrlc.org/press_releases_new/Release012213.html.

9. "Abortion Restriction Sustained," *Eugene Register-Guard*, April 19, 2007.

10. "Slip Opinion for Gonzales v. Carhart," Supreme Court of the United States, updated April 18, 2007, http://www.supremecourtus.gov/opinions/06pdf/05-380.pdf.

11. Ruth Bader Ginsburg, "Ginsburg, J., dissenting," Supreme Court of the United States, Gonzales v. Carhart," accessed June 12, 2013, http://www.law.cornell.edu/supct/html/05-380.ZD.html.

12. Ginsburg, "Ginsburg, J., dissenting."

13. "Partial Birth Abortion Q & A," National Right to Life, accessed June 12, 2013, http://www.nrlc.org/abortion/facts/pbafacts.html.

14. "The Pain of the Unborn Child," National Right to Life, accessed June 12, 2013, http://www.nrlc.org/abortion/Fetal_Pain/.

15. "Obama and 168 House Members Defend Single-Sex Abortion," National Right to Life, accessed May 15, 2012, http://www.nrlc.org/.

16. "Targets of Domestic Terror," National Organization for Women, accessed January 13, 2010, http://www.now.org/issues/abortion/.

17. "NOW Denounces Justified Terrorism Defense in Wichita Murder Trial," updated January 13, 2010, http://www.now.org/press/01-10/01-13.html.

18. "Speak Out against Anti-Abortion Terrorism," National Organization for Women, accessed June 12, 2013, http://www.now.org/issues/abortion/.

19. Emily Le Coz, "State Abortion Laws Restrict Women's Access to Reproductive Health Care," *Huffington Post*, accessed July 18, 2012, http://www.huffingtonpost.com/2012/07/18/state-abortion-laws_n_1684825.html.

20. Rachel Benson Gold and Elizabeth Nash, "Troubling Trend: More States Hostile to Abortion Rights as Middle Ground Shrinks," *Guttmacher Policy Review* 15, no. 1 (2012), accessed June 1, 2012, http://www.guttmacher.org/pubs/gpr/15/1/gpr150114.html.

21. Mary Spaulding Balch, *The Circuit Rider Blog*, updated October 22, 2010, http://wesleysocialgospel.blogspot.com/2010_10_01_archive.html.

22. Quoted in Le Coz, "State Abortion Laws Restrict Women's Access to Reproductive Health Care."

23. Terry O'Neill, "Forty Years after Ruling, Support for 'Roe v. Wade' Growing in the Face of Ongoing Attacks: Statement of NOW President Terry O'Neill," updated January 22, 2013, http://now.org/press/01-13/01-22.html.

24. "Mission," Guttmacher Institute, accessed June 13, 2013, http://www.guttmacher.org/about/mission.html.

25. "Abortions in the United States: Statistics and Trends," National Right to Life Committee, accessed June 13, 2013, http://www.nrlc.org/abortion/facts/abortionstats.html.

26. Lawrence B. Finer, Lori F. Frohwirth, Lindsay A. Dauphinee, Susheela Singh, and Ann M. Moore, "Reasons U.S. Women Have Abortions: Quantitative and Qualitative Perspectives," *Perspectives on Sexual and Reproductive Health* 37, no. 3 (2005): 110, The Guttmacher Institute, accessed June 14, 2010, http://www.agi-usa.org/about/index.html. Citations to "Reasons U.S. Women Have Abortions" are to this text.

27. "Thinking about Adoption," Planned Parenthood, accessed June 12, 2013, http://www.plannedparenthood.org/health-topics/pregnancy/adoption-21520.htm?__utma=1.514028599.1265658222.1.

28. "Alternatives to Abortion," National Right to Life, accessed June 12, 2013, http://www.nrlc.org/abortion/ASMF/asmf15.html. See also Pam Belluck, "Pregnancy Centers Gain Influence in Anti-Abortion Arena," *New York Times*, January 4, 2013, http://www.nytimes.com/2013/01/05/health/pregnancy-centers-gain-influence-in-anti-abortion-fight.html?pagewanted=all&_r=0. Belluck points out that "abortion rights advocates have long called some of [the approaches of these centers] deceptive or manipulative." According to her, thirteen states now provide direct funding to these centers, and in 2011 the state of Texas increased such funding while cutting funding for family planning.

29. StandupGirl.com, accessed June 12, 2013, http://www.standupgirl.com/.

30. "History," Public Conversations Project, accessed June 12, 2013, http://www.publicconversations.org/who/history.

31. Anne Fowler et al., "Talking with the Enemy," *Boston Globe*, January 28, 2001, http://pubpages.unh.edu/~jds/BostonGlobe.htm.

32. "Us and Them," *O, Opra Magazine*, November 2005, accessed June 12, 2013, http://www.oprah.com/omagazine/Us-and-Them.

33. Common Ground Network for Life and Choice, accessed June 13, 2013, http://www.cpn.org/topics/families /prolife.html; National Association for Community Mediation, accessed June 13, 2013, http://www.nafcm.org/.

34. "History," Public Conversations Project.

35. Toni Morrison, *Beloved* (New York: Plume, 1987), 272.

# Epilogue

## *The Statue of Liberty*

The Statue of Liberty is a powerful emblem of freedom. With its blank, yet resolute stare, its placement at the edge of a continent and its sheer size, it seems to insist on the tangible presence of freedom: a promise, a threat, and an absolute. Rising like a goddess from the primal forces of earth, air, and water, it holds up to us the fourth element, fire, as if to say, "Do not dare to look away!"

This statue expresses the two concepts of freedom questioned in these pages: enlightenment and autonomy. Its original title, "Freedom Enlightening the World," is explicit about the connection to enlightenment.[1] To be in the presence of freedom is to become enlightened, and anywhere in the world the truth it confers can and will be felt. The torch in the statue's right hand reinforces this message. To penetrate its light is to understand liberty, once and for all. The torch is held high, above all else, as if the statue itself is answerable to a higher power, to liberty itself. The torch seems to reach across the Atlantic Ocean and beyond, inviting everyone, everywhere, to embrace freedom.

The Statue of Liberty also expresses freedom as autonomy, the ability to be left alone to do as we please, as long as we do not hurt anyone else. The broken chains folded into the drapery of the figure's gown call to mind a slave's shackles that have been broken, once and for all. The individual is now liberated, curtailed only by law, as represented by the tablets in the statue's left hand. On these tablets is inscribed "July 4, 1776," the date of the signing of the Declaration of Independence. The statue balances the illuminating torch in its right hand with the restraining tablets in its left, where it pays homage to the founding document that connects autonomy with enlightenment by listing the right to liberty among the truths that are held to be self-evident.

From a dialogic perspective, the Statue of Liberty's celebration of freedom as enlightenment and autonomy, concepts that result from centuries of efforts to unify key ideas, expresses our human ability to negotiate the push and pull of forces for unity and chaos. At the same time that it celebrates enlightenment and autonomy, it invites us to question them. The many details we see in photographs or in person—the statue's massive presence, the torch, gown, broken chains and tablets—are registered by different people and different generations in conflicting ways that raise as many questions as they answer. Does the statue mean what the sculptor, or those who paid to erect it, meant? Can enlightenment clash with autonomy? In the age of mass media, what does it mean to be left alone? If my idea of harm conflicts with yours, which one of us is enlightened? The questions it generates could lead to chaos. Thus this statue calls on us to navigate each other's ways of thinking about freedom, balancing forces for unity and chaos, as we help construct its meaning.

In 1876, when the French sculptor Frederic-Auguste Bartholdi lacked funds to complete his creation, he traveled to Philadelphia and New York to display its gigantic hand holding the torch, a trip that succeeded in generating both excitement and financial support.[2] But it took the engineering know-how of the designer of the Eiffel tower, the combined resources of the citizens of France and America, as well as a transatlantic journey with 350 pieces loaded into 214 crates, to assemble and erect the statue in 1886, a full decade after the 100th anniversary of the Declaration of Independence it celebrated.[3] The complicated history of the statue's genesis, funding, dedication, and custodial care is as much a part of its meaning as the theories of liberty it celebrates.

In 1903, when immigrants arrived by ship at Ellis Island, they saw a bronze plaque mounted inside the lower level of the statue's pedestal, engraved with the last five lines of "The New Colossus," a sonnet by Emma Lazarus. She had written it in 1883, in order to help raise money for the construction of the pedestal. Her poem captured for generations the promise of a new life in a new world. In it the welcoming Mother of Exiles is contrasted with the threatening Colossus of Rhodes, one of the seven wonders of the ancient world:

> Not like the brazen giant of Greek fame
> With conquering limbs astride from land to land;
> Here at our sea-washed, sunset gates shall stand
> A mighty woman with a torch, whose flame
> Is the imprisoned lightning, and her name
> Mother of Exiles. From her beacon-hand
> Glows world-wide welcome; her mild eyes command

The air-bridged harbor that twin cities frame,
"Keep, ancient lands, your storied pomp!" cries she
With silent lips. "Give me your tired, your poor,
Your huddled masses yearning to breathe free,
The wretched refuse of your teeming shore,
Send these, the homeless, tempest-tossed to me,
I lift my lamp beside the golden door!"[4]

A statue that was erected as a rebuke to European tyrants and a symbol of Roman *Libertas,* is now given a new voice. This voice asks tyrants not to embrace liberty at home, but to send their "refuse" across the Atlantic. Never mind that the conditions immigrants met in the New World were often squalid, dangerous, or alienating. In her glowing narrative, Lazarus sees the statues eyes as "mild," not blank.

For tourists today, the Statue of Liberty remains a coveted destination, but it is not at all clear whether her right arm holds up the torch as a beacon of truth, a cage for "imprisoned lightening," or a weapon. Lazarus's image of the Mother of Exiles has endured for many, but it has also been challenged by those with a more ironic sensibility. They see the statue not as a welcoming presence, but as a hostile guardian, daring immigrants to try to penetrate closed U.S. borders.[5] An enormous bystander in the immigration debate, the Statue of Liberty generates uneasy questions. What place should immigrants have in twenty-first century America? Should they be free to live wherever they want, as long as they don't hurt anyone? Does their very presence threaten the livelihoods of U.S. workers? What are the self-evident truths?

Others see the Statue of Liberty as a tribute to slaves freed in the Civil War. So many websites have been devoted to the claim that the model for the Statue of Liberty was a black woman, that the National Park Service commissioned ethnographers to evaluate the evidence. They concluded that although "the statue's design almost certainly evolved from an earlier concept Bartholdi proposed for a colossal monument in Egypt," which used drawings of Egyptian women as models, "there is no evidence that Bartholdi's 'original' design was perceived by white American supporters or the United States government as representing a black woman."[6]

Amidst competing narratives, the silent statue continues to provoke us to respond to her blank stare, much as Dostoevesky's silent Christ provoked the Grand Inquisitor. In the process, the meaning of freedom that she expresses becomes a product not just of her stare, her gown, her broken chains, her tablets and her torch, but also of the questions we think to ask when we confront her massive presence. For the Statue of Liberty, freedom encompasses not just enlightenment and autonomy, but also our ability to question these concepts as we engage in the two-sided act of bearing witness to her as a work of art, politics and history. We can meet her gaze with prejudices and fears that drive us to take refuge in polarized enclaves, but she will keep staring as us, inviting us to respond to the dialogic imperative to become more free the better able we are to see from the perspectives of others.

## NOTES

1. "America's Proud History Based on Freedom, Equality," Indystar.com, accessed October 1, 2013 http://www.indystar.com/article/20070704/OPINION/707040384/America-s-proud-history-based-freedom-equality.

2. Robert McNamara, "The Hand and Torch of the Statue of Liberty on Display," accessed October 1, 2013 http://history1800s.about.com/od/tothenewworld/ig/The-Statue-of-Liberty/Torch-of-the-Statue-of-Liberty.htm.

3. "Statue of Liberty," National Park Service, accessed August 28, 2013 http://www.statueofliberty.org/Statue_History.html.

4. Emma Lazarus, "The New Colossus," About.com, accessed October 1, 2013 http://history1800s.about.com/od/tothenewworld/a/The-New-Colossus-By-Emma-Lazarus.htm.

5. Holly Thomas, "What Does it Mean That Ellis Island Shuttered its Doors?," Public History Productions, November 12, 2012 http://www.publichistoryproductions.com/category/anti-immigration/.

6. Joseph, Rebecca M., Brooke Rosenblatt, and Carolyn Kinebrew, "National Park Service Summary Report: The Black Statue of Liberty," September, 2000 http://www.nps.gov/stli/historyculture/black-statue-of-liberty.htm.

# Appendix A: Theoretical Roots of Dialogic Freedom

Mikhail Bakhtin never imagined a thing called dialogic freedom, and some might argue that he would never have sanctioned my political application of his ideas. When he referred to freedom explicitly, he described it either as autonomy or as a kind of enlightened disinterestedness, the very concepts of negative and positive liberty that I challenge in these pages. I argue, though, that his thoughts about freedom do not stop at autonomy and disinterestedness, and that a careful reading of his writings uncovers assumptions about the human condition and decision making that lead step by step to dialogic freedom. Chapter 1 explores four aspects of that concept: a context of others; freedom as a two-sided act; forces for unity and chaos; and navigating the perspectives of others. Here I widen the discussion to include other scholars' approaches to Bakhtin's views about freedom, the ways in which Bakhtin invites us to rethink these approaches, and the significant but confusing role that the word "unity" played in his thoughts about freedom. Rethinking Bakhtin's explicit ideas about freedom and unity encourages us to see in the sideshadow of these comments the roots of dialogic freedom.[1]

## AUTONOMY AND DISINTERESTEDNESS

In the Autumn 1998 issue of *New Literary History*, Thomas Pavel, Michael André Bernstein, Caryl Emerson, and Gary Saul Morson consider the implications of Mikhail Bakhtin's thinking for our understanding of freedom. All distance Bakhtin from utopian Hegelian claims for freedom as enlightenment, a concept Hannah Arendt associates with Montesquieu, in the tradition of Parmenides and Plato, and defines as "being able to do what one ought to will."[2] Isaiah Berlin identifies this perspective with "positive liberty" and "the severe authoritarianism of Plato's guardians and Soviet elites."[3] The NLH contributors reject this utopianism in favor of the philosophical tradition of freedom as autonomy (as opposed to determinism), within which they situate Bakhtin. Thomas Pavel sees a dichotomy between "existential liberalism . . . the governing principle of contemporary middle-class Americans, academics included," which he sees as "the freedom to take charge of one's own existence and change its course as one sees fit," and "conservatism," which to him involves various forms of teleological determinism.[4] In this dichotomy he aligns Bakhtin with those who seek to "take charge of one's own existence."

Gary Saul Morson, navigating carefully between the Scylla of determinism and the Charybdis of license, emphasizes that Bakhtin's "prosaic view of freedom sees choice as severely restricted at every moment by numerous social, psychological, and historical constraints. . . . We choose in a highly specific situation, which has been shaped by countless forces we know and do not know."[5] Note the word "shaped" here, rather than "determined." Something can be shaped by something else, as a snowball is shaped by the one who throws it (my example, not Morson's). Other factors—the age of the thrower (child, adult?), weather, opportunity, the rules of the game, chance, clothing—enter the picture, not to mention mood and situation. The first to throw, or in retaliation? In fun? In anger? All these "determining" factors weigh in. Yet, there is always a significant element of choice. "Prosaic freedom" acknowledges the absence of absolute autonomy without conceding determinism. Morson explains that "freedom does not require an unrestricted or unlimited menu of choices; it is entirely sufficient if more than one alternative exists" (NLH, 684). He avoids insisting that freedom be absolute. In fact, he adds, following John Stuart Mill, "Freedom . . . actually demands constraints" (NLH, 685). The fascination with alternatives and possibilities has led Morson and Bernstein to coin the term "sideshadowing," which describes "real but unactualized possibilities in an undeterministic world" (NLH, 678), "a middle realm of real possibilities that could have happened even if they did not."[6] Their discussion of freedom thus expands to include choices not made. According to Morson, "sideshadowing encourages—from the 'side'—the shadow of an alternative present" (NF, 11). Moreover, it "conveys the sense that actual events might just as well not have happened," giving us a "glimpse of unrealized but realizable possibilities," thus reducing the illusion of "inevitability" (NF, 118).

> Sideshadowing therefore counters our tendency to view current events as the inevitable products of the past. Instead, it invites us to inquire into the other possible presents that might have been and to imagine a quite different course of events. If only that chance had not happened, if only a different choice had

been made, if only a favorable sequence of events had not been interrupted or had been interrupted a moment later—what would have happened then? (NF, 118)

Morson focuses on the ability of sideshadowing to undermine determinism by liberating the human mind from the tyranny of expectations. It is just this sense of sideshadowing I call on to help me explain how dialogic freedom constitutes an "unrealized but realizable" alternative to Bakhtin's explicit discourse on freedom.[7]

According to Morson, Dostoevsky creates many characters whose "checked impulses" and "aborted possibilities" veer away from "events that might have happened" (NF, 120–21), demonstrating that at any moment events could take a quite unexpected turn, unexpected even to Dostoevsky, and that events which occur are not at all inevitable. Furthermore, according to Morson, the novelist uses sideshadowing to cast doubt on crucial plot elements: Did Fyodor Karamazov's first wife die from starvation, or typhus? Was Karamazov's reaction joy, or sorrow, or both? (NF, 138). Morson sees sideshadowing as Dostoevsky's "weapon against psychological determinism" (NF, 140), one that emphasizes his characters' responsibility for their choices, hence their freedom. Here, Morson once again presents freedom as moral autonomy, but not license; it is freedom from determinism, yet limited by the social, psychological, and historical constraints of the prosaic world. According to him, sideshadowing and the moral autonomy it presumes "encourages the sort of intellectual pluralism we find in the thought of Isaiah Berlin" (NF, 140). Thus, he draws an implicit link between Bakhtin's philosophical concept of freedom as autonomy and Berlin's political "ideal of freedom to choose ends without claiming eternal validity for them, and the pluralism of values connected with this."[8] This implicit connection suggests that in the sideshadow of Bakhtin we can look for "realizable but unrealized possibilities" that lead to dialogic freedom.

In *Mikhail Bakhtin: An Aesthetic for Democracy*, intellectual historian Ken Hirschkop also draws political inferences from Bakhtin's writings. Like Morson, he considers the implications of the idea of freedom as autonomy. In so doing, however, he is critical not only of Bakhtin, whom he finds in some ways incoherent, but also of Bakhtin's Russian and American readers. He rebukes Russian readers for "religiously guided interpretations."[9] On the other hand, he rejects the Americans Morson and Emerson for espousing "a familiar right-liberal belief in the overarching importance of personal responsibility," then goes on to reject also "left-liberal critics" who "use 'dialogue' as a keystone for a case about the virtues of cultural difference" (8). Hirschkop sees in all these readers a tendency to create an ahistorical Bakhtin. He argues that to say "language itself is inherently 'dialogical'" naturalizes the concept in such a way as "not only to legitimate existing structures of power but to ornament them with the fine drapery of the aesthetic." He dismisses the Americans and their work as "no more than the reflected image of the self-understanding of American liberalism" (9). He recommends that instead of looking at "tendencies within language itself . . . we should be looking into the historical situation which gives rise to 'heteroglossia'" (22). If we do, we will discover "the relative failure of the dialogues which actually take place [in the political sphere], the moment at which communication which fulfills the ordinary prerequisites for being dialogue nonetheless falls short of the democratic project" (57). With systematic rigor Hirschkop seeks to answer the question: "Does the definition of democracy itself have an inner connection to a style of language?" (16).

Pursuing Bakhtin to his Kantian roots, Hirschkop's critique of both Bakhtin and his readers rests on his own analysis of autonomy not as individual choice but as an "intersubjective accomplishment" (240), directly related to "the subject's ability to act responsibly" (241). More than either Kant or Bakhtin, however, Hirschkop emphasizes the importance of a historical context in which intersubjectivity is not absolute but rather evolves historically. He criticizes Bakhtin for negating historical evolution in a religious way, by displacing human responsibility onto God (241–43). He criticizes Bakhtin's American readers for negating historical evolution in a secular way, by focusing on the "dialogic nature of language." He advocates instead historically situating both language and the operations of language in the novel. In the process, he advocates an idea of responsibility that "cannot be disentangled from the roles we play in an actual social world, roles or positions which determine the depth and limits of our responsibilities" (242). Following Bakhtin's emphasis on "eventness" and prosaic life as a project to be achieved, Hirschkop observes that "democracy is constantly fought for and defended, not instituted once and for all" (34). The emphasis here is not on the democrat's willingness to resort to violence, but rather on the ongoing challenge of creating democracy moment by moment, in the midst of accidents, responses, opportunities, and choices that could easily lead in a different direction. The fragility of freedom as something never securely achieved once and for all, always in the historical process of becoming, is central to both Hirschkop's discussion and to mine.

In Hirschkop's critique of Bakhtin, however, autonomy remains the gold standard of human freedom:

> While Bakhtin may have been wrong to displace all responsibility into an absolute and religious form, he was right to claim that responsibility, and the achievement of personality, is its own reward. Subjects whose ability to act autonomously is acknowledged receive more than the direct pay-off of the desired end: they are recognized as competent subjects, and, by being so recognized, they become historical actors, whose achievements fit into a narrative which will transcend their own lives. (243)

Whatever his criticisms of the shortcomings of Bakhtin's "bourgeois" fascination with the "medieval public square" (250), Hirschkop focuses on autonomy, the ability to claim responsibility for action and to achieve desired ends (as do Morson and Bernstein), as the central feature of Bakhtin's concept of freedom. Thus, despite his criticism of the Americans, Hirschkop agrees with Morson, Emerson, and Bernstein (and for that matter, with Bakhtin himself) on the most essential point: that Bakhtin's interest in the subject of freedom is mainly philosophical, not political. He quotes Bakhtin's supplemental notes to the study of Rabelais to illustrate Bakhtin's affinity for what Arendt would classify as a philosophical concept of "disinterestedness": "The highest sphere of disinterestedness, absolutely sober and free being, to such heights of fearless consciousness where he is least of all liable to be muddied by any kind of sensual arousal" (291).

Here, Bakhtin's emphasis on liberation from the bondage of the senses conjures up a philosophical Bakhtin, reminiscent of the tradition Arendt associates with Montesquieu and "being able to do what one ought to will."[10] This philosophical Bakhtin is congruent with the familiar image of the persecuted intellectual under Stalin.

Bakhtin himself gives ample evidence to support this reading. Thus I bring a reluctant Bakhtin to the conversation; in fact, choices that he explicitly rejects, that lurk in the sideshadows of his thinking, are at the heart of dialogic freedom. In *The First Hundred Years of Mikhail Bakhtin*, Caryl Emerson classifies Bakhtin with Hellenistic philosophers like Epicurus, for whom "an individual's responsibility was personal integrity realized through withdrawal from public life."[11] Since the "heroic martyrdom of Socrates's sort would not register on a diffuse and corrupt body politic" (25), the wise path was to steer clear of politics and any discussion of political freedom. Here Emerson follows an Arendtian analysis of philosophical freedom as a withdrawal from politics. To illustrate the degree to which Bakhtin learned to avoid politics, Emerson presents Bakhtin's reminiscences about the 1917 revolutions, in which he describes himself as "utterly apolitical" (22). According to Michael Holquist's foreword to *Toward a Philosophy of the Act*, "the shock of his arrest during Stalin's terror made Bakhtin extremely cautious in later years."[12] Ken Hirschkop puts it most strongly: "Bakhtin was virtually worthless as a political thinker in the strict sense," because of "his disdain for the ordinary business of politics, the distribution and mechanisms of power" (274). It comes down to a choice between "dull convention or spectacular isolation," and either way the "need for freedom" was "blocked by the force of the state" (290), which was why Bakhtin embraced "disinterestedness" and considered himself philosophically above the fray. This does not mean that Bakhtin holds no value for us as a political thinker, but rather that he was cautious about being considered one. Hirschkop describes that caution in terms of Bakhtin's experience of Stalinism, "a first-hand experience of expressive popular politics" (107). Bakhtin saw in "the ideal of a single consciousness" a discourse that was anything but free. Even if a whole nation could agree upon a single ideal and thus consider it democratically established, that would not make its citizens free. Speaking for Bakhtin, Hirschkop concludes: "A democracy which is no more than a shared or agreed consciousness, or a commonly held, but 'consummated' culture, has already surrendered its intersubjective and experimental character, and with it, the future" (107). If the only political world Bakhtin knew insisted upon such a shared, monological vision, how could he possibly investigate the implications of the dialogical within this political context? He had already been arrested. Some of his best friends were already dead. What did the future hold for a political Bakhtin?

## BAKHTIN THE AESOPIAN

To take Bakhtin from the philosophical isolation where various readers have found him, contemplating freedom as autonomy and disinterestedness, to a more political sphere where he enters the conversation with Aristotle, Tocqueville, Arendt, Mill, and Berlin, and where we will find dialogic freedom, takes some doing. We begin with nineteenth-century Russia. According to Emerson, Bakhtin was heir to a tradition of "Aesopian language," developed "to outwit the unfree authoritarian word." In *The First Hundred Years of Mikhail Bakhtin*, Emerson explains that this tradition assumes that no one speaks or writes straight, and that every officially public or published text (by definition censored) has a "'more honest,' multilayered, hidden subtext that only insiders can decode" (8). That Bakhtin's idol, Dostoevsky, indulged in such evasive writing in the legend of the Grand Inquisitor, we can be sure (in that it purports to be about religious, not political tyranny), but Bakhtin himself is not easy to pin down. There is still considerable disagreement about whether or not he published texts under the names of Voloshinov and Medvedev,[13] and whether or not these "disputed" texts, the apparent work of professed Marxists, were Aesopian attacks on Marx or Stalin. In *Mikhail Bakhtin*, Michael Holquist and Katerina Clark see political implications in Bakhtin's most pervasive "literary" language, arguing that "Bakhtin's discussions of such scholarly matters as monologue versus dialogue and the relations between authors and their characters may be read as latent political commentaries having a special relevance to his own time and place."[14] We do know that "under Stalinist conditions of repression, when people were forced to lie or die, Bakhtin wrote: 'Even a word that is known to be false is not absolutely false. . . . It always presupposes an instance that will justify and understand it, even if in the form, 'anyone in my position would have lied too.'"[15] This justification for Aesopian language can only add fuel to the debate about disputed texts and cast doubt on Bakhtin's claim to be "disinterested." At the very least it suggests that there is a sideshadow to Bakhtin's disinterestedness, a "glimpse of unrealized but realizable possibilities" (NF, 118). To put the point in slightly different terms, in what sense should we take the claim to be philosophically disinterested, within a context in which every writer is by definition political, in that the political apparatus completely controls access to the dissemination of ideas, and this apparatus must be anticipated as an "addressee" in whatever the writer chooses to say or not to say?

Morson has argued effectively for inclusion of Bakhtin within the Russian counter-tradition of intellectuals critical of the apocalyptic, utopian intellegensia, the politically correct precursors of Stalin, for whom "the truth was already given and the role of thinkers was consequently reduced to that of propagandists."[16] Morson presents a "prosaic Bakhtin," kindred spirit to the contributors of *Landmarks: A Collection of Articles on the Russian Intelligentsia,*[17] in which "seven remarkable Russian thinkers" in 1909 "attacked the intelligentsia's automatic habit of radicalism," recommended tolerance, and "refused to consider politics as the solution to all problems, even political ones" (36). Rejecting nihilism, determinism, and "the 'mystique' of revolution" (37), these critics favored such "bourgeois" values as "personal moral improvement" (36). According to Morson, it was Bakhtin's project to sketch out the non-deterministic alternative called for by the contributors of *Landmarks.* Thus, "above all, Bakhtin wanted to give body and weight to an understanding of the world in which real selves create, exercise choice, take responsibility, and develop unexpectedly while interacting with a social world that is also uncertain" (54). Bakhtin considered this mission ethical rather than political, and Morson agrees, arguing that Bakhtin "refused to identify the ethical with the political. Politicism, as this equation might be called, was for Bakhtin simply another form of reductionism fatal to true ethical sensibility" (33). I argue, however, that Bakhtin's affinities with the Aesopian intellectuals of *Landmarks* encourage us to explore the sideshadows of his avoidance of the political. When we do this, we discover within the precincts of concepts like "word is a two-sided act," "answerability," the tension between centripetal and centrifugal forces, and "epistemological layers of meaning," an arena for dialogic freedom.

## IN THE SIDESHADOW: A POLITICAL BAKHTIN

Aristotle's concept of the political, which I discuss in chapter 1, has at its heart exactly the participatory aspect of citizenship denied to the politicians and creative artists purged by Stalin. It would seem that participatory citizenship, the merits of which have been extolled by communitarians as a Tocquevillian "large free school"[18] and disdained by libertarians as a source of indoctrination, was just what Bakhtin eschewed. After all, he wrote mainly about aesthetic questions—author and hero, genres, carnival, the novel—and avoided discussing politics. Yet, at the heart of this aesthetic orientation is an idea of language and life that is so fundamentally social and political, in the Aristotelian sense, that it carries with it implications that drag Bakhtin into a discussion of freedom that is political. Late in his career, Bakhtin reveals in *Speech Genres* a vision of language that is fundamentally social:

> Everything that pertains to me enters my consciousness, beginning with my name, from the external world through the mouths of others (my mother, and so forth). . . . I realize myself initially through others: from them I receive words, forms, and tonalities for the formation of my initial idea of myself. . . . Just as the body is formed initially in the mother's womb (body), a person's consciousness awakens wrapped in another's consciousness. (SG, 138)

Here Bakhtin lives in the shadow of Aristotle's acorn and oak, maintaining not just that we are all social beings in our interactions with others, but that even in our "inner selves," our very consciousness, we are social beings. In the beginning "everything . . . enters my consciousness . . . from the external world." The first words are received from others, hence in some sense determined by them, even as a person's individual consciousness comes into existence. According to Bakhtin, consciousness of these original connections to others is a prerequisite of freedom: "The better a person understands the degree to which he is externally determined (his substantiality), the closer he is to understanding and exercising his real freedom" (SG, 139). Even as Bakhtin recognizes a deterministic element in this connection to others, he sees it as a prerequisite for "real freedom."

This example of mother and child was not new to Bakhtin in *Speech Genres*. He had explored it in detail much earlier, in "Author and Hero in Aesthetic Activity," where he discussed the mother's role in determining her infant's identity:

> The child receives all initial determinations of himself and of his body from his mother's lips and from the lips of those who are close to him. It is from their lips, in the emotional-volitional tones of their love, that the child hears and begins to acknowledge his own *proper name* and the names of all the features pertaining to his body and to his inner states and experiences. The words of a loving human being are the first and most authoritative words about him; they are the words that for the first time determine his personality *from outside*, the words that *come to meet* his indistinct inner sensation of himself, giving it a form and a name in which, for the first time, he finds himself and becomes aware of himself as a *something*. Words of love and acts of genuine concern come to meet the dark chaos of my inner sensation of myself.[19]

In this early philosophical text, Bakhtin presents the mother as the first authoritative presence in a person's life. "All initial determinations" come from her lips. More precisely, her words "come to meet" the infant's sensation of self, "giving it a form and a name." Her authoritative words and kisses, which are an unquestioned and unifying presence, answer the grunts and coos that arise from the indistinct chaos of first sensations. Surprisingly, in the excerpt from *Speech Genres*, written long after dialogism had become central, Bakhtin presents this relationship in terms of one consciousness wrapped in another, while in the earlier essay, where he was most interested not in dialogue but in the distinctions between "authoritative" and "internally persuasive" discourse, Bakhtin presents the mother's "determining" words as addressed to and called forth by the child—words that "come to meet" his indistinct inner sensations. We see that long before the word *dialogic* becomes central to his discourse, Bakhtin presents the dialogic relationship between mother and child as a human being's first form-giving experience. Her "emotional-volitional tones of love" are called forth by the infant and directed toward him. The child "receives all initial determinations," yet in this experience the child codetermines the mother's loving words by needing them, even as the mother codetermines the child's identity by responding to "his indistinct inner sensation of himself" that lodges in "dark chaos." Even if she has already settled on a name in advance of his birth, the child, by responding, "begins to acknowledge his own *proper name*." Only when he responds to it is that name really his. In this idealized and logo-centric vision of how life begins, "acts of genuine concern" imply that for Bakhtin not just words but choices are codetermined as the infant calls forth and responds to the mother's embrace.

To be sure, this domestic scene of infant and mother is part of a household realm that Aristotle would separate from the public realm of the *polis*. Yet, the dialogic aspects of the mother-child relationship establish for Bakhtin a foundation for other relationships that move beyond the household to a more public world. In this public world the isolated individual is unthinkable. In his revisions of the Dostoevsky book, Bakhtin describes "nonself-sufficiency, the impossibility of the existence of a single consciousness. I am conscious of myself and become myself only while revealing myself for another, through another, and with the help of another."[20] The mother-child relationship has been replaced by the myriad daily relationships among friends, lovers, workers, and citizens, but the dialogic core remains. The presence of others in some sense determines the individual, even though the consciousness of that individual is unique. Holquist and Clark agree with Bakhtin that his view of human experience should not be seen as narrowly deterministic, for although "meaning is context bound . . . context is boundless" (MB, 218). They explain that Bakhtin's concept of liberty "is grounded not in the will of a monologic God, the inevitable course of history, or the desire of men, but rather in the dialogic nature of language and society" (MB, 11). That "dialogic nature" has been the subject of much debate, but Clark and Holquist link it to the idea that words happen as actions "wrapped in contextual layers" (MB, 13) and that meaning is an activity, not a fact. Holquist further explores this "dialogic nature of language," asserting that for Bakhtin "the very capacity to have consciousness is based on otherness.[21] Holquist explains that "conceiving being dialogically means that reality is always experienced, not just perceived, and further that it is experienced from a particular position" (21). Thus the very ideas of self and consciousness, which one might consider the characteristics of isolated, autonomous beings, depend on a social context.

Bakhtin takes issue with Saussure and semiotics for regarding language as a system of signs encoded and decoded, as information transmitted from one singular consciousness to another. He presents language instead as action taking place between speakers and listeners— present, imagined, anticipated, loved, hated, ignored, existing in myriad relationships. When language is described as a "two-sided act," it is this quality that is emphasized. Language experienced from a particular position that presupposes an "other" is at the heart of Bakhtin's idea of freedom. What Gary Saul Morson and Caryl Emerson refer to in *Mikhail Bakhtin: Creation of a Prosaics* as "genuine freedom," the ability "to remake themselves and take responsibility for their actions," requires a social context within which responsibility can be assumed.[22] This context can never be "finalized," because "the act of finalizing, defining, or accounting for another 'causally and genetically' and 'secondhand' is . . . a fundamental threat to the essence of selfhood, which lies in the ability to render untrue all finalizing definitions" (91). Thus, for Bakhtin freedom is linked to action, selfhood, language, and consciousness, all seen in relationship to living among other human beings, in a project that is never complete. In this sense freedom is for Bakhtin dialogic.

## THE PROBLEM OF UNITY

A key aspect of dialogic freedom described in chapter 1 is the tension between unifying and fragmenting forces in our daily lives and in the decisions we make. Throughout Bakhtin's career he was fascinated by the push and pull of these centrifugal and centripetal forces, and this fascination led to a number of discussions of the meaning of the word "unity." The word turned out to be so problematic for him—so able to be used in diametrically opposed and hence confusing ways—that he eventually abandoned it altogether. Early in his career, in *Toward a Philosophy of the Act*, he uses the word "unity" in two diametrically opposed ways, one centripetal, the other centrifugal. He describes the "theoretical unity" posited by abstract thought (TPA,

7), which, like the centripetal "domain of culture," produces unified explanations. He contrasts this "theoretical unity" with the "unity" of "once-occurrent answerable life" (TPA, 8), which corresponds to the centrifugal uniqueness of "lived and experienced life." Another early philosophical work, "Author and Hero in Aesthetic Activity," echoes this same distinction: "Cognition constructs a unitary and universally valid world, a world independent in every respect from the concrete and unique position which is occupied by this or that individual" (AH, 23). Bakhtin explains the distinction between these two conceptions of unity: "The affirmation of a judgment as a true judgment is an assigning of it to a certain theoretical unity, and this unity is not at all the unique historical unity of my life" (TPA, 4). Bakhtin came to be frustrated with the term "unity," partly because it could be used in these two opposite, hence potentially confusing ways. Eventually he concluded that "the very word *unity* should be discarded as being overly theoreticized" (TPA, 37). For our purposes, the important thing to take from these ruminations is Bakhtin's lifelong fascination with the significance of this tug of war between the desire to unify meaning culturally or abstractly, which is a project human beings undertake—"a unity set as a task" (AH, 16)—and the resistance to this impulse by the lived events of prosaic life—the unity of "once-occurrent answerable life" (TPA, 8). In terms of dialogic freedom, we see the value of recognizing the impossibility of avoiding this struggle between unity and chaos, even as we confront the necessity to make choices within this challenging context.

The theoretical impulse, which Bakhtin saw as a centripetal force for abstract explanation and finalization, was a side of the equation that he came to question more and more throughout his life, culminating in his critique of formalism and his endorsement of the novel as the genre best suited to the expression of unfinalizability. Early in his career, however, he had regarded as a good thing the author's aesthetic impulse to consummate (or finalize) the hero in a unified image, and Bakhtin's analysis of the author-hero relationship in "Author and Hero in Aesthetic Activity" can contribute to our understanding of the tensions between centripetal and centrifugal forces. Bakhtin began by observing that when I look at another human being I can see things he cannot see (behind him, what his body looks like from outside), and vice versa: "I shall always see and know something that he . . . cannot see himself: parts of his body that are inaccessible to his own gaze (his head, his face and its expression), the world behind his back" (AH, 23). The "excess" of my seeing allows me to "render the other complete precisely in those respects in which he cannot complete himself by himself" (AH, 24). My position outside the other makes it possible for me to see things the other cannot see and for the other to see things about me that I cannot see. In the process, the "surplus" each of us enjoys allows us to "complete" each other for each other. We depend upon each other to unify our own images of ourselves. Note that

Bakhtin is talking at this point not about authors of books and the characters they create, but about people in daily life contemplating each other. In this process, the "excess of my seeing must 'fill in' the horizon of the other human being who is being contemplated. . . . I must empathize or project myself into this other human being, see his world . . . as *he* sees this world . . . and then, after returning to my own place, 'fill in' his horizon" (AH, 25), hence creating a "consummating environment for him, which renders the other "complete" (AH, 24). In this description not of what novelists do but of what you and I do every day in the two-sided act of thinking about each other, Bakhtin uses words like "fill in," "complete," and "consummating" to describe the centripetal task of creating identity.

In tension with this consummating task is the uniqueness of every lived moment, which in its infinite variety constitutes a centrifugal force for chaos. Even here, though, Bakhtin has his finger in the dike against relativism. Though the individual experiences the uniqueness of every "once-occurrent" lived moment, and this uniqueness could be seen as a centrifugal force for chaos, according to Bakhtin, the very uniqueness of each moment, instead of freeing the individual from all constraints, removes every alibi against taking responsibility for that unrepeatable moment. "It is precisely the choice of purpose, the place within the event of being, for which moral self-activity is answerable, and in this respect it is free" (AH, 119). Even though (or *be-cause*) each moment is unique and can never be adequately accounted for by an all-encompassing theory, we are all answerable for the decisions we make moment by moment, and in that answerability (not in cutting loose from all restraint) lies our capacity for freedom. Paradoxically, to Bakhtin the world of abstraction—a world we usually associate with unifying theories that give meaning to life—is actually the source of relativism. To him, the world of "the good, the beautiful, etc." is a "domain of endless questions" which provides "no principle for choice; everything that *is* could also *not* be, could be different" (TPA, 43). To counterbalance this centrifugal tendency within the world of abstraction and theory, "what is necessary is the initiative of an actually performed act," the "ought-to-be" of a socially embedded individual. For Bakhtin, individuals are responsible for the choices they make and the actions they take in a world of others, no matter how many ideological crosscurrents and unique events threaten to create chaos. This answerability that we all experience every moment of every day is at the heart of the concept of dialogic freedom as a two-sided act, chosen within a field of unifying and fragmenting forces along a continuum of minimal to maximal layers of knowing that are never final.

# NOTES

1. The ideas in this appendix draw in part from my discussion of dialogic freedom in "Dialogic Freedom: In the 'Sideshadow' of Bakhtin," *Modern Philology* 106, no. 4.(2009): 648–76, used with permission from the University of Chicago Press.

2. Hannah Arendt, "What Is Freedom," in *Between Past and Future: Eight Exercises in Political Thought* (1954; repr., New York: Viking Press, 1968), 161.

3. Isaiah Berlin, "Two Concepts of Liberty," in *Four Essays on Liberty* (1958; repr., London: Oxford University Press, 1969), 152.

4. Thomas Pavel, "Freedom, from Romance to the Novel: Three Anti-Utopian American Critics," *New Literary History* 29, no. 4 (1998): 591. Citations to this issue of *New Literary History* use the abbreviation NLH.

5. Gary Saul Morson, "Contingency and Freedom, Prosaics and Process," NLH, 684.

6. Morson, *Narrative and Freedom: The Shadows of Time* (New Haven, CT: Yale University Press, 1994), 6. Citations to *Narrative and Freedom* are to this text, with the abbreviation NF.

7. I use the concept of "sideshadowing" in my essay "Dialogic Freedom: In the 'Sideshadow' of Bakhtin."

8. Berlin, "Two Concepts of Liberty," 172.

9. Ken Hirschkop, *Mikhail Bakhtin: An Aesthetic for Democracy* (New York: Oxford University Press, 1999), 6.

10. See note 2 above.

11. Caryl Emerson, *The First Hundred Years of Bakhtin* (Princeton, NJ: Princeton University Press, 1997), 25.

12. Michael Holquist, "Foreword," in Mikhail Bakhtin, *Toward a Philosophy of the Act*, ed. Vadim Liapunov and Michael Holquist; trans. Vadim Liapunov (Austin: University of Texas, 1993), vii. Citations to *Toward a Philosophy of the Act* are to this edition, with the abbreviation TPA.

13. Texts published under the names of Ivan Ivanovich Kanaaev, Valentin Volosinov, and Pavel Medvedev are attributed to Mikhail Bakhtin by some scholars, but to one of these three authors by others. For a discussion of this dispute about attribution, and my decision to refer to the authorship of the disputed texts as Bakhtin/Another Author, see chapter 1, note 12.

14. Michael Holquist and Katerina Clark, *Mikhail Bakhtin* (Cambridge, MA: Harvard University Press, 1984), 81. Citations to *Mikhail Bakhtin* are to this text, with the abbreviation MB.

15. Caryl Emerson, *First Hundred Years*, 124, quoting "Aesthetics of Verbal Creativity," from *Speech Genres and Other Late Essays,* ed. Caryl Emerson and Michael Holquist; trans. Vern McGee (Austin: University of Texas Press, 1986), 127. Citations to *Speech Genres and Other Late Essays* are to this text, with the abbreviation SG.

16. Gary Saul Morson, "Prosaic Bakhtin: *Landmarks,* Anti-Intelligensialism, and the Russian Countertradition," in *Bakhtin in Contexts: Across the Disciplines* (Evanston, IL: Northwestern University Press, 1995), 51.

17. Morson quotes Vekhi/*Landmarks: A Collection of Articles about the Russian Intelligentsia,* ed. and trans. Marshall S. Shatz and Judith E. Zimmerman (Armonk, NY: Sharpe, 1994).

18. Alexis de Tocqueville, *Democracy in America,* trans. Henry Reeve (New York: Schocken, 1974), 140.

19. Mikhail Bakhtin, "Author and Hero in Aesthetic Activity," in *Art and Answerability: Early Philosophical Essays by M. M. Bakhtin,* ed. Michael Holquist and Vadim Liapunov; trans. Vadim Liapunov (Austin: University of Texas Press, 1990), 49–50. Citations to "Author and Hero in Aesthetic Activity" are to this text, with the abbreviation AH.

20. Mikhail Bakhtin, *Problems of Dostoevsky's Poetics,* ed. and trans. Caryl Emerson (Minneapolis: University of Minnesota Press, 1984), 287.

21. Michael Holquist, *Dialogism: Bakhtin and His World* (London: Routledge, 1994), 18.

22. Gary Saul Morson and Caryl Emerson, *Mikhail Bakhtin: Creation of a Prosaics* (Stanford, CA: Stanford University Press, 1990), 92.

# Appendix B: Discussion Guide for Teachers, Students, and Book Groups

This discussion guide is divided into two parts: a one-day discussion guide for the entire book, and a general guide for multiple discussions of individual chapters and the literature they feature.

## ONE-DAY DISCUSSION GUIDE

1. Do you agree that today when most people talk about freedom they most often think of it as autonomy or as enlightenment? If so, give examples of these types of freedom and discuss their importance in your life. If not, give examples of other types of freedom.

2. Which work of literature did you enjoy reading about most in this book? Pick a favorite passage from it that deals with freedom. Can you identify in it elements of freedom as autonomy or enlightenment? Other types of freedom? What details in the passage make you interpret it the way you do? (Take turns sharing passages and leading the discussion.)

3. Do you think you understand the definition of dialogic freedom introduced in this book? *Dialogic freedom: a two-sided act, chosen within a field of unifying and fragmenting forces along a continuum of minimal to maximal layers of knowing that are never final.* If you had to explain this idea to a friend, what would you say? What example would you give? How is this idea of freedom different from freedom as autonomy or enlightenment?

4. Consider the example I give in chapter 1: "Will you marry me?," which I argue suggests different decisions, depending on who asks the

question and who gets asked. Can you think of another question that calls for a choice or action, which can mean different things and call for different actions, depending on the relationship between the one who asks and the one who is being asked? Pose this question to someone else in your group, and discuss what this experiment tells you about the dialogic nature of choice. (Break into groups of two to do this, then report back to the group as a whole.)

5. Think of a situation involving a decision (buying a gun, smoking pot, deciding whom to marry, etc.) that you think involves freedom, and identify how freedom as autonomy or enlightenment enters the picture. What elements of the situation you imagine illustrate the dialogic nature of freedom? Can all three kinds of freedom be present at once?

6. Think of an important decision (quitting a job, moving to another country, buying a house, having or not having a child, etc.) and list the voices in your head you feel most answerable to (spouse? friend? God? "the law"? reason? justice? science? family? etc.). These are your superaddressees. Which of these voices is most important to you? Are any of them in conflict for you (spouse v. friend? "the law" v. family? God v. science? etc.). How do you resolve these conflicts? Do you pioritize? Do you ignore some voices? Where do you experience the most intense conflicts?

7. Do you think the abortion discussion in chapter 10 was a good application of the concept of dialogic freedom to a current hot-button issue? Why or why not?

8. What other issues do you think would be interesting to discuss from the perspective of dialogic freedom? Brainstorm hot-button issues.

9. Pick a hot-button issue and try to discuss it from a dialogic perspective. Identify the key ideas and arguments of the polarized opponents on this topic. What are the best arguments on both sides? How does each side demonize the other? Identify the values that inform your own views on this topic—the voices that you feel answerable to. What conflicts do you feel within yourself about this issue? To focus your discussion, use the two questions the Public Conversations Project poses: (1) What events or other personal life experiences may have shaped your current views and feelings about this topic? and (2) Do you experience mixed feelings, value conflicts, uncertainties, or other dilemmas within your own perspective? When you share with others your answers to these questions, what common ground do you discover?

10. Can you improve the definition of dialogic freedom given in this book? How would you change it?

## GENERAL GUIDE FOR MULTIPLE DISCUSSIONS

Begin with the overview discussion questions above, spending as many days of discussion as you need to move through the list, saving questions 8–10 for later. Follow up, over the next weeks or months, with discussions of the individual works of literature featured in this book. Read each work in its entirety, including all eight if you have time and inclination. End by discussing one or more current hot-button topics and trying to improve on the definition of dialogic freedom presented here, by answering questions 8–10.

In a book group these discussions could take place monthly over the course of a year; in a high school or college classroom they could be spread out over a semester. The important thing is to read the relevant works of literature, discussing all the interesting things about them—many of which may have nothing at all to do with freedom—but also looking for opportunities to discuss freedom. For example, the opening of the *Iliad* involves a breakdown of communication between Agamemnon, the leader of the Greek army that is attacking Troy, and Achilles, who is the greatest warrior in that army. In this tense encounter between two stubborn men, all kinds of choices are being made. What are they? We can think about these decisions in terms of freedom as autonomy (Achilles and Agamemnon both want to do as they please), or in terms of freedom as enlightenment (neither of them may understand what is best for their people—by the way, what *is* best for their people?). We can also think about their decisions in terms of dialogic freedom. What voices and values do they each answer to? How do the expectations these warriors have about each other influence what they say and how they react? What values do they share? Why can't they work out their differences? The answers to these questions will suggest how dialogic freedom operates or fails to operate in this situation.

Find and discuss other situations in the *Iliad* where important decisions are being made. Bring to your meetings specific passages that you would like to talk about. Discuss the similarities and differences between the way people in this epic seem to have thought about freedom thousands of years ago and how we think about it today.

Go through a similar process with the other works of literature presented in this book. You can also put these works into dialogue with each other by considering how individual characters from different works, or how the authors of those works, might agree or disagree with each other, or with you, about the nature of freedom. As you discuss these texts, you can use each chapter in this book as a point of departure. Kick off your discussion with one of the passages I quote and see where it takes you. Don't be afraid to disagree completely with the way I interpret a passage, or with the ideas about freedom I express in each chapter. The point is to present reasons to explain the conclusions you reach, and to find evidence in these works of literature to support your interpretations.

You will also find references in the footnotes to books and essays about each work of literature. Whether or not you consult them, remember that they are there, and that they often take one side or another in controversies about how these works should be interpreted. If you would like to expand your reading list to include works of political theory, I highly recommend Aristotle's *Politics,* John Stuart Mill's *On Liberty,* Isaiah Berlin's "Two Concepts of Liberty," and Hannah Arendt's "What Is Freedom?" These works are all listed in the bibliography. If you would like to delve deeper into the thinking of Mikhail Bakhtin, I recommend starting with his book about Dostoevsky (also listed in the bibliography), which is the most accessible of his works. If you are interested in a more interdisciplinary approach to discussion, you could alternate works of literature with works of political theory, week by week, or month by month.

Reading for and with dialogic freedom is a challenge, but it is also fun. As your discussions evolve, you may well come up with a better definition for this concept than I have presented. In any case, your discussions should prepare you well to confront whatever hot-button topics you choose to focus on in your final meetings. At that point I hope you will return to the two questions posed by the Public Conversations Project (referenced above) and use them to structure your discussion. Above all, I hope that your exploration of dialogic freedom, through reading and discussing the literature presented in these pages, helps you develop new tools for navigating the perspectives of others and balancing the forces for unity and chaos as you coauthor decisions in a polarized world.

# Glossary

**addressee**. Listener taken into consideration by a speaker: anticipated, dreaded, loved, feared, disdained, etc.

**apophatic**. Having to do with the belief that God can be known to humans only in terms of what he is not, as in "God is unknowable."

**centrifugal**. Fragmenting, tending toward chaos.

**centripetal**. Unifying, tending toward order.

**dialogic freedom**. A two-sided act, chosen within a field of unifying and fragmenting forces along a continuum of minimal to maximal layers of knowing that are never final.

**epistemological layers**. Different ways of knowing reality through the experiences and perspectives of different professions, nationalities, phases of life, genders, etc. Physicians, musicians, auto mechanics, athletes, criminals, and priests could be said to navigate different epistemological layers of reality. They know the world in part by the experiences they have. A physician might have trouble knowing the world as an athlete might, and vice versa.

**eventness**. Moment by moment unfolding of life.

**finalize**. Complete, consummate, fill in, unify, explain once and for all.

**heteroglossia**. Diversity of social speech; different vocabularies of people in different professions or situations. Examples: the jargon of medical doctors, plumbers, musicians, bicyclists, young people, travelers, prisoners, scientists, lawyers, literary critics. Bakhtin defined *heteroglossia* as "specific points of view on the world" (*The Dialogic Imagination: Four Essays by M.M. Bakhtin*, ed. Michael Holquist; trans. Caryl Emerson and Michal Holquist [Austin: University of Texas Press, 1981], 291).

**indirect free style** (or **free indirect discourse**). A style of narration in which the thoughts of the narrator and the thoughts of a character become indistinguishable. Example: *He laid down his bundle and thought of his life. Just what pleasure had he found, since he came into this world?*

**lacuna**. Gap; a missing section of text.

**liminal**. On the border.

**monologic**. The product of a stable, unified ideology or undisputed ideal. Example: the ancient Greek heroic ideal.

**polyphonic**. The product of many different voices or perspectives.

**sideshadow**. A term coined by Gary Saul Morson and Michael Bernstein to describe a realm of real possibilities that could happen but do not; sideshadowing encourages "from the side" an alternative present and conveys the sense that actual events might just as well not have happened.

**speech genres**. See *heteroglossia*.

**superaddressee**. The perfect listener, real or imagined, who can understand or judge the speaker absolutely. Examples: God, "the law," "justice," "the people."

# Bibliography

Adler, Joyce. "The Monastic Slaver: Images and Meaning in 'Benito Cereno.'" In *Critical Essays on Herman Melville's "Benito Cereno."* Edited by Robert Burkholder. New York: Hall, 1992.

Ahearn, John. "Singing the Book: Orality in the Reception of Dante's *Comedy.*" In *Dante: Contemporary Perspectives*, edited by Amilcare Fannucci. Toronto: University of Toronto Press, 1997.

Allen, Elizabeth Cheresh, and Gary Saul Morson, eds. *Freedom and Responsibility in Russian Literature: Essays in Honor of Robert Louis Jackson.* Evanston, IL: Northwestern University Press, 1995.

Arendt, Hannah. *Between Past and Future: Eight Exercises in Political Thought.* 1954. Reprint, New York: Viking Press, 1968. See especially "What Is Freedom?"

Aristotle. *Politics.* Translated by H. Rackham. Cambridge, MA: Harvard University Press; London: William Heinemann Ltd., 1944. Perseus Digital Library. Accessed April 17, 2012, text:1999.01.0126.

———. *Politics.* In *Introduction to Aristotle*, edited by Richard McKeon; translated by Benjamin Jowett. New York: Modern Library, 1947.

———. *Politics.* Edited by Gregory R. Crane. Perseus Digital Library Project. Accessed February 1, 2009. http://www.perseus.tufts.edu.

———. *The Politics of Aristotle.* Translated by Ernest Barker. London: Oxford University Press, 1958.

Associated Press. "Sides in Gun Debate Taciturn." *Eugene Register-Guard*, December 31, 2012.

Bakhtin, Mikhail. *Art and Answerability: Early Philosophical Essays by M. M. Bakhtin.* Edited by Michael Holquist and Vadim Liapunov; translated by Vadim Liapunov. Austin: University of Texas Press, 1990. See especially "Author and Hero in Aesthetic Activity."

———. *The Bakhtin Reader: Selected Writings of Bakhtin, Medvedev, Voloshinov.* Edited by Pam Morris. London and New York: Arnold, 1994. See especially Bakhtin/Volosinov, *Marxism and the Philosophy of Language.*

———. *The Dialogic Imagination: Four Essays by M. M. Bakhtin.* Edited by Michael Holquist; translated by Caryl Emerson and Michael Holquist. Austin: University of Texas Press, 1981. See "From the Prehistory of Novelistic Discourse," "Epie and Novel," and "Discourse in the Novel."

———. *Problems of Dostoevsky's Poetics.* Edited and translated by Caryl Emerson. Minneapolis: University of Minnesota Press, 1984. See especially "Appendix II: Toward a Reworking of the Dostoevsky Book."

————. *Speech Genres and Other Late Essays*. Edited by Caryl Emerson and Michael Holquist; translated by Vern McGee. Austin: University of Texas Press, 1986. See especially "The Problem of the Text."

————. *Toward a Philosophy of the Act*. Edited by Vadim Liapunov and Michael Holquist; translated by Vadim Liapunov. Austin: University of Texas Press, 1993.

Berdyaev, Nicholas. *Dostoevsky*. Translated by Donald Attwater. Cleveland, OH: Meridian Books, 1965.

Berlin, Isaiah. *Four Essays on Liberty*. 1958. Reprint, London: Oxford University Press, 1969. See especially "Two Concepts of Liberty."

Bevington, David. *The Necessary Shakespeare*. New York: Longman, 2002.

Blake, William. *The Complete Poetry of William Blake*. Edited by David Endman. New York: Doubleday, 1988.

Branch, Watson G., ed. *Melville: The Critical Heritage*. London: Routledge, 1974.

Bulman, James. *The Merchant of Venice: Shakespeare in Performance*. New York: Manchester University Press, 1991.

Cardwell, Guy. "Melville's Gray Story: Symbols and Meaning in 'Benito Cereno.'" In *Modern Critical Views: Herman Melville*. Edited by Harold Bloom. New York: Chelsea House, 1986.

Caretti, Lanfranco. "Canto V: Il canto di Francesca." In Dante, *Dante Alighieri: Cultura, Politica, Poesia: Antologia della critica dantesca*. Edited by Tommaso Di Salvo. Florence: La Nuova Italia Editrice, 1987.

Catteau, Jacques. "The Paradox of the Legend of the Grand Inquisitor in *The Brothers Karamazov*." In *Dostoevsky: New Perspectives*. Edited by Robert Louis Jackson. Englewood Cliffs, NJ: Prentice-Hall, 1984.

Corns, Thomas N., ed. *A Companion to Milton*. Oxford: Blackwell, 2001.

Dante Alighieri. *Dante Alighieri: Cultura, Politica, Poesia: Antologia della critica dantesca*. Edited by Tommaso Di Salvo. Florence: La Nuova Italia Editrice, 1987.

————. *Dante Alighieri's Divine Comedy: Verse Translation and Commentary*. Vol. 2. Translated by Mark Musa. Bloomington: Indiana University Press, 1996.

————. *Dante's Inferno*. Translated by John D. Sinclair. New York: Oxford University Press, 1961.

————. *Dante's Inferno: Translations by Twenty Contemporary Poets*. Edited by Daniel Halperin. Hopewell, NJ: The Ecco Press, 1993.

————. *The Divine Comedy I: The Inferno*. Translated by Mark Musa. Middlesex, UK: Penguin, 1971.

————. *The Inferno of Dante*. Translated by Robert Pinsky. New York: Noonday, 1994.

————. *The Letters of Dante*, ed. and trans. Paget Toynbee (Oxford: Clarendon Press, 1920).

————. *The Portable Dante*. Edited by Mark Musa. New York: Penguin, 1995. See especially *La Vita Nuova*.

Davis, Mike. *Reading the Text That Isn't There: Paranoia in the Nineteenth-Century American Novel*. New York: Routledge, 2005. See especially "Rhetorical Razors: 'Lurking Significance' in the 'Vexatious Coincidence' of 'Benito Cereno.'"

Delano, Amasa. *A Narrative of Voyages and Travels, in the Northern and Southern Hemispheres: Comprising Three Voyages Round the World, Together with a Voyage of Survey and Discovery in the Pacific Ocean and Oriental Islands* (Boston: E. G. House, 1817). In *Melville's Benito Cereno: An Interpretation with Annotated Text and Concordance*. Edited by William D. Richardson. Durham, NC: Carolina Academic Press, 1987.

Dostoevsky, Fyodor. *The Brothers Karamazov*. Translated by Ralph Matlaw. New York: Norton, 1976.

————. *The Brothers Karamazov*. Translated by Richard Pevear and Larissa Volokhonsky. New York: Vintage, 1991.

————. *Notebooks for The Brothers Karamazov*. Edited and translated by Edward Wasiolek. Chicago: University of Chicago Press, 1971.

————. *Notes from Underground. The Grand Inquisitor*. Translated by Ralph Matlaw. New York: Dutton, 1960.

Eliot, T. S. "Vita Nuova." In *Selected Essays*. New York: Harcourt, 1950.

Emerson, Caryl. *The First Hundred Years of Bakhtin*. Princeton, NJ: Princeton University Press, 1997.

———. "Word and Image in Dostoevsky's Worlds," in *Freedom and Responsibility in Russian Literature: Essays in Honor of Robert Louis Jackson*, edited by Elizabeth Cheresh Allen and Gary Saul Morson. Evanston, IL: Northwestern University Press, 1995.

Empson, William. *Milton's God*. 1961. Reprint, London: Cambridge University Press, 1981.

Fannucci, Amilcare A., ed. *Dante: Contemporary Perspectives*. Toronto: University of Toronto Press, 1997.

Feltenstein, Rosalie. "Melville's 'Benito Cereno.'" *American Literature* 19 (1947): 245–55.

Finer, Lawrence B., Lori F. Frohwirth, Lindsay A. Dauphinee, Susheela Singh, and Ann M. Moore. "Reasons U.S. Women Have Abortions: Quantitative and Qualitative Perspectives," in *Perspectives on Sexual and Reproductive Health* 37, no. 3 (2005).

Fish, Stanley. *How Milton Works*. Cambridge, MA: Harvard University Press, 2001.

———. *Surprised by Sin*. 1967. Rev. ed. Cambridge, MA: Harvard University Press, 1998.

Foley, John Miles. "Epic as Genre." In *The Cambridge Companion to Homer*, edited by Robert Fowler. London: Cambridge University Press, 2004.

Ford, Andrew. "Epic as Genre." In *A New Companion to Homer*, ed. Ian Morris and Barry Powell. New York: Brill, 1997.

Frank, Joseph. *Dostoevsky: The Mantle of the Prophet, 1871–1881*. Princeton, NJ: Princeton University Press, 2002.

———. *Dostoevsky: The Years of Ordeal, 1850–1859*. Princeton, NJ: Princeton University Press, 1990.

Franklin, H. Bruce. "'Apparent Symbol of Despotic Command': Melville's *Benito Cereno*." In *Critical Essays on Herman Melville's "Benito Cereno."* Edited by Robert Burkholder. New York: Hall, 1992.

———. "Past, Present, and Future Seemed One." In *Critical Essays on Herman Melville's "Benito Cereno."* Edited by Robert Burkholder. New York: Hall, 1992.

Freccero, John. "Notes on Canto V." In *The Inferno of Dante*. Translated by Robert Pinsky. New York: Noonday, 1994.

Girard, René. "To Entrap the Wisest." In *Shakespeare: An Anthology of Criticism and Theory, 1945–2000*. Edited by Russ McDonald. Malden, MA: Blackwell, 2004.

Gross, John. *Shylock: A Legend and Its Legacy*. New York: Simon & Schuster, 1992.

Hardwick, Elizabeth. *Herman Melville*. New York: Viking, 2000.

Herman, Peter. *Destabilizing Milton: Paradise Lost and the Poetics of Incertitude*. New York: Macmillan, 2005.

Hersh, Seymour. "Torture at Abu Ghraib." *New Yorker*, May 10, 2004.

Hirschkop, Ken. *Mikhail Bakhtin: An Aesthetic for Democracy*. New York: Oxford University Press, 1999.

Holquist, Michael. *Dialogism: Bakhtin and His World*. London: Routledge, 1994.

———. "Foreword." In Mikhail Bakhtin, *Toward a Philosophy of the Act*. Edited by Vadim Liapunov and Michael Holquist; translated by Vadim Liapunov. Austin: University of Texas, 1993.

———. "Introduction." In *The Dialogic Imagination: Four Essays by M. M. Bakhtin*. Edited by Michael Holquist; translated by Caryl Emerson and Michael Holquist. Austin: University of Texas Press, 1981.

Holquist, Michael, and Katerina Clark. *Mikhail Bakhtin*. Cambridge, MA: Harvard University Press, 1984.

Homer. *The Iliad*. Translated by Robert Fagles. New York: Penguin, 1990.

———. *The Iliad*. Translated by Richmond Lattimore. Chicago: University of Chicago Press, 1951.

———. *The Odyssey*. Translated by Robert Fagles. New York: Penguin, 1996.

House, Elizabeth. "Toni Morrison's Ghost: The Beloved Who Is Not Beloved." *Studies in American Fiction* 18 (1990): 17–26.

Jackson, Robert Louis. *Dialogue with Dostoevsky: The Overwhelming Question*. Stanford, CA: Stanford University Press, 1993.

Jones, Malcolm. *Dostoevsky and the Dynamics of Religious Experience.* London: Anthem Press, 2005.

Kafka, Franz. *The Diaries of Franz Kafka, 1910–1913.* Edited by Max Brod; translated by Joseph Kresh. New York: Schocken, 1948.

———. *The Diaries of Franz Kafka 1914–1923.* Edited by Max Brod; translated by Martin Greenberg. New York: Schocken, 1949.

———. "In der Strafkolonie," in *Erzählungen.* Berlin: Schocken Verlag, 1946.

———. "In the Penal Colony," in *Franz Kafka: The Complete Stories.* Edited by Nahum Glatzer; translated by Willa Muir and Edwin Muir; foreword by John Updike. New York: Schocken, 1971.

———. *Letters to Friends, Family, and Editors.* Translated by Richard Winston and Clara Winston. New York: Schocken, 1977.

Kaplan, Sidney. "*Benito Cereno*: An Apology for Slavery." In *Melville's Benito Cereno: A Text for Guided Research.* Edited by John P. Runden. Lexington, MA: Heath, 1965.

Kaplan, Thomas. "Sweeping Limits on Guns Become Law in New York." *New York Times,* January 15, 2013.

Karcher, Carolyn. "The Riddle of the Sphinx: Melville's 'Benito Cereno' and the Amistad Case." In *Critical Essays on Herman Melville's "Benito Cereno."* Edited by Robert Burkholder. New York: Hall, 1992.

———. *Shadow over the Promised Land: Slavery, Race, and Violence in Melville's America.* Baton Rouge: Louisiana State University Press, 1980.

Kirkpatrick, Robin. *Dante's Inferno: Difficulty and Dead Poetry.* Cambridge, UK: Cambridge University Press, 1987.

Knox, Bernard. "Introduction." In *The Iliad*, trans. Robert Fagles. New York: Penguin, 1990.

Kolb, Clayton. *Kafka's Rhetoric: The Passion of Reading.* Ithaca, NY: Cornell University Press, 1989.

Kristofferson, Kris. "Me and Bobby McGee." Recorded by Janis Joplin, *Pearl.* New York: Columbia Records, 1971.

Lateiner, Donald. "The *Iliad*: An Unpredictable Classic." In *The Cambridge Companion to Homer*, edited by Robert Fowler. London: Cambridge University Press, 2004.

Leatherbarrow, W. J. *A Devil's Vaudeville: The Demonaic in Dostoevsky's Major Fiction.* Evanston, IL: Northwestern University Press, 2005.

Lewis, C. S. *The Allegory of Love.* New York: Oxford University Press, 1958.

Locke, John. *The Second Treatise of Government.* Edited by Thomas P. Peardon. Indianapolis: Bobbs-Merrill, 1952.

Lynn-George, Michael. *Epos: Word, Narrative, and the Iliad.* Atlantic Highlands, NJ: Humanities Press International, 1988.

Masson, David. "A Brief Life of Milton." In John Milton, *Paradise Lost.* Edited by Scott Elledge. New York: Norton, 1975.

Matusik, Martin Beck. *Radical Evil and the Scarcity of Hope.* Bloomington: Indiana University Press, 2008.

Mayer, Jane. "A Deadly Interrogation: Can the CIA Legally Kill a Prisoner?" *New Yorker,* November 14, 2005.

Mazzotta, Giuseppe. "Why Did Dante Write the Comedy? Why and How Do We Read It? The Poet and the Critics." In *Dante Now: Current Trends in Dante Studies*, ed. Theodore J. Cachey. Notre Dame, IN: University of Notre Dame Press, 1995.

Melville, Herman. "Benito Cereno." In *"Billy Budd" and Other Tales.* New York: Signet, 1998.

Mill, John Stuart. *On Liberty.* Edited by David Spitz. New York: Norton, 1974.

Miller, Robin Feuer. *The Brothers Karamazov: Worlds of the Novel.* New York: Twayne, 1992.

Miller, Timothy, ed. *The Critical Response to John Milton's Paradise Lost.* London: Greenwood Press, 1997.

Milton, John.. *Paradise Lost.* Edited by Thomas H. Luxon. The Milton Reading Room. Accessed March 2012.http://www.dartmouth.edu/~milton.

Mochulsky, Konstantin. *Dostoevsky: His Life and Work.* Princeton, NJ: Princeton University Press, 1967.

Morrison, Toni. *Beloved.* New York: Plume, 1987.

Morson, Gary Saul. *Bakhtin in Contexts: Across the Disciplines.* Evanston, IL: Northwestern University Press, 1995. See especially "Prosaic Bakhtin: *Landmarks,* Anti-Intelligensialism, and the Russian Countertradition."

———. "Contingency and Freedom, Prosaics and Process," *New Literary History* 29, no. 4 (1998): 673–86.

———. *Narrative and Freedom: The Shadows of Time.* New Haven, CT: Yale University Press, 1994.

Morson, Gary Saul, and Caryl Emerson. *Mikhail Bakhtin: Creation of a Prosaics.* Stanford, CA: Stanford University Press, 1990.

———. *Rethinking Bakhtin: Extensions and Challenges.* Evanston, IL: Northwestern University Press, 1989.

Nagy, Gregory. *Homeric Questions.* Austin: University of Texas Press, 1996.

Parker, Deborah. "Interpreting the Commentary Tradition to the *Comedy.*" In *Dante: Contemporary Perspectives.* Toronto: University of Toronto Press, 1997.

Parry, Milman. *The Making of Homeric Verse.* New York: Oxford University Press, 1967.

Pascal, Roy. *Kafka's Narrators: A Study of His Stories and Sketches.* Cambridge, UK: Cambridge University Press, 1982.

Pavel, Thomas. "Freedom, from Romance to the Novel: Three Anti-Utopian American Critics." *New Literary History* 29, no. 4 (1998): 579–98.

Peradotto, John. "Modern Theoretical Approaches to Homer." In *A New Companion to Homer,* ed. Ian Morris and Barry Powell. New York: Brill, 1997.

Petrarch. "Letters on Familiar Matters." In *Critical Essays on Dante.* Edited by Giuseppe Mazzotta. Boston: Hall, 1991.

Plato. *Great Dialogues of Plato.* Translated by W. H. D. Rouse. New York: New American Library, 1956.

Pope, Alexander. "Epistle I of Horace." In *The Works of Alexander Pope Esq.* London, 1751.

Postelthwaite, Norman. *Homer's Iliad: A Commentary on the Translation of Richmond Lattimore.* Exeter, UK: University of Exeter Press, 2000.

Reeve, F. D. *The White Monk: An Essay on Dostoevsky and Melville.* Nashville, TN: Vanderbilt University Press, 1989.

Richardson, Nicholas. *The Iliad: A Commentary.* Vol. 6, Books 21–24. Cambridge, UK: Cambridge University Press, 1993.

Richardson, William D., ed. *Melville's Benito Cereno: An Interpretation with Annotated Text and Concordance.* Durham, NC: Carolina Academic Press, 1987.

Gray, Richard. "Disjunctive Signs: Semiotics, Aesthetics, and Failed Mediation in 'In der Strafkolonie.'" In *A Companion to the Works of Franz Kafka.* Edited by James Rolleston. Rochester, NY: Camden House, 2002.

Rozanov, Vasily. *Dostoevsky and the Legend of the Grand Inquisitor.* Translated by Spencer E. Roberts. 1891. Reprint, Ithaca, NY: Cornell University Press, 1972.

Rumpersad, Arnold. "Melville and Race." In *Herman Melville: A Collection of Critical Essays.* Edited by Myra Jehlen. Englewood Cliffs, NJ: Prentice Hall, 1994.

Runrich, John P. *Milton Unbound.* New York: Cambridge University Press, 1996.

Scanlan, Joseph. *Dostoevsky the Thinker.* Ithaca, NY: Cornell University Press, 2002.

Scholes, Robert. *Protocols of Reading.* New Haven, CT: Yale University Press, 1991.

Schuman, Sharon. "Authorizing Meaning in *The Merchant of Venice.*" *Text and Performance Quarterly* 22, no. 1 (2002): 47–62.

———. "Dialogic Freedom: In the 'Sideshadow' of Bakhtin," *Modern Philology* 106, no. 4 (2009): 648–76.

Shakespeare, William. *First Folio of Shakespeare Facsimile.* New York: Norton, 1968.

———. *The Merchant of Venice.* In *The Norton Shakespeare.* Edited by Stephen Greenblatt. New York: Norton, 1997.

———. *The Merchant of Venice.* Longman Cultural Edition. Edited by Lawrence Danson. New York: Longman, 2005.

Shapiro, James. *Shakespeare and the Jews.* New York: Columbia University Press, 1996.

Shatz, Marshall S., and Judith E. Zimmerman, eds. and trans. *Landmarks: A Collection of Articles about the Russian Intelligentsia*. Armonk, NY: Sharpe, 1994.

Sinclair, John D., "Notes on Canto V." In *Dante's Inferno*. Translated by John Sinclair. New York: Oxford University Press, 1961.

Spanos, William. *Herman Melville and the American Calling: The Fiction after Moby-Dick, 1851–1857*. Albany: State University of New York Press, 2008.

Spitz, David. "Freedom and Individuality: Mill's *Liberty* in Retrospect." In John Stuart Mill, *On Liberty*. Edited by David Spitz. New York: Norton, 1974.

Stewart, Patrick. "Performing Shylock." In *Players of Shakespeare: Essays in Shakespearean Performance by Twelve Players with the Royal Shakespeare Company*. Edited by Philip Brockbank. Cambridge, UK: Cambridge University Press, 1985.

Sundquist, Eric. "'Benito Cereno' and New World Slavery." In *Critical Essays on Herman Melville's "Benito Cereno."* Edited by Robert Burkholder. New York: Hall, 1992.

———. "Suspense and Tautology in 'Benito Cereno,'" in *Modern Critical Interpretations of Billy Budd, Benito Cereno, Bartleby, and Other Tales*. Edited by Harold Bloom. New York: Chelsea House, 1987.

Swan, Charley. "'Benito Cereno: Melville's De(con)struction of the Southern Reader." In *Critical Essays on Herman Melville's "Benito Cereno."* Edited by Robert Burkholder. New York: Hall, 1992.

Terras, Victor. *Reading Dostoevsky*. Madison: University of Wisconsin Press, 1998.

Thiher, Allen. *Franz Kafka: A Study of the Short Fiction*. Boston: Twayne, 1990.

Tocqueville, Alexis de. *Democracy in America*. Vol. 2. Translated by Henry Reeve. New York: Schocken, 1974.

Vanderbildt, Kermit. "'Benito Cereno': Melville's Fable of Black Complicity." In *Critical Essays on Herman Melville's "Benito Cereno."* Edited by Robert Burkholder. New York: Hall, 1992.

Virgil. *The Aeneid of Virgil*, translated by Allen Mandelbaum. New York: Bantam, 1971.

Volosinov, V. N. *Marxism and the Philosophy of Language*. Translated by Ladislaw Matejka and I. R. Titunik. New York and London: Seminar Press, 1973.

von Maltzahn, Nicholas. "Milton's Readers." In *The Cambridge Companion to Milton*. 2nd ed. Edited by Dennis Danielson. Cambridge, UK: Cambridge University Press, 1999.

Waldock, A. J. A. *Paradise Lost and Its Critics*. Cambridge, UK: Cambridge University Press, 1966.

Weil, Simone. "The *Iliad*, Poem of Might." In *The Simone Weil Reader*, ed. George A. Panichas. New York: David McKay, 1977.

Wellek, René, ed. *Dostoevsky: A Collection of Critical Essays*. Englewood Cliffs, NJ: Prentice Hall, 1962.

Winters, Ivor. *In Defense of Reason*. New York: Routledge, 1947. See especially "'Benito Cereno': A Late Masterpiece."

Wolff, Cynthia Griffin. "Margaret Garner: A Cincinnati Story," *Massachusetts Review* 32, no. 3 (1991): 417–40.

Worthen, W. B. *Shakespeare and the Authority of Performance*. New York: Cambridge University Press, 1997.

Zagarell, Sandra. "Reenvisioning America: Melville's 'Benito Cereno.'" In *Critical Essays on Herman Melville's "Benito Cereno."* Edited by Robert Burkholder. New York: Hall, 1992.

Zunder, William, ed. *Paradise Lost: Contemporary Critical Essays*. New York: St. Martin's Press, 1999.

# Index

# About the Author

**Sharon Schuman** earned a PhD in English literature from the University of Chicago and taught at Deep Springs College, Willamette University, and the University of Oregon. Her interest in freedom grew naturally from team-teaching interdisciplinary seminars with political theorists, including John Schaar, R. Jeffrey Lustig, and Robert Hawkinson. In 2009 she introduced the concept of dialogic freedom in "Dialogic Freedom: In the Sideshadow of Bakhtin," which appeared in *Modern Philology*. Beyond academia, she writes essays on contemporary issues for newspapers throughout Oregon, travels with her husband, and performs concerts as a violinist with Chamber Music Amici.

CPSIA information can be obtained at www.ICGtesting.com
Printed in the USA
BVOW02*1728051213

338201BV00002B/9/P